momma *and the* meaning of life:

Tales of Psychotherapy

IRVIN D. YALOM

piatkus

To Saul Spiro, psychiatrist, poet, artist.
With gratitude for our forty years of friendship—
forty years of sharing life, books, the creative enterprise, and
unwavering skepticism about the meaning of the whole shebang.

PIATKUS

First published in the United States by Basic Books,
a member of the Perseus Books Group
First published in the UK in 1999 by
Judy Piatkus (Publishers) Limited
First paperback edition published in 2000
This edition published 2006
Reprinted 2006, 2008, 2009, 2010, 2011, 2012, 2013 (twice)

A CIP catalogue record for this book
is available from the British Library.

ISBN 978-0-7499-2748-6

Printed and bound by CPI Group (UK) Ltd, Croydon, CR0 4YY

Papers used by Piatkus are from well-managed forests
and other responsible sources.

MIX
Paper from
responsible sources
FSC
www.fsc.org   FSC® C104740

Piatkus
An imprint of
Little, Brown Book Group
100 Victoria Embankment
London EC4Y 0DY

An Hachette UK Company
www.hachette.co.uk

www.piatkus.co.uk

Contents

Acknowledgments

My thanks to all who have read, made suggestions, or contributed in some instrumental way to the final form of this manuscript: Sara Lippincott; David Spiegel; David Vann; Jo Ann Miller; Murray Bilmes; Ann Arvin; Ben Yalom; Bob Berger; Richard Fumosa; and my sister, Jean Rose. I am, as always, lovingly indebted to my wife, Marilyn Yalom, in more ways than I can say. And indebted as well to my editor, Phoebe Hoss, who in this work, as in so many other books, has mercilessly prodded me to write to the best of my ability.

❦

Momma and the Meaning of Life

*D*usk. Perhaps I am dying. Sinister shapes surround my bed: cardiac monitors, oxygen canisters, dripping intravenous bottles, coils of plastic tubing—the entrails of death. Closing my lids, I glide into darkness.

But then, springing from my bed, I dart out of the hospital room smack into the bright, sunlit Glen Echo Amusement Park, where, in decades past, I spent many summer Sundays. I hear carousel music. I breathe in the moist, caramelized fragrance of sticky popcorn and apples. And I walk straight ahead—not hesitating at the Polar Bear Frozen Custard stand or the double-dip roller coaster or the Ferris wheel—to take my place in the ticket line for the House of Horrors. My fare paid, I wait as the next cart swivels around the corner and clanks to a halt in front of me. After stepping in and pulling down the guard rail to lock myself snugly into place, I take one last look about me—and there, in the midst of a small group of onlookers, I see her.

I wave with both arms and call, loud enough for everyone to hear, "Momma! Momma!" Just then the cart lurches forward and strikes the double doors, which swing open to reveal a black gaping maw. I lean back as far as I can and, before being swallowed by the darkness, call again, "Momma! How'd I do, Momma? How'd I do?"

Even as I lift my head from the pillow and try to shake off the dream, the words clot in my throat: "How'd I do, Momma? Momma, how'd I do?"

But Momma is six feet under. Stone-cold dead for ten years now in a plain pine casket in an Anacostia cemetery outside Washington, D.C. What is left of her? Only bones, I guess. No doubt the microbes have polished off every scrap of flesh. Maybe some strands of thin gray hair remain—maybe some glistening streaks of cartilage cling to the ends of larger bones, the femur and the tibia. And oh yes, the ring. Nestled somewhere in bone dust must be the thin silver filigree wedding ring my father bought on Hester Street shortly after they arrived in New York, steerage class, from the Russian shtetl half a world away.

Yes, long gone. Ten years. Croaked and decayed. Nothing but hair, cartilage, bones, a silver filigree wedding ring. And her image lurking in my memories and dreams.

Why do I wave to Momma in my dream? I stopped waving years ago. How many? Maybe decades. Perhaps it was that afternoon over half a century ago, when I was eight and she took me to the Sylvan, the neighborhood movie theater around the corner from my father's store. Though there were many empty seats, she plunked herself down next to one of the neighborhood toughs, a boy a year older than I. "That seat's saved, lady," he growled.

"Yeah, yeah! Saved!" my mother replied contemptuously as she made herself comfortable. "*He's* saving seats, the big shot!" she announced to everyone within earshot.

I tried to vanish into the maroon velvet seat cushion. Later, in the darkened theater, I summoned courage, turned my head slowly. There he was, now sitting a few rows back next to his friend. No mistake, they were glaring and pointing at me. One of them shook his fist, mouthed, "Later!"

Momma ruined the Sylvan Theater for me. It was now enemy territory. Off limits, at least in daylight. If I wanted to keep up with the Saturday serial—*Buck Rogers, Batman, The Green Hornet, The Phantom*—I had to arrive after the show started, take my seat in the darkness, at the very rear of the theater, as close to an escape door as possible, and depart just before the lights went on again. In my neighborhood nothing took precedence over avoiding the major calamity of being *beaten up*. To be punched—not hard to imagine: a bop on the chin, and that's it. Or slugged, slapped, kicked, cut—same thing. But *beaten up—ohmygod*. Where does it end? What's left of you? You're out of the game, forever pinned with the "got beat up" label.

And waving to Momma? Why would I wave now when, year after year, I lived with her on terms of unbroken enmity? She was vain, controlling, intrusive, suspicious, spiteful, highly opinionated, and abysmally ignorant (but intelligent—even I could see that). Never, not once, do I remember sharing a warm moment with her. Never once did I take pride in her or think, I'm so glad she's my momma. She had a poisonous tongue and a spiteful word about everyone—except my father and sister.

I loved my Aunt Hannah, my father's sister: her sweetness, her unceasing warmth, her grilled hot dogs wrapped in crisp bologna slices, her incomparable strudel (its recipe forever lost to me, as her son will not send it to me—but that's another story). Most of all I loved Hannah on Sundays. On that day her delicatessen near the Washington, D.C., Navy Yard was closed, and she put free games on the pinball machine and let me play for hours. She never objected to my putting small wads of paper under the front legs of the machine to slow the pinballs' descent so I could run up higher scores. My adoration of Hannah sent

3

my momma into a frenzy of spiteful attacks on her sister-in-law. Momma had her Hannah litany: Hannah's poverty, her aversion to working in the store, her poor business sense, her cloddish husband, her lack of pride and ready acceptance of all hand-me-downs.

Momma's speech was abominable, her English heavily accented and larded with Yiddish terms. She never came to my school for parents' day or for PTA meetings. Thank God! I cringed at the thought of introducing my friends to her. I fought with Momma, defied her, screamed at her, avoided her, and, finally, in my midadolescence, stopped speaking to her altogether.

The great puzzle of my childhood was, How does Daddy put up with her? I remember wonderful moments on Sunday mornings when he and I played chess and he gaily sang along with records of Russian or Jewish music, his head swaying in time to the melody. Sooner or later the morning air was shattered by Momma's voice screeching from upstairs, "Gevalt, Gevalt, enough! *Vay iz mir*, enough music, enough noise!" Without a word my father would rise, turn off the phonograph, and resume our chess game in silence. How many times I prayed, Please, Dad, please, just this once, punch her out!

So why wave? And why ask, at the very end of my life, "How'd I do, Momma?" Can it be—and the possibility staggers me—that I have been conducting my entire life with this lamentable woman as my primary audience? All my life I have sought to escape, to climb away from my past—the shtetl, the steerage, the ghetto, the tallis, the chanting, the black gabardine, the grocery store. All my life I have stretched for liberation and growth. Can it be that I have escaped neither my past nor my mother?

Those friends who have had lovely, gracious, supportive mothers—how I envy them. And how odd that they are not bound to their mothers, neither phoning, visiting, dreaming, nor even thinking about them frequently. Whereas I have to purge my mother from my mind many times a day and even now, ten years after her death, often reflexively reach for a phone to call her.

Oh, I can understand all this intellectually. I have given lectures on the phenomenon. I explain to my patients that abused children often find it hard to disentangle themselves from their dysfunctional families, whereas children grow away from good, loving parents with far less conflict. After all, isn't that the task of a good parent, to enable the child to leave home?

I understand it, but I don't like it. I don't like my mother visiting me every day. I hate it that she has so insinuated herself into the interstices of my mind that I can never root her out. And most of all, I hate that at the end of my life I feel compelled to ask, "How'd I do, Momma?"

I think of the overstuffed chair in her Washington, D.C., retirement home. It partially blocked the entrance to her apartment and was flanked by sentinel tables stacked with at least one copy, sometimes more, of each of the books I had written. With over a dozen books and an additional two dozen foreign-language translations, the stacks teetered dangerously. All it would take, I often imagined, was one middling-respectable earth tremor to bury her up to her nose under the books of her only son.

Whenever I visited I would find her stationed in that chair with two or three of my books in her lap. She weighed them, smelled them, caressed them—everything but read them. She was too blind. But even before her vision failed she could not have comprehended them: her only education had been in a naturalization class to become a U.S. citizen.

I am a writer. And Momma can't read. Still, I turn to her for the meaning of my life's work. To be measured how? On the odor, the sheer heft of my books? The cover design, the slick dry-grease Teflon feel of the jackets? All my painstaking research, my leaps of inspiration, my fastidious searching for the correct thought, the elusive graceful sentence: these she never knew.

The meaning of life? The meaning of *my* life. The very books stacked and swaying on Momma's table contain pretentious responses to such questions. "We are meaning-seeking creatures," I wrote, "who must deal with the inconvenience of being hurled into a universe that intrinsically has no meaning." And then to avoid nihilism, I explained, we must embark on a double task. First, we invent or discover a life-meaning project sturdy enough to support a life. Next, we must contrive to forget our act of invention and persuade ourselves that we have not invented but discovered the life-meaning project—that it has an independent "out there" existence.

Though I feign accepting without judgment each person's solution, I secretly stratify them into brass, silver, and gold. Some people are goaded throughout life by a vision of vindictive triumph; some, swaddled in despair, dream only of peace, detachment, and freedom from pain; some dedicate their lives to success, opulence, power, truth; others search for self-transcendence and immerse themselves in a cause or another being—a loved one or a divine essence; still others find their meaning in a life of service, in self-actualization, or in creative expression.

We need art, Nietzsche said, lest we perish from the truth. Hence I consider creativity as the golden path and have turned my entire life, all my experiences, all my imaginings, into some smoldering inner compost heap out of which I try to fashion, from time to time, something new and beautiful.

But my dream says otherwise. It contends that I have devoted my life to quite another goal—winning the approval of my dead momma.

This dream indictment has power: too much power to ignore, too disturbing to forget. But dreams are, I have learned, neither inscrutable nor immutable. For most of my life I have been a dream tinkerer. I have learned how to tame dreams, to take them apart, to put them together. I know how to squeeze out dream secrets.

And so, letting my head fall back upon my pillow, I drift off, rewinding the dream reel back to the cart in the House of Horrors.

The cart stops with a jerk, slamming me against the guard rail. A moment later, it's reversing direction and slowly backing up through the swinging doors and out again into the Glen Echo sunlight.

"Momma, Momma!" I call, both arms waving. "How'd I do?"

She hears me. I see her plowing her way through the crowd, flinging people to right and left. "Oyvin, what a question," she says, unlocking the guard rail and pulling me out of the cart.

I look at her. She seems about fifty or sixty, is strong and stocky, and is effortlessly carrying a bulging, embroidered, wooden-handled shopping bag. She is homely but does not know it and walks with her chin raised as though she were beautiful. I notice the familiar folds of flesh hanging from her upper arm and the stockings bunched and tied just above her knees. She gives me a big wet kiss. I feign affection.

"You did good. Who could ask for more? All those books. You made me proud. If only your father were here to see."

"What do you mean I did good, Momma? How do you know? You can't read what I've written—your vision, I mean."

"I know what I know. Look at these books." She opens the shopping bag, removes two of my books, and begins to fondle them tenderly. "Big books. Beautiful books."

I feel unnerved by her handling my books. "It's what's *in* the books that's important. Maybe they just contain nonsense."

"Oyvin, don't talk *narishkeit*—foolishness. Beautiful books!"

"Carrying around that bag of books all the time, Momma, even in Glen Echo? You're making a shrine of them. Don't you think—"

"Everybody knows about you. The whole world. My hairdresser tells me her daughter studies your books in school."

"Your hairdresser? That's it, the final test?"

"Everybody. I tell everybody. Why shouldn't I?"

"Momma, don't you have anything better to do? What about spending your Sunday with your friends: Hannah, Gertie, Luba, Dorothy, Sam, your brother Simon? What are you doing here at Glen Echo anyway?"

"You ashamed I should be here? You were always ashamed. Where else should I be?"

"I only mean we're both all grown up. I'm over sixty years old. Maybe it's time we should each have our own private dreams."

"Always ashamed of me."

"I didn't say that. You don't listen to me."

"Always thought I was stupid. Always thought I didn't understand anything."

"I didn't say that. I always said you didn't know everything. It's just the way you—the way you—"

"The way I what? Go ahead. You started—say it—I know what you're going to say."

"What am I going to say?"

"No, Oyvin, *you* say it. If I tell you, you'll change it."

"It's the way you don't listen to me. The way you talk about things you don't know anything about."

"Listen to you? I don't listen to *you*? Tell me, Oyvin, you listen to me? Do you know about me?"

"You're right, Momma. Neither of us has been good at listening to the other."

"Not me, Oyvin, I listened good. I listened to the silence every night when I came home from the store and you don't bother to come upstairs from your study room. You don't even say hello. You don't ask me if I had a hard day. How could I listen when you didn't talk to me?"

"Something stopped me; there was such a wall between us."

"A wall? Nice to say to your mother. A wall. I built it?"

"I didn't say that. I only said there was a wall. I know I retreated from you. Why? How can I remember? This was fifty years ago, Momma, but everything you said to me was, I felt, some sort of reprimand."

"*Vos?* Reperand?"

"I mean criticism. I had to stay away from your criticism. Those years I was feeling bad enough about myself as it was, and I didn't need more criticism."

"What did you have to feel bad about? All those years—Daddy and I working in the store for you to study. Till midnight. And how many times did you phone for me to bring home something for you? Pencils or paper. Remember Al? He worked in the liquor store. The one who got his face cut during a robbery?"

"Of course I remember Al, Momma. The scar all the way down the front of his nose."

"Well, Al would answer the phone and always holler, right across the crowded store, 'It's the king! The king is calling! Let the king go buy his own pencils. The king could use a little exercise.' Al was jealous; his parents gave him nothing. I never paid attention to what he said. But Al was right; I treated you like a king. Any time you called, day or night, I'd leave Daddy with a store full of customers and run down the block to Mensch's Five & Dime. Stamps, too, you needed. And notebooks, and ink. And then ballpoint pens. All your clothes smeared with ink. Like a king. Not criticism."

"Ma, we're talking now. And that's good. Let's not accuse each other. Let's understand. Let's just say I *felt* criticized. I know you said good things about me to others. You bragged about me. But you never said it to me. To my face."

"Not so easy to talk to you then, Oyvin. And not just for me, for everybody. You knew everything. You read everything. Maybe people were a little afraid of you. Maybe me too. *Ver veys?* Who knows? But let me tell you something, Oyvin, I had it voise than you. First, you never said anything nice about me either. I kept house; I cooked for you. Twenty years you ate my food. You liked it, I know. How did I know? Because the plates and pots were always empty. But you never told me. Not once in your life. Huh? Once in your life?"

Ashamed, I can only bow my head.

"Second, I knew that you didn't say anything nice behind my back—at least *you* had that, Oyvin, you knew that behind your back I bragged about you to others. But I knew you were ashamed of me. Ashamed all the way through—in front of me and behind my back. Ashamed of my English, my accent. Of everything I didn't know. And the things I said wrong. I heard the way you and your friends made fun of me—Julie, Shelly, Jerry. I heard everything. Huh?"

I bow my head lower. "You never missed anything, Momma."

"How could I know anything that's in your books? If I had a chance, if I could have gone to school, what I could have done with my head, my *saychel!* In Russia, in the shtetl, I couldn't go to school—only the boys."

"I know, Momma, I know. I know you would have done as well as me in school if you'd had the chance."

"I got off the boat with my mother and father. I was only twenty. Six days a week I had to work in a sewing factory. Twelve hours a day. Seven in the morning to seven at night, sometimes eight. And two hours earlier, at five in the morning, I had to walk my father to his newspaper stand next to the subway and help him unpack the papers. My brothers never helped. Simon went to accountancy school. Hymie drived a cab—never came home, never sent money. And then I married Daddy and moved to Washington, and until I was old, I worked side by side with him in the store twelve hours a day and cleaned the house and cooked too. And then I had Jean, who never gave me one minute trouble. And then I had you. And you were not easy. And I never stopped working. You saw me! You know! You heard me running up and down the stairs. Am I lying?"

"I know, Momma."

"And all those years, as long as they lived, I supported Bubba and Zeyda. They had nothing—the few pennies my father made from the paper stand. Later we opened a candy store for him, but he couldn't work—the men had to pray. You remember Zeyda?"

I nod. "Faint memories, Momma." I must have been four or five . . . a sour-smelling tenement building in the Bronx . . . throwing scraps of bread and balls of tinfoil down five stories to the chickens in the courtyard . . . my grandfather, all in black, tall black yarmulke, white wild beard stained with gravy, his arms and forehead wrapped in black cords, mumbling prayers. We couldn't converse—he spoke only Yiddish—but he pinched my cheek hard. Everyone else—Bubba, Momma, Aunt Lena—working, running up and down the stairs all day to the store, unpacking and packing, cooking, cleaning feathers from chickens, scales from fish, dusting. But Zeyda didn't lift a finger. Just sat and read. Like a king.

"Every month," Momma keeps on, "I took the train to New York and brought them food and money. And later, when Bubba was in the nursing home, I paid for the home and visited her every two weeks—you remember, sometimes I took you on the train. Who else in the family helped? Nobody! Your Uncle Simon would come every few months and bring her a bottle of 7 Up, and my next visit all I would hear about was your Uncle Simon's wonderful 7 Up. Even when she was blind, she'd lie there just holding the empty 7 Up bottle. And not only Bubba I helped, but everyone else in the family—my brothers, Simon and Hymie, my sister, Lena, Tante Hannah, your Uncle Abe, the greenhorn, who I brought from Russia—everybody, the whole family, was supported by that *schmutzig*, dirty, little grocery store. Nobody helped me—ever! And no one ever thanked me."

Taking a deep, deep breath, I utter the words: "I thank you, Momma. I thank you."

That isn't too hard. Why has it taken me fifty years? I take her arm, maybe for the first time. The fleshy part just above the elbow. It feels soft and warm, something like her warm *kichel* dough just before baking. "I remember your telling Jean and me about Uncle Simon's 7 Up. That must have been hard."

"Hard? You're telling me. Sometimes she'd drink his 7 Up with a piece of my *kichel*—you know what a job making *kichel* is—and all she'd talk about was the 7 Up."

"It's good to talk, Momma. It's the first time. Maybe I've always wanted it, and that's why you stay in my mind and my dreams. Maybe now it will be different."

"Different how?"

"Well, I'll be able to be more myself—to live for the purposes and causes that I choose to cherish."

"You want to get rid of me?"

"No—well, not in that way, not in a bad way. I want the same for you too. I want you to be able to rest."

"Rest? Did you ever see me rest? Daddy napped every day. Ever see me nap?"

"What I mean is you should have your *own* purpose in life—not *this*," I say, poking her shopping bag. "Not my books! And I should have my own purpose."

"But I just explained," she replies, moving her shopping bag to her other hand, away from me. "These aren't only *your* books. These are *my* books too!"

Her arm, which I'm still clutching, is suddenly cold, and I release it.

"What do you mean," she goes on, "I should have my purpose? These books *are* my purpose. I worked for you—and for them. All my life I worked for those books—*my* books." She reaches into her shopping bag and pulls out two more. I cringe, afraid she is going to hold them up and show them to the small crowd of bystanders who have now gathered around us.

"But you don't get it, Momma. We've *got* to be separate—not fettered by one another. That's what it is to become a person. That's exactly what I write about in those books. That's how I want my children—all children—to be. Unfettered."

"*Vos meinen*—unfeathered?"

"No, no, *unfettered*—a word that means free or liberated. I'm not getting through to you, Momma. Let me put it this way: every single person in the world is fundamentally alone. It's hard, but that's the way it is, and we have to face it. So I want to have my own thoughts and my own dreams. You should have yours too. Momma, I want you out of my dreams."

Her face tightens sternly, and she steps back away from me. I rush to add, "*Not* because I don't like you but because I want what's good for all of us—for me and for you too. You should have your own dreams in life. Surely you can understand that."

"Oyvin, still you think I understand nothing and that you understand everything. But I look, too, into life. And death. I understand about death—more than you. Believe me. And I understand about being alone—more than you."

"But Momma, you don't *face* being alone. You stay with me. You don't leave me. You wander about in my thoughts. In my dreams."

"No, Sonny."

"Sonny": I haven't heard that name for fifty years, had forgotten that that's what she and my father often called me.

"It's not the way you think it is, Sonny," she continues. "There's some things you don't understand, some things you've got turned upside down. You know that dream, the one with me standing there in the crowd, watching you in the cart waving to me, calling to me, asking me how you did in life?"

"Yes, of course I remember my dream, Momma. That's where this all started."

"*Your* dream? That's what I want to say to you. That's the mistake, Oyvin—your thinking I was in *your* dream. That dream was *not* your dream, Sonny. It was *my* dream. Mothers get to have dreams too."

2

Travels with Paula

As a medical student I was taught the fine art of looking, listening, and touching. I looked at vermilion throats, bulging eardrums, and the serpentine arterial rivulets in the retina. I listened to the hiss of mitral murmurs, the gurgling tubas of the intestines, the cacophony of respiratory rales. I felt the slippery edges of spleens and livers, the tautness of ovarian cysts, the marbled hardness of prostatic cancer.

Learning *about* patients—yes, that was the business of medical school. But to learn *from* patients—that aspect of my higher education came much later. Perhaps it began with my professor, John Whitehorn, who often said, "Listen to your patients; let them teach you. To grow wise you must remain a student." And he meant much more than the banal truth that the good listener learns more about the patient. He meant quite literally that we should allow our patients to teach us.

A formal, awkward, courtly man whose gleaming pate was fringed with a fastidiously clipped crescent of gray hair, John Whitehorn was the distinguished chairman of the Johns Hopkins Department of Psychiatry for thirty years. He wore gold-rimmed spectacles and had no superfluous features—not a wrinkle in his face, or in the brown suit he wore every day of the year (he must have, we surmised, two or three identical ones in his closet). And no superfluous expressions: when he lectured his lips moved; all else—hands, cheeks, eyebrows—remained remarkably still.

During my third year of psychiatric residency five classmates and I spent every Thursday afternoon making rounds with Dr. Whitehorn. Beforehand we had lunch in his oak-paneled office. The fare was simple and unvarying—sandwiches of tuna, cold cuts, and cold Chesapeake Bay crab cake, followed by fruit salad and flattened pecan pie—but served with Southern elegance: linen tablecloth, glistening silver trays, bone china. The lunch conversation was long and leisurely. Though each of us had calls to return and patients clamoring for attention, there was no way to rush Dr. Whitehorn, and ultimately even I, the most frenetic of the group, learned to put time on hold. In these two hours we had the opportunity to ask our professor anything: I remember asking him about such matters as the genesis of paranoia, a physician's responsibility to the suicidal, the incompatibility between therapeutic change and determinism. Though he responded fully, he clearly preferred other subjects: the accuracy of Persian archers, the comparative quality of Greek versus Spanish marble, the major blunders of the battle of Gettysburg, his improved periodic table (he was originally trained as a chemist).

After lunch Dr. Whitehorn began interviewing in his office the four or five patients on his service while we silently observed. It was never possible to predict the length of each interview. Some lasted fifteen minutes; many continued for two or three hours. I most clearly remember the summer months, the cool, darkened office, the orange- and green-striped awnings blocking out the fierce Baltimore sun, the awning posts encircled by magnolia climbers whose fleecy blossoms dangled just outside the window. From the corner window I could just spot the edge of the house staff tennis court. Oh, how I ached to play in those days! I fidgeted and daydreamed about aces and volleys as the shadows inexorably lengthened across the court. Only when dusk had swallowed the very last strands of tennis twilight did I relinquish all hope and fully give my attention to Dr. Whitehorn's interviews.

His pace was leisurely. He had plenty of time. Nothing interested him as much as a patient's occupation and avocation. One week he would be encouraging a South American planter to talk for an hour about coffee trees; the next week it might be a history professor discussing the failure of the Spanish Armada. You would have thought his paramount purpose was to understand the relationship between altitude and the quality of the coffee bean or the sixteenth-century political motives behind the Spanish Armada. So subtly did he shift into more personal domains that I was always surprised when a suspicious, paranoid patient suddenly began to speak frankly about himself and his psychotic world.

By allowing the patient to teach him, Dr. Whitehorn related to the *person*, rather than the pathology, of that patient. His strategy invariably enhanced both the patient's self-regard and his or her willingness to be self-revealing.

A cunning interviewer, one might say—yet "cunning" it was not. There was no duplicity: Dr. Whitehorn genuinely wanted to be taught. He was a collector and had in this manner accumulated an astounding treasure trove of factual curios over the years. "You and your patients both win," he would say, "if you let them teach you enough about their lives and interests. Learn about their lives; you will not only be edified but you will ultimately learn all you need to know about their illness."

Fifteen years later, in the early 1970s, Dr. Whitehorn was dead, I had become a professor of psychiatry, and a woman named Paula with advanced breast cancer entered my life to continue my education. Though I didn't know it at the time, and though she never acknowledged it, I believe that from the very beginning she assigned herself the task of mentoring me.

Paula had called for an appointment after having heard from a social worker in the oncological clinic that I was interested in forming a therapy group of patients with terminal disease. When she first entered my office, I was instantaneously captivated by her appearance: by the dignity in her bearing; by her radiant smile, which gathered me in; by her shock of short, exuberantly boyish, glowing white hair; and by something I can only call luminosity that seemed to emanate from her wise and intensely blue eyes.

She caught my attention with her first words: "My name is Paula West," she said. "I have terminal cancer. But *I am not a cancer patient.*" And indeed, in my travels with her through many years, I never regarded her as a patient. She went on to describe in clipped, precise fashion her medical history: cancer of the breast diagnosed five years earlier; surgical removal of that breast; then cancer of the other breast, that breast also removed. Then came chemotherapy with its familiar awful entourage: nausea, vomiting, total loss of hair. And then radiation therapy, the maximum permitted. But nothing would slow the spread of her cancer—to skull, spine, and the orbits of her eyes. Paula's cancer demanded to be fed, and though the surgeons tossed it sacrificial offerings—her breasts, lymph nodes, ovaries, adrenal glands—it remained voracious.

When I imagined Paula's nude body, I saw a chest crisscrossed with scars, without breasts, flesh, or muscle, like the rib planks of some shipwrecked galleon, and below her chest a surgically scarred abdomen, all supported by thick, ungainly, steroid-thickened hips. In short, a fifty-five-year-old woman sans breasts, adrenals, ovaries, uterus, and, I'm sure, libido.

I have always relished women with firm, graceful bodies, full breasts, and a readily apparent sensuality. Yet a curious thing happened to me the first time I met Paula: I found her beautiful and fell in love with her.

We met weekly for a few months in an irregular contractual arrangement. "Psychotherapy," an observer might have said, for I entered her name in my professional appointment book and she sat in the patient's chair for the ritual fifty minutes. Yet our roles were always blurred. The question of fees, for example, never arose. From the very beginning I knew this was no ordinary professional contract and found myself reluctant to mention money in her presence—it would have been vulgar. And not only money but other such tasteless issues as carnality, marital adjustment, or social relationships.

Life, death, spirituality, peace, transcendence: those were the topics we discussed; those were Paula's only concerns. Mostly we talked about death. Each week four of us, not two, met in my office—Paula and I, her death and my own. She became my courtesan of death: she introduced me to it, taught me how to think about it, even to befriend it. I came to understand that death has had a bad press. Though there is little joy to be found in it, still death is not a monstrous evil that drags us off to some unimaginably terrible place. I learned to demythologize death, to see it for what it is—an event, a part of life, the end of further possibilities. "It's a neutral event," Paula said, "which we've learned to color with fear."

Every week Paula entered my office, flashed the broad smile I adored, reached into her large straw bag, lifted her journal to her lap, and shared her reflections and dreams of the past week. I listened hard and tried to respond appropriately. Whenever I voiced doubts about whether I was being helpful, she seemed puzzled; then, after a moment's pause, she smiled as if to reassure me and turned again to her journal.

Together we relived her entire encounter with cancer: the initial shock and disbelief, the mutilation of her body, her gradual acceptance, her getting used to saying, "I have cancer." She described her husband's loving care and that of close friends. I could easily understand that: it was hard not to love Paula. (Of course I never declared my love until much later, at a time when she was not to believe me.)

Then she described the horrible days of her cancer's recurrence. That phase was her Calvary, she said, and the stations of the cross were the trials experienced by all patients with recurrence: radiotherapy rooms with doomsday metallic eyeball suspended aloft, impersonal harried technicians, uncomfortable friends, aloof doctors, and, most of all, the deafening hush of secrecy everywhere. She cried when she told me about calling her surgeon, a friend of twenty years, only to be informed by his nurse that there were to be no further appointments because the doctor had nothing more to offer. "What is wrong with doctors? Why don't they understand the importance of sheer presence?" she asked me. "Why can't they realize that the very moment they have nothing else to offer is the moment they are most needed?"

The horror in learning of one's sickness unto death, I learned from Paula, is intensified many times over by the withdrawal of others. The isolation of the dying patient is exacerbated by the foolish charade of those who attempt to conceal the approach of death. But death cannot be concealed; the clues are ubiquitous: the nurses speak in hushed tones, the rounding doctors often pay attention to the wrong parts of the body, the medical students tip-toe into the hospital room, the family smiles bravely, visitors attempt cheeriness. A patient with cancer once told me that she knew death was near when her doctor, who previously had always concluded his physical exam with a playful pat on her fanny, instead ended his exam with a warm handshake.

More than death, one fears the utter isolation that accompanies it. We try to go through life two by two, but each of us must die alone—no one can die our death with us or for us. The shunning of the dying by the living prefigures final absolute abandonment. Paula taught me how the isolation of the dying works two ways. The patient cuts herself off from the living, not wanting to drag family or friends into her horror by revealing her fears or her macabre thoughts. And friends shrink away, feeling helpless, awkward, uncertain of what to say or do, and reluctant to get too close to a preview of their own deaths.

But Paula's isolation was now at an end. If nothing else, I was constant. Though others had abandoned Paula, I would not. How good that she had found me! How could I have known then that the time would come when she would consider me her Peter, denying her not once but many times?

She could find no suitable words to describe the bitterness of her isolation, a period she often referred to as her Garden of Gethsemane. Once she brought me a lithograph drawn by her daughter in which several highly stylized silhouette figures are stoning a saint, a single tiny crouching woman whose frail arms cannot protect her from the hail of granite. It still hangs in my office, and whenever I see it I think of Paula saying, "I am that woman, helpless before the onslaught."

It was an Episcopal priest who helped her find her way out of the Garden of Gethsemane. Familiar with the wise aphorism of Nietzsche, the Antichrist, "He who has a 'why' can put up with any 'how,'" the priest reframed her suffering. "Your cancer is your cross," he told her. "Your suffering is your ministry."

That formulation—that "divine illumination," as Paula called it—changed everything. As she described her acceptance of her ministry and her dedication to easing the suffering of individuals stricken with cancer, I began to understand my assigned role: she wasn't my project, I was *hers*, the object of her ministry. I could help Paula but not through support, interpretation, or even caring or fidelity. My role was to allow her to educate me.

Is it possible that someone whose days are limited, whose body is infiltrated with cancer, can experience a "golden period"? Paula did. It was she who taught me that embracing death honestly permits one to experience life in a richer, more satisfying manner. I was skeptical. I suspected that her talk of a "golden period" was overdone, her typical spiritual hyperbole. "Golden? Really? Oh, come now, Paula, how can there be anything golden about dying?"

"Irv," Paula chided, "that's the wrong question! Try to understand that what's golden is not the dying but the full living of life in the face of death. Think of the poignancy and preciousness of last times: the last spring, the last flight of dandelion fluff, the last shedding of wisteria blossoms.

"The golden period is also," Paula said, "a time of great liberation—a time when you have the freedom to say *no* to all trivial obligations, to devote yourself wholly to whatever you most care about—the presence of friends, the changing seasons, the rolling swell of the sea." She was deeply critical of Elizabeth Kübler-Ross, medicine's high priestess of death, who, failing to recognize the golden stage, had developed a negativistic clinical approach. Kübler-Ross's "stages" of dying—anger, denial, bargaining, depression, acceptance—never failed to arouse Paula's ire. She insisted, and I am certain that she was correct, that such rigid categorizing of emotional responses leads to a dehumanization of both patient and doctor.

Paula's golden period was a time for intense personal exploration: she had dreams of wandering through enormous halls and discovering in her house new, unused rooms. And it was a time of preparation: she had dreams of cleaning her house from basement to attic and of reorganizing bureaus and closets. She prepared her husband efficiently and lovingly. There were times, for example, when she felt strong enough to shop and cook but deliberately refrained in order to train him to be more self-sufficient. Once she told me that she was very proud of him because he had for the first time referred to "my" rather than "our" retirement. At such times I sat wide-eyed in disbelief. Was she on the level? Did such virtue really exist outside the Dickensian world of Peggotty, Little Dorrit, Tom Pinch, and the Boffins? Psychiatric texts rarely discuss the personality trait of "goodness" except to label it a defense against darker impulses, and at first I questioned her motives while poking around as unobtrusively as possible for flaws and chinks in the facade of saintliness. Finding none, I eventually concluded that it was no facade and, calling off my search, allowed myself to bask in Paula's grace.

Preparation for death, Paula believed, is vital and requires explicit attention. Upon learning that her cancer had spread to her spine, Paula prepared her thirteen-year-old son for her death by writing him a letter of farewell that moved me to tears. In her final paragraph she reminded him that the lungs in the human fetus do not breathe, nor do its eyes see. Thus, the embryo is being prepared for an existence it cannot yet imagine. "Are we not, too," Paula suggested to her son, "being prepared for an existence beyond our ken, beyond even our dreams?"

I have always been baffled by religious belief. As long as I can remember, I have regarded it as self-evident that religious systems develop in order to provide comfort and soothe the anxieties of our human condition. One day when I was twelve or thirteen and working in my father's grocery store, I talked of my skepticism about the existence of God with a World War II soldier who had just returned from the European front. In response, he gave me a crinkled, faded picture of the Virgin Mary and Jesus that he had carried with him throughout the Normandy invasion. "Turn it over," he said. "Read the back. Read it aloud."

"'There are no atheists in foxholes,'" I read.

"Right! There are no atheists in foxholes," he repeated slowly, shaking his finger at me with every word. "Christian God, Jew God, Chinese God, any other God—but *some* god, by God! Can't do without it."

Given to me by a total stranger, that crinkled picture fascinated me. It had survived Normandy and who knows how many other battles. Perhaps, I thought, it was an omen; perhaps divine providence had finally found me. For two years I carried that picture in my wallet, every so often pulling it out and pondering it. And then one day I asked, "So? What if it *is* true that there are no atheists in foxholes? If anything, that supports the skeptical position: *of course* belief increases when fear is greatest. That's the very point: fear begets belief; we need and want a god, but wishing doesn't make it so. Belief, no matter how fervent, how pure, how consuming, says nothing whatsoever about the reality of God's existence. The next day, in a bookstore, I drew the now powerless picture out of my wallet and—I was careful with it, for it deserved respect—inserted it between the leaves of a book titled *Peace of Mind*, where perhaps some other embattled soul might find it and make better use of it.

Although the idea of dying had long filled me with dread, I came to prefer the raw dread to some belief whose chief appeal lay in its very absurdity. I have always hated the impregnable declaration, "I believe *because* it is absurd." Yet, as a therapist, I keep such sentiments to myself: I know that religious faith is a powerful source of comfort and never tamper with a belief if I have no better replacement.

My agnosticism has rarely wavered. Oh, perhaps a few times in school during morning prayer, I would feel queasy at the sight of all my teachers and classmates, heads bowed, whispering to the patriarch above the clouds. Has everyone but me gone mad? I wondered. And then there were those newspaper photos of the beloved Franklin Delano Roosevelt attending church every Sunday—those gave me pause: FDR's beliefs had to be taken very seriously.

But what of Paula's views? What of her letter to her son, of her belief in a purpose awaiting us that we cannot anticipate? Freud would have been amused at Paula's metaphor—and in the religious arena, I have always agreed with him entirely. "Wish fulfillment, pure and simple," he would have said. "We wish to *be*, we dread *nonbeing*, and we invent pleasant fairy tales in which all our wishes come true. The unknown purpose awaiting us, the enduring soul, Heaven, immortality, God, reincarnation—all illusions, all sweeteners to cut the bitters of mortality."

Paula always responded gently to my skepticism and softly reminded me that though I thought her beliefs were implausible, they were impervious to disproof. Despite my doubts, I liked Paula's metaphors and listened to her preachifying with more tolerance than I had ever listened to anyone before. Perhaps it was simply barter, I trading a small corner of my skepticism for a closer snuggle with Paula's grace. At times I even heard myself mouthing little phrases such as: "Who knows?" "Where, after all, does certainty lie?" "Can we ever really know?" I envied her son. Did he realize how blessed he was? How I longed to be the son of such a mother.

Around this time I attended the funeral service of a friend's mother in which the priest offered a story of consolation. He described a congregation of people on a shore who sadly wave good-bye as a ship sails away. The ship diminishes in size until only the tip of its mast is visible. When that too vanishes, the onlookers murmur, "She's gone." At that very instant, however, somewhere far away, another group of people are scanning their horizon and, seeing the tip of a mast appear there, exclaim, "She's come!"

"A silly fable," I might have snorted in my pre-Paula days. Yet now I felt less condescending. As I looked around at my fellow mourners, I felt for a brief moment at one with them, bonded together in illusion, all of us glowing at the image of the ship nearing the shores of a new life.

Before Paula, no one had been quicker than I to ridicule the flaky California landscape. The New Age horizon went on forever: Tarot, I Ching, body work, reincarnation, Sufi, channeling, astrology, numerology, acupuncture, scientology, Rolfing, holotrophic breathing, past-lives therapy. People have always needed these pathetic beliefs, I used to think. They answer a deep longing, and some people are too weak to stand alone. Let them have their fairy tales, poor children! Now I expressed my opinions more gently. Softer phrases now came to my lips: "Who can tell?" "Maybe!" "Life is complex and unknowable."

After Paula and I had met for many weeks, we began to make concrete plans to form a group for dying patients. Nowadays, such groups are commonplace and much discussed in magazines and television, but in 1973 there was no precedent: dying was as heavily censored as pornography. Hence, we had to improvise every step of the way. The beginning posed a major hurdle. How to start such a group? How to recruit group members? With a classified ad: "Wanted! Dying people"?

But Paula's network of her church, hospital clinics, and home-care organizations began to yield potential group members. The Stanford renal dialysis unit referred the first, Jim, a nineteen-year-old with severe kidney disease. Though he must have known that his life span was short, he had little interest in deepening his acquaintance with death. Jim avoided eye contact with Paula and me and, for that matter, any form of engagement—with anyone. "I'm a man without a future," he said. "Who would want me as a husband or a friend? Why keep facing the pain of rejection? I've talked enough. Been rejected enough. I'm doing okay without anyone." Paula and I saw him only twice; he did not return for a third session.

Jim, we concluded, was too healthy. Renal dialysis offers too much hope, postponing death so long that denial takes root. No, we needed the doomed, the short-timers on death row, those without hope.

Then Rob and Sal came through our door. Neither of them met our qualifications precisely: Rob often denied that he was dying, and Sal claimed that he had already come to terms with his illness and needed no help from us. Rob, only twenty-seven, had lived for six months with a highly malignant brain tumor. Lurching in and out of denial, he would insist, at one moment, "You'll see, I'll be backpacking in the Alps in six weeks" (I don't believe poor Rob had ever been east of Nevada), and, a few moments later, curse his paralyzed legs for preventing him from searching for his life insurance policy: "I've got to find out whether the benefits to my wife and kids will be canceled if I commit suicide."

Although we knew the group was not large enough, we started with four members—Paula, Sal, Rob, and I. Since Sal and Paula needed no help and I was the therapist, Rob became the group's raison d'être. But Rob obstinately refused to give us much satisfaction. We tried to offer him comfort and guidance while respecting his choice to deny. Supporting denial, however, is an unsatisfying, duplicitous endeavor, especially when what we wanted was to help Rob accept his dying and get the most out of what life he had left. None of us looked forward to our meetings. After two months Rob's headaches grew more severe, and one night he died quietly in his sleep. I doubt we were useful to him.

Sal greeted death in a very different manner. His spirit expanded as his life drew to a close. His imminent death flooded his life with a meaning he had never previously known. Multiple myeloma, an extraordinarily painful bone-invasive cancer, was Sal's disease; he had fractured many bones and was encased in a full body cast from neck to thigh. So many people loved Sal that it was hard to believe he was only thirty. Like Paula, he had been, at a time of greatest despair, transformed by the stunning idea that his cancer was his ministry. This revelation determined everything Sal did subsequently in life, even his agreeing to enter the group: he felt it might provide a forum to help others find some transcendent meaning in their illness.

Although Sal entered our group six months too early, when it was still too small to give him the audience he deserved, he found other platforms—primarily high schools, where he addressed troubled teenagers. "You want to corrupt your body with drugs? Want to kill it with booze, with grass, with cocaine?" his voice thundered through the auditorium. "You want to smash your body in autos? Kill it? Throw it off the Golden Gate Bridge? You don't want it? Well, then, *give me your body!* Let me have it. I need it. I'll take it—I want to live!"

It was an extraordinary appeal. I trembled when I heard him speak. The force of his delivery was augmented by the particular power that we always give to the words of the dying. The students listened in silence, sensing, as I did, that he was speaking truly, that he had no time for game playing or pretense or fear of consequences.

Evelyn's arrival in the group a month later provided Sal with another opportunity to work at his ministry. Sixty-two years old, embittered, and gravely ill with leukemia, Evelyn was wheeled into the group with a blood transfusion in process. She was candid about her illness. She knew she was dying: "I can accept that," she said, "it no longer matters. But what *does* matter is my daughter. She is poisoning my final days!" Evelyn reviled her daughter, a clinical psychologist, as "a vindictive, unloving woman." Months earlier they had had a bitter and foolish argument after her daughter, caring for Evelyn's cat, had fed it the wrong food. Since then they had not spoken to each other.

After hearing her out, Sal spoke to her simply and passionately. "Listen to what I have to say, Evelyn. I'm dying too. What does it matter what your cat eats? What does it matter who gives in first? You know you don't have much time left. Let's stop pretending. Your daughter's love is the most important thing in the world to you. Don't die, please don't die, without telling her that! It will poison her life, she'll never recover, and she'll pass on the poison to *her* daughter! Break the cycle! Break the cycle, Evelyn!"

The appeal worked. Although Evelyn died a few days later, the ward nurses told us that, swayed by Sal's words, she had had a tearful reconciliation with her daughter. I was very proud of Sal. It was our group's first triumph!

Two more patients joined, and after several months Paula and I were persuaded that we had learned enough to begin working with larger numbers of patients. Now she began to recruit in earnest. Her contacts with the American Cancer Society soon generated a number of referrals. After we had interviewed and accepted seven new patients, all with breast cancer, we officially opened our group for business.

At our first full-sized group meeting Paula surprised me when she began the session by reading aloud an old Hasidic tale:

A rabbi had a conversation with the Lord about Heaven and Hell. "I will show you Hell," said the Lord and led the rabbi into a room containing a large round table. The people sitting around the table were famished and desperate. In the middle of the table was an enormous pot of stew which smelled so delicious that the rabbi's mouth watered. Each person around the table held a spoon with a very long handle. Although the long spoons just reached the pot, their handles were longer than would-be diners' arms: thus, unable to bring food to their lips, no one could eat. The rabbi saw that their suffering was terrible indeed.

"Now I will show you Heaven," said the Lord, and they went into another room, exactly the same as the first. There was the same large round table, the same pot of stew. The people, as before, were equipped with the same long-handled spoons—but here everyone was well nourished and plump, laughing and talking. The rabbi could not understand. "It is simple, but it requires a certain skill," said the Lord. "In this room, you see, they have learned to feed each other."

Although Paula's independent decision to start the session by reading the parable threw me off balance, I let it pass. That's her way, I thought, knowing that we had not yet worked out our roles and our collaboration in the group. Besides, her judgment was impeccable—it remains to this day the most inspired beginning of a group I have ever witnessed.

What to name the group? Paula suggested the "Bridge Group." Why? Two reasons. First, the group created a bridge from one cancer patient to another. Second, it was a group where we put our cards on the table. Hence, the Bridge Group. A typical Paula touch.

Our "flock," as Paula called it, grew rapidly. New, terror-stricken faces appeared every week or two. Paula took the new members in hand, inviting them out to lunch, teaching, charming, and spiritualizing them. Soon we were so large we had to split into two groups of eight, and I introduced some psychiatric residents as coleaders. All the members resisted the splitting; it threatened the integrity of the family. I suggested a compromise: we would meet as two separate groups for an hour and a quarter and then, in the final fifteen minutes, merge so that the two groups could inform one another of the details of their meetings.

The meetings were powerful and dealt, I believe, with issues that were more painful than any group had ever dared to face before. Meeting after meeting, members came in with new metastases, new tragedies; each time we found a way to offer presence and comfort to each stricken person. Occasionally, if someone were too weak, too close to death to attend, we would hold the group meeting in that member's bedroom.

There was no topic too difficult for the group to discuss, and Paula played an important role in every critical discussion. One meeting, for example, began with a member named Eva speaking of envying a friend who that week had very suddenly and unexpectedly died in her sleep of a coronary. "That's the best way to go," Eva proclaimed. But Paula took issue with Eva and suggested that instant death is a tragic death.

I felt embarrassed for Paula. Why, I wondered to myself, is she compelled to commit herself to such ludicrous positions? Who could disagree with Eva's position that dying in your sleep is a good way to go? With her usual persuasiveness, however, Paula gracefully elaborated on her point of view that sudden death is the worst death. "You need time, much unhurried time," she said, "to prepare others for your death—your husband, friends, and, most of all, your children. You need to attend to life's unfinished business. For surely your projects are important enough not to be discarded casually. They deserve to be completed or resolved. Otherwise, what meaning does your life contain?

"Furthermore," she concluded, "dying is a part of life. To miss it, to sleep through it, is to miss one of life's great adventures."

Eva, herself a formidable presence, was, however, to have the final word: "Say what you want, Paula, I still envy my friend's sudden death. I've always loved surprises."

The group soon became well known in the Stanford community. Students—psychiatric residents, nurses, classes of undergraduates—began observing the meetings through the one-way mirror. Sometimes the pain in the group was too much to bear, and students ran from the observation room in tears. But they always returned. Although psychotherapy groups often permit observation by students, permission is always granted grudgingly. But not this group: on the contrary, they welcomed it. Like Paula, the members were eager for students; they felt that they had much to teach, and that their death sentences had made them wise. They had learned one lesson particularly well: that life cannot be postponed; it must be lived *now*, not suspended until the weekend, until vacation, until the children leave for college, until the diminished years of retirement. More than once I heard the lament, "What a pity it is that I had to wait till now, till my body was riddled with cancer, to learn how to live."

At that time I was consumed with the goal of succeeding in the academic world, and my frenzied schedule of research, grant applications, lecturing, teaching, and writing limited my contact with Paula. Was I afraid of getting too close to her? Perhaps her cosmic perspective, her detachment from quotidian goals, threatened the underpinnings of my dedication to success in the academic marketplace. Of course, I saw her weekly in the group, where I was the titular leader and Paula—what was she?—not a cotherapist but something else—a coordinator, or cofacilitator, or liaison. She oriented new members to the group, made certain they were welcomed, shared her personal experiences, phoned all members during the week, took them out to lunch, and was available to anyone in crisis.

Perhaps "spiritual consultant" is the best way to describe Paula's role. She elevated and deepened the group. Whenever she talked, I listened attentively: Paula always had unexpected insights. She taught the members how to meditate, how to reach deep within themselves, how to find a center of tranquillity, how to contain pain. One day, as a meeting was about to close, she surprised me by taking a candle out of her bag, lighting it, and setting it on the floor. "Let's move closer together," she said, stretching our her hands to the member on either side of her. "Look at the candle and meditate for a few moments in silence."

Before I met Paula, I was so deeply ensconced in the medical tradition that I would not have had charitable thoughts about a therapist who ended group sessions with the members holding hands and staring silently at a candle. Yet Paula's suggestion felt so right to the members, and to me, that we began to end each meeting in that fashion. I came to treasure those closing moments and, if I happened to be sitting next to Paula, would give her hand a warm squeeze before I relinquished it. She generally led the meditation aloud, improvising, always with great dignity. I loved her meditations, and to the end of my life, I will hear her quietly instructing us: "Let go, let go of anger, let go of pain, let go of self-pity. Reach into your center, into your quiet, peaceful depths, and open yourself up to love, to forgiveness, to God." Heady stuff for an uptight, free-thinking, medically trained empiricist!

Sometimes I wondered whether Paula had any needs beyond the need to help others. Though I often asked her what the group could do for her, I never got an answer. Sometimes I wondered about her busy pace—she visited several sick patients every day. What drives her? I asked myself, and why does she present her problems only in the past tense? She offers us only her solutions, never her unsolved problems. But I never wondered too long. After all, Paula did have advanced metastatic cancer and had out-lived even the most optimistic statistics. She was energetic, widely loved, widely loving, an inspiration to everyone forced to live with cancer. What more could one ask?

This was the golden period of my travels with Paula. Perhaps I should have let things remain there. But one day I looked around and observed how large the enterprise was getting—group lead-ers, secretarial help to transcribe summaries of intakes and meet-ings, teachers to meet with student observers. Such size needed capital, I decided, and began searching for research funding to keep the group afloat. Since I did not want to think of myself as being in the death profession, I had never charged any of the patients or even inquired about medical insurance. Nonetheless, I was devoting considerable energy and time to the group, and I had a moral obligation to Stanford University to help cover the salary it was paying me. I also felt that my clinical apprenticeship in leading groups of cancer patients was coming to an end; it was time to *do* something with this enterprise, to research it, to evaluate its effectiveness, to publish our results, to spread the word, to encourage similar programs elsewhere in the country. In short, it was time to promote it and to get promoted.

A propitious opportunity appeared when the National Cancer Institute sent out a call for applications for social-behavioral breast cancer research. I applied successfully for a grant enabling me to evaluate the effectiveness of my therapeutic approach to the terminal breast cancer patient. It was a simple, straightforward project. I felt confident that my treatment approach improved the quality of life of the terminally ill patient and that I had only to develop an evaluation component—the administration of questionnaires before members entered the group and at regular intervals thereafter.

Notice that I now begin to make more use of the first-person pronoun: "*I* decided . . . *I* applied . . . *my* treatment approach." As I look back and sift through the ashes of my relationship with Paula, I suspect that these first-person pronouns foreshadowed the corruption of our love. But as I lived through this period, I was unaware of even the most subtle spoilage. I remember only that Paula filled me with light and that I was her rock, the haven for which she had searched before we two were lucky enough to have found each other.

Of one thing I am certain: it was shortly after the funded research officially began that things started to go wrong. First small hairline cracks, then crevices began to appear in our relationship. Perhaps the first clear sign that something was amiss was Paula's telling me one day that she felt exploited by the research project. I thought this a curious remark because I had tried in every way possible to make her role in the project just what she requested: she interviewed all the new candidates for the groups, all women with metastatic breast cancer, and helped in the construction of the evaluation questionnaires. Furthermore, I had made sure she was well paid—far more than the average research assistant and more than she had requested.

A few weeks later, in a disturbing conversation, she told me that she felt overworked and yearned for more time for herself. I felt sympathetic and tried to offer suggestions for reducing her frenetic pace.

Shortly afterward I submitted to the National Cancer Institute my written report of the first stage of the research. Though I made sure to put Paula's name first among the list of the research associates, I soon heard a rumor that she was dissatisfied about the amount of credit she had received. I made the mistake of paying this rumor little heed: it seemed uncharacteristic of Paula.

A short time later I introduced Dr. Kingsley into one of the groups as a cotherapist—a young female psychologist who, though inexperienced in working with cancer patients, was extraordinarily intelligent, well intentioned, and dedicated. Soon Paula sought me out. "That woman," she scolded, "is the coldest, most ungiving person I've ever encountered. Not in a thousand years will she be able to help any of the patients."

I was astonished—both by her gross misperception of the new cotherapist and by her bitter, condemning tone. Why so harsh, Paula? I thought. Why so uncompassionate, so unchristian?

The research grant stipulated that during the first six months of funding I hold a two-day workshop to consult with a panel of six experts in cancer treatment, research design, and statistical analysis. I invited Paula and four other group members to attend as patient consultants. The workshop was pure window dressing, a flagrant waste of time and money. But such is life in the field of federally sponsored contractual research: one simply learns to accommodate these charades. Paula, however, couldn't accommodate. Calculating the amount of money spent in the two-day meeting (approximately $5,000), she railed at me about the immorality of the workshop: "Think of the help that five thousand dollars could provide for cancer patients!"

Paula, I thought, I do love you, but you can be so muddle-headed. "Can't you see," I said, "that compromise is necessary? There's no way that the five thousand dollars can be used for direct patient care. More important, we'll lose our funding if we don't follow federal guidelines for a consultation workshop. If we can persevere, complete the research, and demonstrate the value of our approach to dying cancer patients, we will benefit more patients, many more, than could be directly helped by the five thousand dollars. Let's not be penny-wise and pound-foolish, Paula. Compromise, please," I pleaded, "this one time."

I could sense her disappointment with me. Shaking her head slowly, she replied, "Compromise once, Irv? No such thing as a single compromise. They breed."

During the workshop the consultants all made the contribution for which they had been recruited (and were well paid). One discussed psychological testing to measure depression, anxiety, modes of coping, locus of control; another talked about health care delivery systems; another about community resources.

Paula threw herself fully into the workshop. I assume she felt that with little time left, one doesn't play a waiting game. She acted the Socratic gadfly to the solemn consultant panel. When, for example, they discussed such objective evaluation indices of maladaptive coping as a patient's not getting out of bed, not dressing, withdrawing, and crying, Paula argued that for her, each of these activities was at times a stage of incubation that eventually ushered in another stage, sometimes a period of growth. She rejected the experts' attempts to convince her that when one uses a large enough sample, aggregate scores, and a control group, such considerations can be easily dealt with statistically in the data analysis.

Then came the moment when the workshop participants were asked to suggest important antecedent variables, that is, factors that might predict a person's psychological adjustment to cancer. Dr. Lee, a cancer specialist, wrote these factors on the blackboard as the participants called them out: marital stability, available environmental resources, personality profile, family history. Raising her hand, Paula suggested, "How about courage? And spiritual depth?"

Deliberately, without speaking, Dr. Lee looked over at her, all the while tossing the chalk into the air and catching it a couple of times. Finally he turned and wrote Paula's suggestions on the board. Although I thought them not unreasonable, I knew—and knew that everyone else knew—that as Dr. Lee watched the tumbling chalk, he was thinking, Somebody, anybody, please get that old lady out of here! Later, at lunch, he referred to Paula contemptuously as an evangelist. Although Dr. Lee was an eminent oncologist whose support and referrals were essential to the project, I risked antagonizing him and defended her staunchly by emphasizing her critical importance in the formation and functioning of the groups. Though I failed to alter his impression of her, I felt proud of myself for standing by her.

That evening Paula phoned me. She was furious. "All of the medical professionals at the workshop are automatons, inhumane automatons. We patients who struggle with cancer twenty-four hours a day—what are we to them? I'll tell you: we are nothing more than 'maladaptive coping strategies.'" I spoke with her for a long time and did all I could to mollify her. I tried to suggest gently that she not stereotype the doctors and urged her to be patient. Affirming my loyalty to the principles with which we had started the group, I concluded, "Remember, Paula, none of this makes any difference because I have my own research plan. I'm not going to be controlled by their mechanistic perspective. Trust me!"

But Paula was not to be mollified, nor, as it turned out, would she trust me. The workshop festered in her mind. For weeks she ruminated about it and finally directly accused me of selling out to the bureaucracy. She submitted a minority report of one to the National Cancer Institute, and it did not lack vigor or rancor.

Finally, one day Paula came into my office and announced that she had decided to leave the group.

"Why?"

"Well, I'm just tired of it."

"Paula, there's more to it than that. What's the real reason?"

"I told you, I'm tired of it." No matter how I probed, she continued to insist on that excuse, though we both knew that the real reason was that I had disappointed her. I used all my cunning (and after all my years of practice, I knew a few ways to get around people), but to no avail. Each of my attempts, including some ill-advised bantering and appeals to our long friendship, was greeted by an icy glare. I had no more rapport with her and had to endure the sorrow of a deceptive discussion.

"I'm just working too hard. It's too much for me," she said.

"Isn't that what I've been saying for months, Paula? Cut down all your visits and phone calls to the dozens of patients on your roll. Simply come to the group. The group needs you. And I need you. Surely ninety minutes a week isn't too much."

"No, I can't do things piecemeal. I need a clean break. Besides, the group isn't where I am anymore. It's too superficial. I need to go deeper—to work with symbols, dreams, and archetypes."

"I agree, Paula." By this time I was very sobered. "It's what I want too, and we're just now breaking that ground in the group."

"No, I'm too tired, too drained. Each new patient forces me to relive my own time of crisis, my own Calvary. No, I've decided: next week will be my last meeting."

And so it was. Paula never returned to the group. I asked her to call me at any time if she wanted to talk. She replied that it was also possible for me to call her. Although she wasn't being malicious, her comment shifted the frame and stung me sharply. She never called me again. I phoned her a few times and twice took her to lunch. The first lunch (which was so painful that it was many months before I called her for another) began ominously. Finding the restaurant of our choice crowded, we went across the street to Trotter's, a huge, cavernous structure, utterly without grace, that had had many previous lives: an Oldsmobile dealership, a natural-foods grocery store, a dance parlor. Now it was a restaurant featuring a menu of "dance" sandwiches—the Waltz, the Twist, the Charleston.

No, it was not right; I felt it wasn't right when I heard myself order a Hula sandwich and knew it wasn't when Paula opened her purse, extracted a rock about the size of a small grapefruit, and placed it on the table between us.

"My anger rock," she said. From this point on, my memory is uncharacteristically spotty. Fortunately, I took some notes after our lunch—my conversations with Paula being too important to me to be entrusted to memory.

"Anger rock?" I repeated blankly, transfixed by the lichen-covered boulder sitting on the table between us.

"I've been buffeted about so much, Irv, that I've been swallowed by anger. Now I've learned to put anger away. Into this rock. I had to bring it today. I wanted it here when I met you."

"Why are you angry with me, Paula?"

"I'm no longer angry. There's too little time left to be angry. But I've been hurt; I've been deserted when I needed help most of all."

"I've never deserted you, Paula," I said, but she didn't acknowledge my comment and went on.

"After the workshop I was shattered. Looking at Dr. Lee standing there tossing that chalk in the air, ignoring me, ignoring the human concerns of all patients, I felt the whole world give way under me. Patients are human. We struggle. Sometimes we struggle with great courage against cancer. Often we talk about winning or losing our fight—it *is* a fight. Sometimes we're plunged into despair, sometimes into sheer physical exhaustion, and sometimes we rise above our cancer. We are *not* 'coping strategies.' We are much, much more than that."

"But Paula, that was Dr. Lee—that's not me. That's not the way I felt. I defended you when I spoke to him later; I've told you that. After all our work together, can you believe that I consider you nothing more than a coping strategy? I hate that language and that perspective as much as you do!"

"You know, I'm really not going to return to the group."

"That's not the point, Paula." And it wasn't. It was no longer of urgent concern to me whether she returned to the group. Though she had been a great force there, I had come to realize that she had been almost too powerful and too inspiring: her leaving had made it possible for several other patients to grow and to learn to inspire themselves. "What's most important to me is that you trust me and care for me."

"After the workshop, Irv, I cried for twenty-four hours. I called you. You did not call back that day. Later, when you did, you offered me no comfort. I went to church to pray and had a three-hour talk with Father Elson. *He* listened to me. He always listens to me. I think he saved me."

Damn that priest! I strained to recollect that day three months ago. I vaguely remembered speaking to her on the phone but not her asking for help. I had been certain she was phoning to gripe some more about the workshop, which I'd already discussed with her several times. Too many times. Why couldn't she get it? How often did I have to tell her that the whole damn thing was meaningless, that *I* wasn't Dr. Lee, that *I* hadn't tossed the chalk, that I had defended her against him later, that I was going to continue the group in the same way, that nothing would change except that the group members would be asked to fill out a few questionnaires every three months? Yes, Paula had called me that day, but not then, not ever, had she asked me for help.

"Paula, if you had told me you wanted help for yourself, do you think I'd have refused you?"

"I cried for twenty-four hours."

"But I'm not a mind reader. You told me you wanted to talk about the research and your minority report."

"I cried for twenty-four hours."

And so it went, the two of us speaking past each other. I did my best to reach her. I told her I needed her—for myself, not for the group. Indeed, I did need her. There were issues in my life troubling me at the time, and I yearned for her inspiration and

39

her soothing presence. Once, several months before, I had called Paula one evening, ostensibly to discuss our plans for the group but in reality because my wife was out of town and I was feeling lonely and anxious. After our phone conversation, which went on for over an hour, I felt much better—though slightly guilty for having gotten therapy on the sly.

I thought now about that long, healing phone conversation with Paula. Why hadn't I been more honest? Why hadn't I simply said, "Look here, Paula, can I talk to you tonight? Can you help me—I'm feeling anxious, lonely, driven? I'm having trouble sleeping." No, no, out of the question! I preferred to take my nourishment secretly.

How hypocritical, therefore, for me to have demanded that Paula ask help from me openly. So she'd covertly asked for help, using a cover story about the workshop? So what! I should have tried to comfort her without insisting she genuflect.

As I contemplated Paula's anger rock, I realized how little chance there was of salvaging our relationship. Certainly this was no time for subtlety, and I opened up to her as never before. "I need you," I said, reminding her, as I often had before, that therapists too have needs. "And perhaps," I went on, "I haven't been sensitive enough to your distress. Yet I'm not a mind reader, and haven't you for years refused all my offers to help you?" What I wanted to say was, "Give me another chance. Even if this one time I didn't pick up on your distress, Paula, don't leave forever." But I had come close enough to begging that day. Paula was adamant, and we parted without touching.

I put Paula out of my mind for many months until Dr. Kingsley, the young psychologist to whom she had taken such an irrational dislike, told me of a disagreeable encounter she had had with Paula. Paula had returned to the group Dr. Kingsley was leading (we now had several groups in the project) and—sounding like "Mrs. Cancer," as the psychologist put it—had monopolized the session with a speech. I immediately phoned Paula and invited her to lunch again.

I was surprised at how pleased Paula seemed by my invitation, but as soon as we met—this time at the Stanford Faculty Club, which serves no Hula sandwiches—her agenda became clear. She could talk of nothing but Dr. Kingsley. According to Paula, Dr. Kingsley's cotherapist had invited her to address their group, but as soon as she had begun speaking, Dr. Kingsley had accused her of taking too much time. "You've got to reprimand her," Paula said urgently. "You know teachers can and should be held responsible for the unprofessional behavior of their students." But Dr. Kingsley was my colleague, not my student, and I had known her for years. Not only was her husband a close friend but she and I had led many groups together: knowing her to be a superb therapist, I was certain that Paula's account of her behavior was greatly distorted.

Slowly, far too slowly, it dawned on me that Paula was jealous: jealous of the attention and affection I bestowed on Dr. Kingsley; jealous of my alliance with her and with all the members of the research staff. Naturally Paula had resisted the consultation workshop; naturally she had discouraged any collaboration with other researchers. She would resist any change. All she wanted was to revert to the time when she and I had been alone with our little flock.

What could I do? Her insistence that I choose between her and Dr. Kingsley placed me in an impossible dilemma. "I care for both you *and* Dr. Kingsley, Paula. How can I maintain my own integrity and my collegiality and friendship with Dr. Kingsley without your feeling, once again, abandoned by me?" Though I reached out to her in every way possible, the distance between us grew greater. I could find no proper words; there seemed to be no safe topics. I no longer had the right to ask her personal questions, nor did she evince any interest in my life.

All through lunch she told me stories about terrible mistreatment by her doctors: "They ignore my questions; their medications do more harm than good." She also warned me about a psychologist who was talking to some of the cancer patients who had been in our group: "He's stealing our findings to use in his own book. You'd better protect yourself, Irv."

Paula was obviously deeply troubled, and I was alarmed and saddened by her paranoia. I think my distress must have showed because as I moved to leave, she asked me to stay a few minutes more.

"I have a story for you, Irv. Sit back and let me tell you about the coyote and the locust."

She knew I loved stories. Especially her stories. I listened expectantly.

There was once a coyote who felt overwhelmed by the pressures in his life. All he could see were too many hungry cubs, too many hunters, too many traps. So one day he ran off to be alone. Suddenly he heard the notes of a sweet melody, a melody of well-being and great peacefulness. Following the song to a clearing in the forest, he came upon a large locust sunning himself on a hollow log and singing.

"Teach me your song," the coyote asked the locust. No response. Again he demanded to be taught the song. But the locust remained silent. Finally, when the coyote threatened to gobble him up, the locust acquiesced and sang the sweet song over and over until the coyote had memorized it. Humming his new song, the coyote started back to his family. Suddenly a flock of wild geese flew up and distracted him. When he had recovered his wits he opened his mouth to sing again but found he had forgotten the song.

So he turned back to the sunny clearing in the forest. But by this time the locust had molted, left his empty skin sunning on the same hollow log, and flown onto a tree branch. The coyote wasted no time making sure he had the song permanently inside him. In one gulp he swallowed the locust skin, thinking that the locust was still within. Starting home, again he discovered he did not know the song. He realized he could not learn it from ingesting the locust. He would have to let the locust out and force it to teach him. Taking a knife, he cut into his abdomen to release the locust. He cut so deep that he died.

"And so, Irv," Paula said, giving me her lovely, beatific smile, reaching out for my hand and then whispering into my ear, "you've got to find your own song to sing."

I was very moved: her smile, her mystery, her stretch for wisdom—that was the Paula I loved so much. I liked the parable. It was vintage Paula; it felt like old times. I took the meaning at face value—that I should sing my own song—and pushed away the story's darker, more disturbing implications about my relationship with her. I have refused even to this day to examine it too deeply.

And so we each sang our songs separately. My career progressed: I conducted research, wrote many books, received the academic rewards and promotions I so coveted. Ten years went by. The breast cancer project that Paula had helped launch had long been completed and the findings from it published. We had offered group therapy to fifty women with metastatic breast cancer and found that, compared with thirty-six control patients, the group had vastly improved the quality of the patients' remaining lives. (Years later, in a follow-up study published in *Lancet*, my colleague Dr. David Spiegel, whom I had asked many years before to become the project's principal investigator, ultimately demonstrated that the group had significantly lengthened the lives of the members.) But the group was now history; all of the thirty women in the original Bridge Group and the eighty-six women in the metastatic breast cancer study had died.

All but one. One day in the hospital corridor, a young woman with red hair and a flushed face hailed me and said, "I bear greetings from Paula West."

Paula! Could it be? Paula still alive? And I hadn't even known. I shuddered to think that I had become a person who was unaware whether a spirit like hers still dwelled on earth.

"Paula? How is she?" I stammered. "How do you know her?"

"Two years ago, when I was diagnosed as having lupus, Paula came to visit me and introduced me into her lupus self-help group.

Ever since she's been taking care of me—indeed, the whole lupus community."

"I'm sorry to hear about your illness. But Paula? Lupus? I hadn't heard." What hypocrisy, I thought. How *could* I have heard? Had I even once called her?

"She says it was caused by the medicine she was given for cancer."

"Is she very sick?"

"You never know with Paula. Certainly not too sick to start a lupus support group, to invite all the new lupus patients to lunch, to visit us when we're too ill to leave the house, to arrange a series of medical speakers to keep us apprised of new research in lupus. Also not too sick to launch a medical-ethics-board investigation of her cancer doctors."

Organizing, educating, nursing, agitating, starting up lupus self-help groups, castigating her doctors—sounded like Paula, all right.

I thanked the young woman and later that day dialed Paula's number, which I still knew by heart, even though it had been a decade since I had last called. As I waited for her to answer, I thought of some recent geriatric research that showed a positive correlation between personality style and longevity: cantankerous patients who are paranoid, vigilant, and assertive tend to live longer. Better a feisty, irritating, living Paula, I thought, than a placid dead one!

She seemed pleased by my call and invited me to lunch at her home; the lupus had, she said, made her too sun sensitive to venture out to restaurants in the daytime. I accepted gladly. The day of our lunch I found Paula in her front garden. Wrapped in linen from head to toe and wearing an enormous broad-brimmed beach hat, she was weeding a beautiful patch of tall, fragrant Spanish lavender. "This disease is probably going to kill me, but I'm not going to let it keep me out of my garden," Paula said, clasping my arm and escorting me inside. She led me to a dark purple velvet sofa and, sitting down next to me, immediately began on a serious note. "It's been ages since I've seen you, Irv, but I think of you often. You're much in my prayers."

"I like your thinking of me, Paula. But as for your prayers, you know my shortcomings there."

"Yes, yes, I realize that in this one area you have yet to open your mind. It reminds me," she said, smiling, "that my job with you isn't yet complete. Do you remember the last time we talked about God? It's years ago, but I remember your telling me that my feeling of the holy was not much different from gas pains in the night!"

"Out of context that sounds harsh, even to me. But I didn't mean to be insulting. I only meant that a feeling is merely a feeling. A subjective state can never substantiate an objective truth. A wish, a fear, a sense of awe, of the tremendum, doesn't mean that—"

"Yes, yes," Paula interrupted me with a smile, "I know your hard-line materialist litany. I've heard it many times, and I've always been struck by the amount of passion, of devoutness, of faith you put into it. I remember that in our last conversation you told me you had never had a close friend, never known anyone whose mind you respected, who was a devout believer."

I nodded.

"Well, there's something I should have said to you then: you forgot one friend who is a believer—me! How I wish I could introduce you to the holy! How strange that you phoned now because I've been thinking much about you the last two weeks. I've just returned from a two-week church retreat in the Sierras, and I so much wish I could have taken you with me. Sit back and let me tell you about it.

"One morning we were asked to meditate upon someone who had died, some beloved person from whom we really hadn't parted. I chose to think of my brother, whom I had loved very much but who died at seventeen when I was still a child. We were asked to write a letter of farewell telling that person all the important things we had never said. Next we searched in the forest for an object symbolizing that person to us. Finally we were to bury the object together with the letter. I chose a small granite boulder and buried it in the shade of a juniper. My brother was like a rock—solid, steadfast. If he had lived, he would have supported me. He would never have passed me by."

Paula looked into my eyes as she said this, and I started to lodge a protest. But she put her finger on my lips and continued.

"That night at midnight the monastery bells chimed for the person each of us had lost. There were twenty-four of us on the retreat, and the bells rang twenty-four times. Sitting in my room, hearing the first bell, I experienced, *really* experienced, my brother's death, and a wave of indescribable sadness descended upon me as I thought of all the experiences he and I together had had, and also those we never had. Then a strange thing happened: as the bells continued to toll, each chime brought to mind a member of our Bridge Group who had died. When the chimes stopped, I had remembered twenty-one. And all during the tolling I cried. I cried so hard that one of the nuns heard me, came into my room, put her arms around me, and held me.

"Irv, do you remember them? Do you remember Linda and Bunny—"

"And Eva and Lily." I felt my own tears come as I joined her in recalling the faces and the stories and the pain of our first group members.

"And Madeline and Gabby."

"And Judy and Joan."

"And Evelyn and Robin."

"And Sal and Rob."

Holding one another and rocking gently, Paula and I continued our duet, our dirge, until we had inurned the names of twenty-one of our little family.

"This is a holy moment, Irv," she said, breaking away and looking into my eyes. "Can't you feel the presence of their spirits?"

"I remember them so clearly, and I feel *your* presence, Paula. That's holy enough for me."

"Irv, I know you well. Mark my words—the day will come when you realize how religious you really are. But it's unfair trying to convert you while you're hungry. I'll get lunch."

"Wait one moment, Paula. A few minutes ago, when you said your brother was one who would never have passed you by, was that statement meant for me?"

"Once," said Paula, looking at me with her luminous eyes, "at a time when I needed you badly, you did desert me. But that was then. It's gone. You've come back now."

I was certain I knew the *then* she meant—the time when Dr. Lee had tossed that chalk into the air. How much time had the flight of that chalk taken? One second? Two? But those brief moments were frozen in her memory. I'd need an ice pick to hack them out. I was not so foolish as to try. Instead, I returned to her brother.

"Your saying that your brother was like a rock makes me think of another rock, the anger rock you once placed on the table between us. Do you know that you never, until this day, mentioned your brother to me? But his death helps me understand some things about the two of us. Maybe we've always been a threesome—you, me, and your brother? I wonder if his death is the reason you've chosen to be your own rock—the reason you would never let *me* be your rock? Perhaps his death convinced you that other men would prove frail and unreliable?"

I stopped and waited. How would she respond? In all the years I had known Paula, this was the first time I had offered her an interpretation about herself. But she said nothing. I continued, "I think I'm right, and I think it's good that you went on this retreat, good that you tried to say good-bye to him. Maybe things can be different between you and me now."

More silence. Then, with an enigmatic smile, she stood up, saying, "Now it's time to feed you," and walked into the kitchen.

Was that statement—"Now it's time to feed you"—an acknowledgment that I had just fed her? Damn, it was hard to give her anything!

A moment later, when we sat down to eat, she looked directly at me and said, "Irv, I'm in trouble. Will you be my rock now?"

"Of course," I said, glad to recognize her plea as the answer to my question. "Lean on me. What kind of trouble?" But my pleasure in being allowed at last to help turned quickly to dismay as she began to explain her trouble.

"I've been so outspoken about the doctors that I think I've been medically blacklisted. I can't get good medical care any longer. All the doctors of the Larchwood Clinic are in on it. Yet I can't switch clinics—my insurance forces me to get my treatment there. And with my medical condition, what other insurance company would touch me? I'm convinced they've treated me unethically—their treatment is responsible for my lupus. There's been definite malpractice! They're afraid of me! They write some of my medical notes in red ink so they can quickly identify and remove them from my chart in case of a subpoena. They're using me as a guinea pig. They deliberately withheld steroids until it was too late. Then they abused the dosage.

"I honestly think they want me out of the way," Paula continued. "I spent this entire week composing a letter exposing them to the medical board. Yet I haven't mailed it—mainly because I began to worry about what will happen to the doctors and to their families if they lose their licenses. On the other hand, how can I allow them to continue injuring patients? I cannot compromise. I remember once telling you that a compromise cannot exist alone: it breeds, and before long you have lost what you most dearly believe. And silence here, now, is a compromise! I've been praying for guidance."

My dismay rose. Maybe there was some small crystal of truth in Paula's charges. Maybe some of her doctors were, like Dr. Lee many years before, so put off by her manner as to dismiss her. But charts written in red ink, guinea-pig trials, withholding necessary medication? These were absurd accusations, and I was certain they were signs of paranoia. I knew some of these doctors and believed in their integrity. Once again she had placed me in the position of having to choose between *her* strong beliefs and *my* strong beliefs. More than anything, I did not want her to believe I was deserting her. Yet how could I stay with her?

I felt trapped. Finally, after all these years, Paula was making a direct appeal to me. I could see only one way to respond: to consider her a highly disturbed individual and treat her—"treat" in the dark, false sense of the word, in the sense of "handling." That had been what I had always wanted to avoid with Paula—with anyone, for that matter—because "handling" someone is to relate to him or her as an object and, thus, is the antithesis of *being with* that person.

So I empathized with her dilemma. I listened, probed gently, and kept my opinions to myself. Finally I suggested that she write a softer letter to the medical board: "Honest but softer," I said. "Then the doctors will get only a reprimand rather than a license forfeiture." All this, of course, was in bad faith. No medical board in the world was going to take her letter seriously. No one was going to believe that all the clinic physicians were conspiring against her. There was no possibility of either reprimand or revocation of license.

She lapsed into thought, weighing my advice. I believe she felt my caring for her, and I hoped she would not know that I was being false. Finally she nodded. "You've given me good, sound counsel, Irv. It's just what I needed." I felt painfully the irony that it was only now, when I had acted in bad faith, that she considered me helpful and trustworthy.

Despite her sensitivity to the sun, Paula insisted on walking with me to my car. She put on her sun hat, wrapped herself in her veil and linens, and, as I started the ignition, leaned into the car window to give me a last hug. As I drove away I looked back through the rearview mirror. Silhouetted against the sun, her hat and linen wrapping gleaming with light, Paula was incandescent. A breeze came up. Her clothes fluttered. She seemed a leaf, trembling, twisting on its stem, readying itself for the fall.

In the ten years before this visit, I had dedicated myself to my writing. I turned out book after book—a productivity due to a simple strategy: I put the writing first and let nothing and no one interfere with it. Guarding my time as fiercely as a mother bear guards her cubs, I eliminated all but absolutely essential activities.

Even Paula fell into the nonessential category, and I did not take the time to call her again.

Several months later my mother died, and while I was flying to her funeral, Paula slipped into my mind. I thought of her farewell letter to her dead brother—the letter containing all the things she had never said to him. And I thought of what I had never said to my mother. Almost everything! My mother and I, though loving one another, had never spoken directly, heart to heart, as two people reaching out with clean hands and clear minds. We had always "treated" each other, spoken past each other, each of us fearing, controlling, deceiving the other. I'm certain that's why I had always wanted to speak honestly and directly to Paula. And why I hated being forced to "treat" her falsely.

The night after the funeral, I had a powerful dream.

My mother and many of her friends and relatives, all dead, are seated very quietly on a flight of stairs. I hear my mother's voice calling—shrieking—my name. I am particularly aware of Aunt Minny, sitting on the top stair, who is very still. Then she begins to move, slowly at first, then more and more quickly until she is vibrating faster than a bumblebee. At that point everyone on the stairs, all the big people of my childhood, all dead, begin to vibrate. My Uncle Abe reaches out to pinch my cheek, clucking, "Darling Sonny," as he used to do. Then others reach out for my cheeks. At first affectionate, the pinching grows fierce and painful. I awake in terror, cheeks throbbing, at three A.M.

The dream depicted a duel with death. First, I am called by my dead mother and see all the dead of my family sitting in eerie stillness on the stairs. Then I try to negate deathly quiescence by infusing the dead with the movement of life. I especially note my Aunt Minny, who had died the year before after a cataclysmic stroke had left her completely paralyzed for several months, unable to move a muscle in her body aside from her eyes. In the dream Minny begins to move but quickly veers out of control and into frenzy. Next I try to alleviate my dread of the dead by imagining them affectionately pinching my cheeks. But that dread breaks through once again, the pinching grows fierce and malignant, and I am overwhelmed with death anxiety.

The image of my aunt vibrating like a bumblebee haunted me for days. I couldn't shake it loose. Perhaps, I thought, it is a message telling me that my own frenzied life pace is but a clumsy attempt to quell death anxiety. Is the dream not telling me to slow down and attend to the things I really value?

The idea of *value* brought Paula back to my mind. Why hadn't I called her? She was one who had faced death and stared it down. I remembered the way she had guided the meditation at the end of our meetings: her eyes fixed on the candle flame, her sonorous voice leading all of us into deeper, quieter regions. Had I ever told her how much those moments meant to me? So many things I had never said to her. I would say them now. On the flight home from my mother's funeral, I resolved to renew my friendship with her.

But I never did. Too much to do: wife, children, patients, students, writing. I wrote my page a day and ignored all else—friends, mail, phone calls, invitations to lecture. Everything, all the other parts of my life, would wait until the book was finished. And Paula too would have to wait.

Paula, of course, did not wait. A few months later I received a note from her son—the boy I had envied for having Paula as a mother, the son to whom years before she had so wonderfully written of her approaching death. He wrote simply, "My mother died, and I am certain she would have wanted me to let you know."

3

Southern Comfort

I put in my time. Five years. For five years I led a daily therapy group on a psychiatric ward. At ten every morning I left my cozy book-lined office in the Stanford University Medical School, bicycled over to the hospital, entered the ward, winced at my first breath of sticky, Lysol-laced air, and poured my coffee from the staff caffeinated urn (no caffeine for the patients, nor tobacco, alcohol, or sex—all part of an effort, I suppose, to discourage them from settling too comfortably and for too long into the hospital). Then I arranged the chairs into a circle in the multipurpose room, unpocketed my baton, and for eighty minutes conducted a group therapy meeting.

Though the ward had twenty beds, my meetings were small, sometimes only four or five patients. I was picky about my clientele and opened my doors only to higher-functioning patients. The ticket of admission? *Orientation times three:* time, place, and person. My group members had only to know *when* it was and *who* and *where* they were. While I didn't object to members being psychotic (as long as they were quiet about it and did not interfere with the work of others), I did insist that each member be able to talk, pay attention for eighty minutes, and acknowledge the need for help.

Every prestigious club has entrance criteria. Perhaps my requirements for membership made my therapy group—the "agenda group," as it was called for reasons I shall explain later—more desirable. Those without the ticket of admission—the more disturbed, regressed patients? Off with them to "communication group," the other group on the ward, which held shorter, more structured, less demanding meetings. And, of course, there were always those in social exile, those who were too intellectually impaired, distracted, belligerent, or manic to be accommodated in any group at all. Often some agitated patients in social exile would be permitted to attend the communication group after medication had settled them down, perhaps in a day or two.

"Permitted to attend": that phrase would crack a smile in the face of even the most withdrawn patient. No! Let me be honest. Never in hospital history has there been a sighting of disturbed patients pounding on the doors of the group therapy room, demanding admission. A far more familiar scene is the pregroup roundup, the posse of attendants and white-cloaked nurses galloping through the ward, rousting members out of their hiding places in closets, johns, and showers, and herding them into the group room.

The agenda group had a distinct reputation: it was tough and challenging and, worst of all, had no corners—no place to hide. There was never any gate-crashing on the ward. An upper-level patient would not be caught dead in the communication group. Occasionally some confused lower-functioning patient would stumble into the agenda group meeting, but once he learned where he was fear would glaze his eyes, and no one would have to escort him out. Although it was technically possible to graduate from the lower- to the upper-level group, few patients ever stayed in the hospital long enough for that to happen. Thus was the ward covertly stratified: everyone knew his or her place. But no one ever talked about it.

Before I began to lead groups in the hospital, I used to think outpatient groups were challenging. It is not easy to lead a group of seven or eight needy outpatients with major problems in relating to others, and at the end of a meeting I would feel tired, often depleted, and marvel at the therapists who had the stamina to lead another group meeting immediately afterward. Yet once I began working with groups of hospitalized patients, I looked back with much nostalgia to those good old outpatient group therapy days.

Imagine an outpatient group—a cohesive meeting of cooperative, highly motivated patients; a quiet, cozy room; no nurses knocking on the door to yank patients out for some lab procedure or medical appointment; no suicidal members with bandaged wrists; no one refusing to talk; no one zonked on medication falling asleep and snoring in the group; and, most important of all, the same patients and the same cotherapist there for each session, week after week, month after month. What luxury! A therapist's nirvana. In contrast, the landscape of my inpatient groups was nightmarish—the continual rapid turnover of members; the frequent psychotic outbursts; the conning, manipulative members; the patients burned out by twenty years of depression or schizophrenia who were never going to get better; the tangible level of despair in the room.

But the real killer, the ball-breaker in this work, was the hospital and insurance industry bureaucracy. Every day surveillance teams of HMO agents would swoop through the wards, nose through hospital charts, and order the discharge of one or another confused, despairing patient who had functioned relatively well the previous day and whose chart had no MD-signed note stating explicitly that he or she was suicidal or dangerous.

Was there really a time, not so long ago, when the care of the patient was paramount? When physicians admitted the sick and kept them in the hospital until they got well? Was all that only a dream? I no longer talk much about it, no longer risk my students' patronizing smiles by prattling on about that golden era when the administrator's job was to help the doctor help the patient.

The bureaucratic paradoxes were maddening. Consider the case of John, middle-aged, paranoid, and mildly retarded. Having once been attacked in a shelter for the homeless, he thereafter avoided state-sponsored shelters and slept outside. John knew the magic hospital-opening words, and often on cold, wet nights, usually around midnight, he would scratch his wrists in front of an emergency room and threaten deeper wounds unless the state found him a safe, private sleeping space. But no agency had the authority to provide twenty dollars for a room, and since the emergency room physician could not be certain—that is, medically and legally certain—that John would not make a serious suicide attempt if he were forced to sleep in the shelter, he spent many nights a year sleeping soundly in a $700-a-day hospital room, courtesy of an inept and inhumane medical insurance system.

The contemporary practice of brief psychiatric hospitalization works only if there is an adequate posthospital outpatient program. Nonetheless, in 1972 Governor Ronald Reagan with one bold, brilliant stroke abolished mental illness in California by not only closing the large state psychiatric hospitals but also eradicating most of the public aftercare programs. As a result hospital staffs were forced, day after day, to go through the charade of treating patients and discharging them back into the same noxious setting that had necessitated their hospitalization. It was like suturing up wounded soldiers and sending them back into the fray. Imagine breaking your ass taking care of patients—initial workup interviews, daily rounds, presentations to the attending psychiatrists, staff planning sessions, medical student workups, writing orders in the hospital charts, daily therapy sessions—knowing all the while that in a couple of days there would be no option but to return them to the same malignant environment that had disgorged them. Back to violent alcoholic families. Back to angry spouses who had long ago run out of love and patience. Back to rag-filled grocery carts. Back to sleeping in moldering cars. Back to the community of cocaine-crazed friends and pitiless dealers awaiting them outside the hospital gates.

Question: How do we healers maintain sanity? Answer: Learn to cultivate hypocrisy.

So that was how I put in my time. First I learned to muffle my caring—the very beacon that had led me to this calling. Next I mastered the canons of professional survival: avoid involvement—don't let patients matter too much. Remember they'll be gone tomorrow. Don't concern yourself with their postdischarge plans. Remember that small is beautiful—settle for small goals—don't attempt too much—don't set yourself up for failure. If therapy group patients learn simply that talking helps, that being closer to others feels good, that they may be of use to others—that's plenty.

Gradually, after several frustrating months of leading groups with new arrivals and discharges every day, I got the hang of it and developed a method of getting the most out of these fragmented group meetings. My most radical step was to change my time frame.

Question: What is the life span of a therapy group on a hospital's psychiatric ward? Answer: One session.

Outpatient groups last for many months, even years; certain problems require time to emerge, to be identified, and to be altered. In long-term therapy there is time to "work through"—to circle problems and to engage them again and again (hence, the waggish term *cyclotherapy*). But in hospital therapy groups there is no stability, no returning to any theme, because the cast of characters changes so rapidly. In my five years on the ward I rarely had the same complement of members for two consecutive meetings, never for three! And there were many, so many, patients I saw only once, who attended only a single session and were discharged the following day. So I became a John Stuart Mill utilitarian group therapist and, in my one-session groups, strove only to offer the greatest good to the greatest number.

Perhaps it was by turning the hospital therapy group into an art form that I was able to remain committed to a task rendered ineffectual by forces beyond my control. I believed that I fashioned wonderful group meetings. Beautiful, artistic meetings. Having discovered early in life that I could not sing, dance, draw, or play an instrument, I had resigned myself to never becoming an artist. But I had a change of mind when I began to sculpt group meetings. Perhaps I had talent after all; perhaps it was just a matter of finding my métier. Patients liked the meetings; the time passed quickly; we experienced tender, exciting moments. I taught others what I had learned. Student observers were impressed. I gave lectures. I wrote a book about my inpatient groups.

And then, as the years passed, I grew bored. The sessions felt repetitious. There was only so much one could do in a single session. It was like being permanently sentenced to the first few minutes of a potentially rich conversation. I yearned for more. I wanted to go deeper, to matter more in the lives of my patients.

So, many years ago, I stopped leading inpatient groups and concentrated on other forms of therapy. But every three months, when new residents came on service, I would bicycle over from my office in the medical school to the inpatient ward for a week at a stretch to teach them to lead inpatient therapy groups.

That was why I had come today. But my heart wasn't in it. I felt heavy. I was still licking my wounds. My mother had died just three weeks before, and her death profoundly influenced what was about to transpire in my therapy group meeting.

Entering the group room, I looked around and immediately spotted the eager young faces of the three new psychiatry residents. As always, I felt a wave of affection toward my students and wanted nothing so much as to give them something—a good demonstration, the type of dedicated teaching and sustenance I had been given when I was their age. But as I surveyed the meeting room, my spirits dropped. It was not simply that the clutter of medical paraphernalia—intravenous stands, indwelling catheters, cardiac monitors, wheelchairs—reminded me that this particular ward specialized in psychiatric patients who had a severe medical illness and hence were likely to be particularly resistant to talking therapy. No, it was the sight of the patients themselves.

There were five in the room, sitting in a row. The head nurse had briefly described their conditions to me on the phone. First there was Martin, an elderly man in a wheelchair with a severe muscle-wasting disease. He was belted into his chair and draped to his waist with a sheet that permitted only a glimpse of his lower legs—fleshless twigs covered by dark, leathery skin. One of his forearms was heavily bandaged and supported by an external frame: no doubt he had slashed his wrist. (I learned later that his son, exhausted and bitter from having nursed him for thirteen years, had greeted his suicide attempt with, "So you botched that too.")

Next to Martin was Dorothy, a woman who had been paraplegic for a year since trying to end her life by leaping from a third-story window. She was in such a depressive stupor that she could barely lift her head.

Then there were Rosa and Carol, two anorexic young women who, both hooked up to IVs, were being fed intravenously because their blood chemistry was unbalanced from self-purging and their weight was dangerously low. Carol's appearance was particularly unsettling: she had exquisite, nearly perfect facial features but almost no covering flesh. Looking at her, sometimes I saw the face of an astonishingly beautiful child, sometimes a grinning skull.

Last there was Magnolia, an unkempt, obese seventy-year-old black woman whose legs were paralyzed and whose paralysis was a medical mystery. Her thick gold-rimmed spectacles had been mended with a small piece of adhesive tape, and a tiny, delicate lace cap was pinned to her hair. I was struck, when she introduced herself, by the way she held my gaze with her creamy brown eyes and by the dignity in her soft Southern drawl. "Ah'm very pleased to meet you, Doctah," she said. "Ah heah good things about you." The nurses had told me that Magnolia, then sitting quietly and patiently in her wheelchair, was often agitated and tore at imaginary insects crawling on her skin.

My first step was to move the members into a circle and to ask the three residents to sit behind the patients, out of their immediate line of vision. I started the meeting in my usual manner by attempting to orient the members to group therapy. I introduced myself, suggested we use first names, and informed them that I would be there for the next four days. "After that, the two residents"—whom I named and pointed out—"will lead the group. The group's purpose," I went on, "is to help each of you learn more about your relationships with others." As I glanced at the human devastation before me— Martin's withered limbs, Carol's death-mask grin, the intravenous bottles feeding Rosa and Carol the vital nutrients they refused to take by mouth, Dorothy's urine bottle holding the urine siphoned from her paralyzed bladder, Magnolia's paralyzed legs— my words seemed puny and foolish. These people needed so much, and "help with relationships" seemed so pitifully little. But what was the point of pretending that groups could do more than they could? Remember your mantra, I kept reminding myself: *small is beautiful. Small is beautiful*—small goals, small successes.

I referred to my inpatient group as the "agenda group" because I always began a meeting by asking each member to formulate an agenda—to identify some aspect of themselves that they wished to change. The group worked better if its members' agendas pertained to relationship skills—especially to something that could be worked on in the here-and-now of the group. Patients who were hospitalized for major life problems were always puzzled by the focus on relationships and failed to see the relevance of the agenda task. I always answered, "I know that troubled relationships may not have been the reason for your hospitalization, but I've found over the years that everyone who has encountered significant psychological distress can profit by improving their mode of relating to others. The important point is that we can get the most out of this meeting by focusing on relationships because *that's what groups do best*. That's the real strength of group therapy."

Formulating a suitable agenda was difficult, and even after attending a few sessions, most group members rarely got the hang of it. But I told them not to sweat it: "My job is to help you." Still, the process generally consumed up to 50 percent of the meeting time. After that I would devote the rest of the time to addressing as many agendas as possible. The demarcation between formulating and addressing an agenda is not always sharp. For some patients, forming an agenda *was* the therapy. To learn simply to identify a problem and to ask for help was therapy enough for many in our brief time together.

Rosa and Carol, the anorexic patients, began. Carol claimed that she had no problems and didn't want to improve her relationships. "On the contrary," she said emphatically, "what I want is *less* contact with others." Only when I commented that I had never known anyone who didn't wish to change *something* about herself did she tentatively offer that she was too often cowed by the anger of others, especially her parents, who tried to force her to eat. Accordingly, she posited, with little conviction, an agenda: "I'll try to be assertive here in the meeting."

Rosa too had no wish to improve her relationships; she too wanted to stay apart. She didn't trust anyone: "People always misunderstand me and try to change me." "Would it be helpful," I inquired, trying to add a here-and-now dimension to the agenda, "for you to be understood in *this* group, *today*?" "It might," she said but warned me that it was hard for her to talk much in groups: "I've always felt that others are better, more important than me."

Dorothy, spittle dripping from her mouth, head deeply bowed to avoid any eye contact, spoke in a despairing whisper and gave me nothing. She said she was too depressed to participate in the group and that the nurses had told her it would be enough for her simply to listen. Nothing there to work with, I realized, and turned to the other two patients.

"I have no hope of anything good ever happening to me again," Martin said. His body was being relentlessly whittled away; his wife, along with everyone else from his past, had died; years had passed since he had last spoken to a friend; his son was sick to death of nursing him. "Doctor, you've got better things to do. Don't waste your time," he said to me. "Let's face it—I'm beyond help. Once I was a good sailor. I could do everything on a boat. Should've seen me scamper to the crow's nest. Nothing I couldn't do there; nothing I didn't know. But now what can anyone give me? What can I give anyone?"

Magnolia put forward this agenda: "Ah'd like to learn to listen better in this group. Don' you think dat would be a good thing, Doctah? Mah momma always tol' me it was important to be a good listener."

Good God! It was going to be a long, long session. How was I going to fill the rest of the time? As I tried to keep my composure, I could feel the edge of panic seeping in. A fine demonstration for the residents this was going to be! Look what I had to work with: Dorothy was not going to talk at all. Magnolia wanted to learn to listen. Martin, whose life was devoid of people, felt he had nothing to offer anyone. (I tagged that: a slight chance of an opening there.) Carol's agenda to be more assertive and not to be cowed by conflict was, I was certain, empty; she was only going through the motions of cooperating with me. Besides, to encourage someone's assertiveness I would need an active group in which I could urge some patients to practice asking for time or to express opinions forthrightly. Today there would be little against which Carol could be assertive. Rosa gave me one tiny ray of hope—her conviction that she was misunderstood and inferior to others. Maybe there was some handhold there; I tagged it too.

I made a start on Carol's fear of assertiveness by asking her to express some criticism, however slight, about the way I was conducting this meeting so far. But she balked, assuring me that she thought I was exceptionally sympathetic and skillful.

I turned to Rosa. There was no one else. To my suggestion that she say more about others being more important than she, she described how she had messed up everything—"my education, my relationships, every opportunity in my life." I tried to bring her comments into the here-and-now (which always increases the power of therapy).

"Look around the room," I suggested, "and try to describe how the other members are more important than you."

"I'll start with Carol," she said, warming to the task. "She's beautiful. I keep looking at her. It's like looking at a great painting. And I'm jealous of her bod. She's flat, she's perfectly proportioned, while me—look at me, I'm fat and bloated. Look at this." Hereupon Rosa pinched her abdomen to show us an eighth-of-an-inch roll of flesh between her thumb and forefinger.

All this was sheer anorexic madness. Rosa, like many anorexics, was so cunning at bundling herself in layers of clothes that it was easy to forget her emaciation. She weighed less than eighty pounds. And it was mad too for her to admire Carol, who was even thinner. A month ago, when I had been on call and paged because Carol had fainted, I had gotten to the ward just as the nurses were carrying her back to her bed. Her hospital gown had opened, exposing her buttocks, through which the heads of her femurs jutted, all but piercing the skin, reminding me of gruesome photographs of survivors liberated from concentration camps. But there was no point in debating Rosa's assessment that she was fat. Body-image distortions of anorexic patients run too deep—I had challenged them on that issue too many times in too many groups and knew that was an argument I could not win.

Rosa continued with her comparisons. Martin and Dorothy were dealing with far more significant problems than hers: "Sometimes," she said, "I wish I had something visibly wrong with me, like paralysis. Then I'd feel more legitimate." That stirred Dorothy into raising her head and making her first (and, as it happened, only) comment in the group: "You want paralyzed legs?" she whispered huskily. "Have mine."

To my great astonishment, Martin rushed in to defend Rosa: "No, no, Dorothy—I got the right name? It *is* Dorothy, isn't it? Rosa didn't mean it like that. I know she didn't mean that she wanted your legs or mine. Look at my legs. Look at 'em. Just look at 'em. Who in their right mind would want 'em?" With his one good hand Martin ripped away the covering sheet and pointed to his legs. Hideously deformed, they ended in two or three gnarled nubbins. The rest of his toes had entirely rotted away. Neither Dorothy nor any of the other group members looked very long at Martin's legs. They repelled me too, despite my medical training.

"Rosa was just using a figure of speech," Martin continued. "She only meant she wanted to have a more obvious disease, something you can see. She didn't mean to minimize our condition. Did you, Rosa? It *is* Rosa, right?"

Martin surprised me. I had allowed his deformity to conceal his acute intelligence. But he was not finished.

"Do you mind if I ask you something, Rosa? I don't mean to be nosy, so you don't have to answer if you don't want to."

"Shoot!" Rosa replied. "But I may not answer it."

"What *is* your condition? I mean, what's wrong with you? You're real skinny, but you don't look sick. Why are you getting that IV?" he asked, gesturing toward it.

"I don't eat. They feed me with this stuff."

"Don't eat? They don't let you eat?"

"No, they *want* me to eat. But I don't want to." Running her fingers through her hair, Rosa seemed to be trying to groom herself.

"Aren't you hungry?" Martin persisted.

"No."

I was fascinated by this interchange. Since everyone always tiptoes around eating-disorder patients (so defensive, so fragile, so much denial), I had never before witnessed an anorexic patient being confronted so boldly.

"I'm always hungry," Martin said. "You should have seen what I had for breakfast today: around twelve pancakes, eggs, two orange juices." He paused, hesitated. "Don't eat? Haven't you ever had an appetite?"

"No. Not as far back as I can remember. I don't like to eat."

"Don't like to eat?"

I could see Martin struggling to get his mind around this concept. He was genuinely baffled—as though he had just met someone who didn't enjoy breathing. "I've always eaten a lot. Always liked to eat. When my folks took me for a ride in the car, they always had peanuts and potato chips. In fact, that was my nickname."

"What was?" asked Rosa, who had turned her chair slightly toward Martin.

"Mr. Crisp. My mom and dad came from England and called potato chips 'crisps.' That's what they called me, Mr. Crisp. They liked to go down to the harbor to watch the big ships come in. 'Come along, Mr. Crisp,' they'd say, 'let's all go for a ride.' And I'd run out to our car—we had the only car on the block. Of course I had good legs then. Just like you, Rosa." Martin leaned forward in his wheelchair and peered down. "You look like you got good legs—a little skinny, though, no meat on 'em. I used to love to run—"

Martin's voice trailed off. Puzzlement furrowed his face as he pulled the sheet around him. "'Don't like to eat,'" he repeated as if to himself. "I always liked food. I think you missed a lot of fun."

At this point Magnolia, who, true to her agenda, had been listening intently to Martin, spoke up: "Rosa, chile, Ah just reminded me of when mah Darnell was small. Sometimes he wouldn't eat either. And you know what Ah used to do? Change the scenery! We'd get in the car and drive into Georgia—we lived right near the border. And he'd eat in Georgia. Lawd, how he ate in Georgia! We used to josh him about his Georgia appetite. Honey"—here Magnolia leaned toward Rosa and dropped her voice to a loud whisper—"maybe you ought to leave California to eat."

Trying to mine something therapeutic from this discussion, I stopped the action (in the jargon, I called for a "process check") and asked the members to reflect upon their own interaction.

"Rosa, how are you feeling about what's happening now in the group, about Martin's and Magnolia's questions?"

"Questions are okay—I don't mind them. And I like Martin—"

"Could you speak directly to him?" I asked.

Rosa turned to Martin. "I like you. I don't know why." She turned back to face me: "He's been here for a week, but today, in this group, is the first time I've spoken to him. It's like we have a lot in common, but I know we don't."

"Do you feel understood?"

"Understood? I don't know. Well, yeah, in a funny sort of way I do. Maybe that's it."

"That's what I saw. I saw Martin trying his best to understand you. And he wasn't trying to do anything else—I didn't hear him try to manage you or tell you what to do, or even tell you that you *ought* to eat."

"It's a good thing he didn't try. It wouldn't have done any good." Here Rosa turned to Carol, and they exchanged bony grins of complicity. I hated their grisly conspiracy. I wanted to shake them so hard their bones rattled. I wanted to shout, "Stop drinking those Diet Cokes! Stay off those goddamn stationary bikes! This is no joke; you two are five or six pounds away from death, and when each of you is finished dying, your entire life will be described in a three-word epitaph: '*I died thin.*'"

But of course I kept these sentiments to myself. It would have done nothing but rupture whatever slender strands of a relationship I had established with them. Instead I said to Rosa, "Are you aware that through your discussion with Martin, you've already filled part of your agenda today? You said you wanted to have the experience of being understood by someone, and Martin seems to have done exactly that."

I then turned to Martin. "How do you feel about that?"

Martin just stared at me. This, I thought, may be the liveliest interaction he has had for years.

"Remember," I reminded him, "you started this meeting by saying you could no longer be of use to anyone. I heard Rosa say you were of use to her. Did you hear that too?"

Martin nodded. I saw that his eyes were glistening and that he was too moved to speak further. Still, it was enough. With only the tiniest of openings, I had done good work with Martin and Rosa. At least we wouldn't walk away empty-handed (and I confess I was thinking of the residents as much as of the patients).

I turned back to Rosa. "How do you feel about what Magnolia is saying to you today? I'm not sure it's possible to leave California to eat, but what I did see was Magnolia stretching out to help you."

"Stretch? I'm surprised to hear you say that," said Rosa. "I don't think of Magnolia stretching. Giving is natural to her, like breathing. She is pure soul. I wish I could take her home with me or go home with her."

"Honey," Magnolia gave Rosa an enormous, toothy smile, "you don't wanna go to *mah* house. Jes' can't fumigate it. They jes' keep comin' back." Apparently, Magnolia was talking about her insect hallucinations.

"You guys should hire Magnolia," Rosa said, turning to me. "She's the one who really helps me. And not just me. Everybody. Even the nurses come to Magnolia with their troubles."

"Chile, you makin' a lot out of nuthin'. You ain't got much. You so skinny you easy to give to. And you got a big heart. Makes folks want to give to you. Feels good to help out. Thas *mah* bes' medicine.

"Thas mah bes' medicine, Doctah," Magnolia repeated, looking over at me. "You jes' let me help out folks."

For a few moments I couldn't say a word. I felt entranced by Magnolia—by those wise eyes, that inviting smile, that bounteous lap. And those arms—just like my mother's arms, with those generous folds of flesh cascading down to obscure her elbows. What would it be like to be held, to be cradled, in those pillowy chocolate arms? I thought of all the pressures in my life—writing, teaching, consulting, patients, wife, four children, financial commitments, investments, and now my mother's death. I need comfort, I thought. Magnolia-comfort—that's what I need, some of Magnolia's big-armed comfort. A refrain from an old Judy Collins song drifted into my mind: "Too many sad times . . . Too many bad times . . . But if somehow . . . you could . . . pack up your sorrows and give them all to me . . . You would lose them . . . I know how to use them . . . Give them all to me."

I hadn't thought of that song for ever so long. Years before, when I first heard Judy Collins's dulcet voice sing out, "Pack up your sorrows and give them all to me," desire stirred deep within me. I wanted to climb right into the radio to find that woman and pour my sorrows into her lap.

Rosa jolted me out of my reverie: "Dr. Yalom, you asked earlier why I thought others here were better than me. Well, you can see now what I mean. You see how special Magnolia is. And Martin too. They both care about others. People—my folks, my sisters—used to tell me I was selfish. They were right. I don't reach out to do anything for anyone. I don't have anything to offer. All I really want is for people to leave me alone."

Magnolia leaned toward me. "That child is so artful," she said.

"Artful"—a strange word. I waited to see what she meant.

"You should see the blanket she's embroidering for me in occupational therapy. Two roses in the center, and around them she's stitching teeny violets, mus' be twenty of 'em, all along the edges. And she did the edges in a delicate red design. Honey," Magnolia turned to Rosa, "will you bring that blanket into group tomorrow? And the picture you was drawin' too?"

Rosa blushed but nodded assent.

Time was passing. I suddenly realized I hadn't explored what the group could offer Magnolia. I had been too enchanted by the promise of her largesse and the memory of that refrain: "You would lose them . . . I know how to use them."

"You know, Magnolia, you should get something from the group too. You started the meeting by saying that what you want from the group is to be a good listener. But I'm impressed, very impressed, with what a good listener you already are. And a good observer too: look at the details you remember about Rosa's blanket. So I don't think you need a lot of help with learning to listen. How else can we help you in this group?"

"Ah don' know *how* dis group can help me."

"I heard a lot of good things said about you today. How does that feel?"

"Well, natchally, dat feels good."

"But Magnolia, I have a hunch you've heard that before—that people have always loved you for how much you give. Why, the nurses were saying that very thing before the group met today—that you've raised a son and fifteen foster children and never stop giving."

"Not now. Ah can't give nuthin' now. Ah can't move mah legs, and those bugs—" She shuddered suddenly, but her soft smile remained. "Ah don't want to go back home no more."

"What I mean, Magnolia, is that it probably isn't too helpful for others to tell you things about yourself that you already know. If we're going to help you here, we need to give you something else. Maybe we've got to help you learn new things about yourself, give you some feedback about your blind spots, things you may not have known."

"Ah done tol' you, Ah gets help by helpin' other folks."

"I know that, and that's one of the things I really like about you. But you know, it feels good to *everyone* to be helpful to others. Like Martin—look what it meant to him to help Rosa by being understanding."

"Dat Martin is sometin'. He don' move too good, but he's got a fine head on his shoulders, a real fine head."

"You *do* help others and you're good at it. You're a marvel, and I agree with Rosa, the hospital *should* hire you. But Magnolia," I hesitated in order to give my words greater impact, "*it would be good for others to be able to help you too*. By being so totally giving,

69

you don't let others get help from helping you. When Rosa said she'd like to go home with you, I was thinking too how great it would be to be comforted by you all the time. I'd like that too. I'd love it. But then, when I thought more about it, I realized I'd never be able to repay your help, to help *you*, because you never complain; you never ask for anything. In fact," I hesitated again, *"I'd never get to have the pleasure of offering you something."*

"Ah nevah thought about it jes' like that." Magnolia nodded thoughtfully. Her smile had vanished.

"But it's true, isn't it? Maybe what we ought to do here in this group is help you learn to complain. Maybe you need the experience of being listened to."

"Mah momma always said I put myself last."

"I don't always agree with mothers. In fact, I don't *usually* agree with them, but in this case I think your mother was right. So why not practice complaining? Tell us, what hurts? What do you want to change about yourself?"

"Mah health ain't so good . . . these things crawlin' around on mah skin. And these legs heah ain't good. Ah can't move 'em."

"That's a start, Magnolia. And I know those are the real problems in your life now. I wish we could do something about those problems here in this group, but groups can't do that. Try to complain about things we might be able to help you with."

"Ah feel bad about mah house. It's nasty. Dey can't, maybe dey *won't*, fumigate it right. Ah don' want to go back there."

"I know you feel bad about your house and your legs and your skin. But those things aren't *you*. They are just things *about* you, not the real, the core you. Look at the center of you. What do you want to change there?"

"Well, Ah ain't real satisfied with mah life. I got mah regrets. Dat what you mean, Doctah?"

"Right on." I nodded vigorously.

She continued, "Ah've disappointed myself. Ah always wanted to be a teachuh. Dat was mah dream. But Ah never did be one. Sometimes Ah gets down, and Ah think Ah never did nuthin'."

"But Magnolia," Rosa implored, "look what you've done for Darnell or for all those foster kids. You call that nothing?"

"Sometime it feel like nuthin'. Darnell ain't gonna do nuthin' with his life, ain't goin' nowhere. He jes' like his father."

Rosa broke in. She seemed alarmed—her pupils were enormous. She spoke to me as though I were a judge and she a lawyer pleading Magnolia's case. "She never had a chance for an education, Dr. Yalom. When she was a teenager her father died and her mother just disappeared for fifteen years."

Suddenly Carol pitched in, also addressing me: "She had to raise her seven brothers and sisters almost alone."

"Not alone. Ah had help—from the pastor, the church, lots of good folk."

Ignoring Magnolia's disclaimer, Rosa addressed me: "I met Magnolia when we were both in the hospital about a year ago, and once, after we were discharged, I picked her up in my car and we rode around all afternoon—through Palo Alto, Stanford, Menlo Park, up into the hills. Magnolia gave me a tour. She pointed out everything to me, not just the important stuff now but also the way this whole county used to be and all the things that happened thirty or forty years ago on some special spot. That was the best ride I ever had."

"How do you feel about what Rosa said, Magnolia?"

Magnolia softened again. "Das good, das good. Dat chile knows I loves her."

"So, Magnolia," I said, "it looks like, despite everything, despite all the odds stacked against you, you became a teacher after all! And a good teacher."

Now things were click—click—clicking in the group. I glanced proudly toward the psychiatry residents. My last comment—a beautiful example of reframing—was a gem. I hoped they had heard it.

Magnolia heard it. She seemed deeply moved and wept for several minutes. We honored the moment by sitting in respectful silence. Magnolia's next comment took me aback. Obviously I had not listened well to her.

"You right, Doctah. You right." Then she added, "You right, but you *ain't* right. Ah had a dream. Ah wanted to be a *real* teachuh, to get paid white teachuh's pay, to have real students, to have them call me 'Mrs. Clay.' Das what *Ah* mean."

"But Magnolia," Rosa persisted, "look at what you *did* do—think of Darnell and those fifteen foster kids who call you Momma."

"Dat got nuthin' to do with what Ah wanted, with mah dreams," said Magnolia, her voice sharp and forceful. "Ah had dreams too, like white folk. Black folk have dreams too! And Ah was very disappointed with mah marriage. Ah wanted a whole-life marriage, an all Ah got was a fourteen-month marriage. Ah was a fool; Ah picked the wrong man. He liked his gin—lot more'n he liked me.

"God is my witness," she continued, turning to me, "Ah nevah before—till this meetin' today—bad-mouthed mah husband. Ah don' want my Darnell to evah hear anythin' bad about his daddy. But Doctah, you right. You right. Ah got complaints. A lot of things Ah wanted Ah nevah got. Nevah got my dream. Sometimes Ah can feel real bitter."

Tears were streaming down her cheeks as she sobbed softly. Then she turned away from the group, stared out the window, and began scratching her skin, at first softly and then with deep, long digs. "Real bitter. Real bitter," she repeated.

I felt disoriented. Like Rosa, I grew alarmed. I wanted the old Magnolia back. And her clawing unnerved me. Was she trying to scrape away the insects? Or her blackness? I wanted to grab her wrists and still her hands before she lacerated her flesh.

A long pause and then: "And they is other things Ah could say too, but they is very personal."

I knew that Magnolia was primed. I had no doubt that with the slightest prod, she would tell us everything. But she had gone far enough for the rest of us. Too far. Rosa's distraught eyes were telling me, "Please, please, no more! Stop this!" And it was enough for me too. I had taken the lid off, but for once I did not want to look inside.

After two or three minutes, Magnolia stopped weeping, stopped scratching. Slowly her smile reappeared and her voice became soft again. "But then Ah figure that the good Lawd has His reasons for giving us each a burden. Wouldn't it be prideful fo' me to try figure out His reasons?"

The group members were silent. Apparently embarrassed, they all—even Dorothy—looked away, out the window. This is, I kept trying to tell myself, good therapy: Magnolia has faced some of her demons and now seems poised on the brink of some important therapeutic work.

Yet I felt I had desecrated her. Perhaps the other members felt that way too. Yet they said nothing. A heavy silence descended. I caught each member's gaze and silently urged each to speak. Perhaps I had read into Magnolia too much earth mother. Perhaps it was only I who had lost an icon. I struggled to put my sense of desecration into words that would be useful to the group. Nothing came. My mind was silent. Giving up, I glumly resigned myself to a tired, scuffed comment I had uttered countless times before in countless group meetings: "Magnolia has said a great deal. What feelings do her words stir up in each of you?"

I hated saying that, hated its ordinariness, its technical banality. Ashamed of myself, I slumped into my chair. I knew precisely how the group members would respond and grimly awaited their formulaic comments:

"I feel I really know you now, Magnolia."

"I feel a lot closer to you now."

"I see you as a real person now."

Even one of the residents, venturing out of his role as silent observer, chipped in: "Me too, Magnolia. I see you as a full person, someone I can relate to. I experience you in three dimensions now."

Our time was up. I had to summarize the session somehow and delivered the obvious, mandatory interpretation: "You know, Magnolia, this has been a tough meeting but a rich one. What I'm aware of is that we started with the issue of your not being able to complain, perhaps not feeling you had the *right* to complain. Your work today has been uncomfortable, but it's the beginning of real progress. The point is that you have a lot of pain inside, and if you can learn to complain about it and deal with it *directly* as you've done today, you won't have to express it in *indirect* ways—for example, through problems with your house, or your legs, perhaps even the feelings about insects on your skin."

Magnolia didn't answer. She just looked straight at me, her eyes still brimming with tears.

"Do you understand what I mean, Magnolia?"

"Ah understan', Doctah. Ah understan' real good." She wiped her eyes with a tiny handkerchief. "Ah'm sorry to be bawlin' so much. Ah didn't tell you before, maybe Ah should've, but tomorrah's the day mah momma died. One yeah ago tomorrah."

"I know what that feels like, Magnolia, I lost *my* mother last month."

I surprised myself. Ordinarily I wouldn't speak so personally to a patient I barely knew. I think I was trying to give her something. But Magnolia didn't acknowledge my gift. The group began to disperse. The doors opened. Nurses entered to help the patients out. I watched Magnolia scratching away at herself as she was wheeled out.

In the discussion following the group meeting, I enjoyed the harvest of my labors. The residents were full of praise. Above all, they were properly impressed by the spectacle of something emerging from what looked like nothing. Despite scant material and little patient motivation, the group had generated considerable interaction: by the meeting's end, members who for the most part had been oblivious of the existence of other patients on the ward were engaged and concerned with one another. The residents were also impressed by the power of my closing interpretation to Magnolia: that if she were to request help explicitly, she would render obsolete her symptoms, which were symbolic, oblique cries for help.

How did you do it? they marveled. At the beginning of the meeting Magnolia seemed so impenetrable. It wasn't difficult, I told them. Find the right key and it's possible to open a door to anyone's suffering. For Magnolia that key had been the appeal to one of her deepest values—her wish to be of service to others. By persuading her that she could help others by allowing them to be helpful to her, I had quickly undermined her resistance.

As we spoke, Sarah, the head nurse, poked her head in the door to thank me for coming. "You've worked your magic again, Irv. Wanna get your heart warmed? Before you leave, take a peek at the patients having lunch, at all those heads closer together. And what did you do to Dorothy? Can you believe she and Martin and Rosa are *talking* together?"

Sarah's words rang in my ears as I biked back to my office. I knew I had every reason to be satisfied with my morning's work. The residents were right: it *had* been a good meeting—a fantastic one—because it not only encouraged members to improve relationships in their lives but, as Sarah's report suggested, also engaged them more fully in all aspects of the ward's therapy program.

Most of all, I had shown them that there is no such thing as a boring or empty patient—or group. Within every patient, and within every clinical situation, lies the chrysalis of a rich human drama. The art of psychotherapy lies in activating that drama.

But why did my good work give me so little personal satisfaction? I felt guilty—as though I had done something fraudulent. The praise I so often pursued didn't sit well with me that day. The students (covertly egged on by me) had imbued me with great wisdom. In their eyes I offered "powerful" interpretations, worked my "magic," led the group in a prescient, sure-handed manner. But I knew the truth: that throughout the meeting I had scrambled and improvised wildly. Both students and patients viewed me as something I was not, as more than I was, more than I could be. It occurred to me that in that respect Magnolia, the archetypal earth mother, and I had much in common.

I reminded myself that small is beautiful. My job was to lead a single group meeting and make it helpful to as many of its group members as possible. And hadn't I done that? I reviewed the group from the perspective of each of the five members.

Martin and Rosa? Yes, good work. I was certain of them. Their agendas for the meeting had, to some degree, been filled: Martin's demoralization, his conviction that he had nothing of value to offer, had been effectively challenged; Rosa's belief that any person unlike herself—that is, any nonanorexic—would misunderstand and attempt to manipulate her had been refuted.

Dorothy and Carol? Though inactive, they had nonetheless appeared engaged. Perhaps they had benefited from spectator therapy: watching someone else work effectively in therapy often primes a patient for good therapeutic work in the future.

And Magnolia? Therein lay the problem. Had I helped Magnolia? Was she helpable? In the head nurse's briefing I had learned that she had not responded to a wide array of psychotropic medication and that everyone, including her case worker of several years, had long ago given up trying to engage her in any insight-oriented psychotherapy. So why had I decided to try once more?

Had I helped her? I doubted it. Although the residents considered my final interpretation "powerful," and indeed, my words had *felt* so as I said them, in my heart I knew that it was all a sham: my interpretation had no real chance of being useful to Magnolia. Her symptoms—the inexplicable paralysis of her legs, the hallucinations of insects on her skin, her delusion that a conspiracy was behind the insect infestation of her home—were grave and far beyond the reach of psychotherapy. Even under the most favorable circumstances—unlimited time with a skilled therapist—psychotherapy would probably offer Magnolia little. And there were zero favorable possibilities here: Magnolia had no money and no insurance and would undoubtedly be discharged to some bare-bones nursing facility without a prayer of obtaining follow-up psychotherapy. My rationale that my interpretation would prime Magnolia for future work was pure illusion.

Given these conditions, how "powerful," then, was my interpretation? Powerful to what end? The power was a phantom; in fact, my persuasive rhetoric was directed not at the forces that shackled Magnolia but at my student audience. She had been a victim to my vanity.

I was closer to the truth now. And yet my disquiet persisted. I turned to the question of why my judgment had been so poor. I had broken a fundamental rule of psychotherapy: do not strip away a patient's defenses if you have nothing better to offer in their stead. And the force behind my actions? Why had Magnolia assumed such importance to me?

The answer to this question lay, I suspected, in my response to my mother's death. I reviewed again the course of the meeting. When had things started to affect me so personally? It was that first sight of Magnolia: that smile, those cushiony forearms. My mother's arms. How they drew me! How I wished to be encircled and comforted by those soft, doughy arms. And that song, that Judy Collins song—how did it go? I searched for the words.

But instead of the song lyrics, the events of a long-forgotten afternoon drifted into mind. On Saturday afternoons when I was about eight or nine and living in Washington, D.C., my friend Roger and I often bicycled to picnic in a park called the Old Soldiers' Home. One day, instead of roasting hot dogs, we conspired to steal a live chicken from a house bordering the park and cook it over a campfire we built in a sunny clearing in the park forest.

But first, the killing—my initiation into the rites of death. Roger took the initiative and bashed the sacrificial chicken with an enormous rock. Though bloodied and crushed, it continued to fight for life. I was horrified. I turned away, unable to bear watching the wretched creature. Things had gone too far. I wanted to undo them. Then and there I lost interest in my project of appearing grown-up. I wanted my mother; I wanted to cycle home so she could hold me. I wanted to reverse time, erase everything, start the day over. But there was no turning back and nothing to do but watch Roger grab the chicken by its battered head and whirl it around like a bolo until, finally, it was still. We must have plucked it, cleaned it, put it on a spit. We must have roasted it over the fire and eaten it. Perhaps with gusto. But, though I remember with an eerie clarity trying to wish away the whole catastrophe, of all we actually did I recall nothing.

Still, the memory of that afternoon gripped me until I freed myself by asking why it had emerged now after so many decades in deep storage. What linked the wheelchair-filled hospital group room with the events played out so long ago around the campfire in a copse of the Old Soldiers' Home? Perhaps the idea of going too far—as I had gone too far with Magnolia. Perhaps some visceral apprehension of the irreversibility of time. Perhaps the aching, the longing, for a mother to protect me from the brute facts of life and death.

Though the aftertaste of the group meeting was still bitter, I felt closer to its source: undoubtedly my deep craving for motherly comfort, fanned by my mother's death, had resonated mightily with Magnolia's earth-mother image. Had I stripped away that image, secularized her, obliterated her power in an effort to face down my yearning for comfort? That song, that earth-mother song—bits of the lyrics now began to return: "Pack up your sorrows and give them all to me. You would lose them. . . . I could use them. . . . " Silly, puerile words. I could remember only faintly the snug, bountiful, warm place into which they had once led me. Now those words no longer worked. Much as I blink at a Vasarely or an Escher illusion to reinstate the alternate image, I tried to flip my mind back to that place—but in vain.

Could I do without that illusion? All my life I had sought comfort in a variety of earth mothers. I paraded them now before me: my dying mother, from whom I wanted something—I don't know what—even as she gasped her last breaths; the many loving black housekeepers, their names long vanished from memory, who held me as infant and child; my sister, herself badly loved, offering me scraps from her dish; the harried teachers who singled me out for praise; my old analyst, who sat loyally—and silently—with me for three years.

Now I understood more clearly how all these feelings—let us call them "countertransference"—had made it almost impossible for me to offer unconflicted therapeutic help to Magnolia. If I had just let her be, just basked in her warmth as Rosa had done, just settled for small goals, then I would have condemned myself for using my patient for my own comfort. As it was, I had challenged her defensive structure and now condemned myself for grandiosity and for sacrificing her for the sake of a teaching demonstration. What I could not, or did not, do was bracket all my feelings and have a real encounter with Magnolia—Magnolia the flesh-and-blood person, not the image I had imposed upon her.

The day following the group meeting, Magnolia was discharged from the hospital, and I chanced to see her waiting in the hospital corridor by the window of the outpatient pharmacy. Aside from her tiny, delicate lace cap and the blue embroidered blanket (Rosa's gift) covering her legs in the wheelchair, she looked ordinary—weary, shabby, indistinguishable from the long gray line of supplicants stretching before and behind her. I nodded to her, but she didn't see me, and I continued on my way. A few minutes later I reconsidered and turned back to find her. Still at the window, she was placing her discharge medications into a worn petit-point bag on her lap. I watched her wheel away toward the hospital exit, where she stopped, opened her purse, took out a small handkerchief, removed her thick gold-rimmed eyeglasses, and daintily wiped away the tears coursing down her cheeks. I went over to her. "Magnolia, hello. Remember me?"

"Your voice sound real familiar," she said, replacing her spectacles. "Now, you jes' wait a minute while Ah get a look at you." She stared at me, blinking two or three times, and then broke into a warm smile. "Doctah Yalom, Ah sure do remembah you. Nice of you to stop and visit. I bin wanting to talk to you, private-like." She pointed to a chair at the end of the corridor. "Ah see a seat for you over there. Ah carry mah own around with me. Would you wheel me over?"

When we had moved and I had sat down, Magnolia said, "You jes' gonna have to oversight mah tears. Ah can' stop bawling today."

Trying to hush my mounting fear that the group session had indeed been destructive, I said gently, "Magnolia, do your tears have anything to do with our group meeting yesterday?"

"The group?" She looked at me incredulously. "Doctah Yalom, you ain't forgotten what Ah tol' you at the end of that meetin'? Today's the day mah momma died—one yeah ago today."

"Oh, of course. Sorry, I'm a little slow at the moment. Guess too much is going on in my own life, Magnolia." Relieved, I downshifted quickly into my professional gear. "You miss her a lot, don't you?"

"Ah do. And you remembah Rosa tol' you mah momma was gone when Ah was growin' up—she jes' showed up one day after being away for fifteen years."

"But then, when she came back, she took care of you? Gave you a lot of momma comfort?"

"A momma's a momma. Ain't got but one of 'em. But you know, Momma didn't take care of me much—other way around—she was ninety when she passed away. No, it weren't that at all—it was more jes' that she was *there*. Ah don' know . . . guess she stood for somethin' Ah needed. You know what Ah mean?"

"I know exactly what you mean, Magnolia. I do indeed."

"Maybe it ain't mah place to say, Doctah, but Ah think you're like me—you miss your momma too. Doctahs need mommas too, jes' like mommas need mommas."

"You're right about that, Magnolia. You've got a good sixth sense—like Rosa said. But you said you were wanting to talk to me?"

"Well, like I already said—about you missing your momma. Dat was one thing. And then about dat group meetin'. Ah jes' wanted to thank you—thas all. I got a lot from that meetin'."

"Can you tell me what you got from it?"

"Ah learned something urgent. Ah learned that Ah'm done with rearin' children. Ah'm done with that—fo'ever. . . . " Her voice trailed off and she looked away, peered down the corridor.

Urgent? Forever?—Magnolia's unexpected words intrigued me. I wanted to keep on talking to her and was disappointed to hear her say, "Oh, look theh, it's Claudia, comin' for me."

Claudia wheeled Magnolia out the front door to the van that was to take her to the nursing home to which she was being discharged. I followed her out to the curb and watched her and her chair being hoisted inside by the lift on the back of the van.

"Good-bye, Doctah Yalom," she said, waving to me. "Take care of yo'self."

Strange, I mused as I watched the van drive away, that I, who have devoted my life to apprehending the world of the other, have not, until Magnolia, truly understood that those whom we transform into myth are themselves myth-ridden. They despair; they mourn the death of a mother; they search for the exalted; they too rage against life and may need to maim themselves to be done with giving.

4

$$\clubsuit$$

Seven Advanced Lessons
in the Therapy of Grief

Long ago Earl, my friend of many years, phoned to tell me that his closest friend, Jack, had just been diagnosed with a malignant, inoperable brain tumor. Before I could commiserate, he said, "Look, Irv, I'm not calling for me—but for someone else. A favor—something really important to me. Look, will you treat Jack's wife, Irene? Jack's going to die an ugly death—perhaps the hardest death life can deal. It doesn't help matters that Irene is a surgeon: she'll know too much, and it'll be agonizing for her to stand and watch helplessly as his cancer eats away his brain. And then she'll be left with a young daughter and a full practice. Her future's a nightmare."

As I listened to Earl's request, I wanted to help. I wanted to give everything he asked. But there were problems. Good therapy requires crisp boundaries, and I knew both Jack and Irene. Not well, it's true, but we'd been at a couple of dinner parties together at Earl's home. I had also once watched a Super Bowl game with Jack and played tennis with him a few times.

All of this I told Earl and wound up, "Treating someone you know socially never fails to get messy. The best way for me to help is to find the best referral—someone who doesn't know the family."

"I knew you'd say that," he replied. "I prepared Irene for that answer. I've been over it with her again and again, but she won't see anyone else. She's pretty strong-willed, and though in general she has little respect for the field of psychiatry, she's got a fix on you. She says she's followed your work and is convinced, God knows why, you're the only psychiatrist smart enough for her."

"Let me sleep on it. I'll call you back tomorrow."

What to do? On the one hand, friendship called: Earl and I had never refused each other anything. But the potential boundary leakage made me queasy. Earl and his wife, Emily, were two of my closest confidants. And Emily, in turn, was Irene's closest friend. I could imagine the two of them in a tête-à-tête talking about me. Yes, no question: I heard alarm signals ringing. But I turned the volume knob way down. I would extract a pledge from both Irene and Emily to build a wall of silence around therapy. Tricky and complex. But if I were as smart as she thought I was, I could handle it.

After I hung up I wondered why I was so willing to ignore the alarm signals. I realized that Earl's request at this particular juncture of my life seemed fateful. A colleague and I had just finished three years of empirical research on spousal bereavement, studying eighty men and women who had recently become widows and widowers. I had interviewed each at length and treated all of them in brief eight-person therapy groups. Our research team had followed their progress for a year, collected a mountain of information, and published several papers in professional journals. I had become persuaded that few people knew more than I about the subject. As a bereavement hotshot, how could I, in good conscience, withhold myself from Irene?

Besides, she had said the magic words—that I was the only one smart enough to treat her. The perfect plug for my socket of vanity.

Lesson 1: The First Dream

A few days later I met with Irene for our first session. Let me say right off the bat that she turned out to be one of the most interesting, intelligent, stubborn, agonized, sensitive, imperious, elegant, hardworking, ingenious, unbending, courageous, attractive, proud, frosty, romantic, and infuriating women I have ever known.

Midway through the first session, she described a dream she'd had the previous night:

I'm still a surgeon, but I'm also a grad student in English. My preparation for a course involves two different texts, an ancient and a modern text, each with the same name. I am unprepared for the seminar because I haven't read either text. I especially haven't read the old, first text, which would have prepared me for the second.

"What else do you remember, Irene?" I asked when she stopped. "You say each text had the same name. Do you know what it was?"

"Oh, yes, I remember it clearly. Each book, the old and the new, was titled *The Death of Innocence.*"

Listening to Irene, I lapsed into reverie. This dream of hers was pure gold, intellectual ambrosia—a gift from the gods. The psychological gumshoe's daydream come true. The reward for patience, the payoff for countless tedious therapy stakeouts with inhibited engineers.

86

It was a dream to make even the most irritable, the most grumpy therapist purr with pleasure. And purr I did. Two texts—an ancient and a new one. Purr, purr. The ancient text needed to understand the new. Purr. Purr. And the title, *The Death of Innocence*. Purr, purr, purr.

It wasn't only that Irene's dream promised an intellectual treasure hunt of the highest order; it was also a *first dream*. Ever since 1911, when Freud first discussed it, a mystique has surrounded the initial dream that a patient reports in psychoanalysis. Freud believed that this first dream is unsophisticated and highly revealing because beginning patients are naive and still have their guards down. Later in therapy, when it is evident that the therapist has highly skilled dream-interpretative abilities, the dreamweaver residing in our unconscious grows cautious, goes on full alert, and takes care thereafter to manufacture more complex and obfuscating dreams.

Following Freud, I often imagined the dreamweaver as a plump, jovial homunculus, living the good life amidst a forest of dendrites and axons. He sleeps by day, but at night, reclining on a cushion of buzzing synapses, he drinks honeyed nectar and lazily spins out dream sequences for his host. On the night before the first therapy visit, that host falls asleep full of conflicting thoughts about the upcoming therapy, and as usual the homunculus goes about his nighttime job blithely weaving those fears and hopes into a simple, transparent dream. Then, with great alarm, the homunculus learns that the therapist has deftly interpreted his dream. The homunculus graciously doffs his chapeau to his able opponent—the therapist who has broken his dream code—but from that time forward takes care to bury the dream meaning ever deeper and deeper in nocturnal disguise.

A foolish fairy tale. Typical nineteenth-century anthropomorphization. The widespread error of concretizing Freud's abstract mental structures into independent, free-willed sprites. If only I didn't believe it!

For decades many have regarded the first dream as a priceless document that represents the translation into dream language of the whole content of the neurosis. Freud went so far as to suggest that the full interpretation of an initial dream would coincide with the entire analysis.

The first dream in my own analysis is fixed in my mind with all the freshness and detail and feeling of the day I dreamed it forty years ago, shortly after beginning my psychiatric residency.

I am lying on a doctor's examining table. The sheet is too small to cover me properly. I can see a nurse inserting a needle into my leg—my shin. Suddenly there's an explosive hissing, gurgling sound—WHOOOOOSH.

The center of the dream—the loud *whoosh*—was immediately clear to me. As a child I was plagued with chronic sinusitis, and every winter my mother took me to Dr. Davis for a sinus draining and flushing. I hated his yellow teeth and his fishy eye, which peered at me though the center of the circular mirror attached to the headband otolaryngologists used to wear. As he inserted a cannula into my sinus foramen, I felt a sharp pain, then heard a deafening *whooooosh* as the injected saline flushed out my sinus. Looking at the quivering, disgusting mess in the semicircular chrome drainage pan, I thought that some of my brains had been washed out along with the pus and mucus.

Just as Freud had suggested, my first dream anticipated layer after layer of years of analytic work: my fears of exposure, of losing my mind, of being brainwashed, of suffering a grievous injury (deflation) to a long, firm body part (depicted as a shinbone).

Freud and many subsequent analysts have cautioned against plunging too quickly into the meaning of the first dream lest early interpretation and exposure to unconscious material overwhelm patients and immobilize our dreamweaving homunculus entirely. Such admonishments have seemed to me directed not so much toward increasing the effectiveness of therapy as toward protecting the parochial self-interest of the analytic discipline, and I've always resisted them.

From the 1940s to the 1960s, a walking-on-eggshells approach to therapy reigned. The precise, delicate phrasing of interventions was the topic of endless arcane debates within analytic institutes. Bombarded with propaganda about the necessity for exquisitely timed and formulated interpretations, novices—full of awe and fear—tiptoed carefully through therapy, stifling their spontaneity—and their effectiveness. I found that such formalism was counter-productive because it interfered with the greater goal of establishing an empathic, authentic relationship to the patient. To me, Freud's warning not to work on dreams until the therapeutic alliance is firmly established seems strangely inverted: working together on a dream is an excellent way to build the therapeutic alliance.

So I plunged right into Irene's dream.

"So you hadn't read either text," I began, "*especially* not the old one."

"Yes, yes, I expected you to ask about that. *Of course*, it doesn't make sense; I know that. But that's exactly the way it was in the dream. I had not read the assignment—I hadn't read either text, but I *especially* hadn't read the ancient one."

"The one that would have prepared you for the new text. Any hunches about the meaning of the two texts in your life?"

"Hardly a hunch," Irene replied. "I know exactly what they mean."

I waited for her to go on but she simply sat in silence, looking out the window. I hadn't yet learned of Irene's irritating trait of not volunteering a conclusion unless I explicitly requested it.

Annoyed, I let the silence last a minute or two. Finally I obliged: "And the meaning of the two texts, Irene, is—"

"My brother's death, when I was twenty, was the ancient text. My husband's death to come is the modern text."

"So the dream is telling us that you may not be able to deal with your husband's death until you deal first with your brother's."

"You got it. Precisely."

The examination of this initial dream anticipated not only the content of therapy but also its *process*, that is, the nature of the therapist-patient relationship. For one thing, Irene was always forthcoming and thoughtful. I never asked a question without receiving an original and comprehensive response. Did she know the titles of the two texts? Indeed she did. Had she any hunches about why she needed to read the ancient text in order to understand the modern one? Of course; she knew precisely what it meant. Even routine questions—"What do you make of this?" or "Where do your thoughts go now, Irene?"—never failed, in five years of therapy, to reap a fertile harvest. Often Irene's responses unnerved me: they were too quick, too precise. They brought to my mind Miss Fernald, my fifth grade teacher, who often said, "Come along, Irvin," as she impatiently tapped her foot, marked time, and waited for me to stop daydreaming and keep up with some class exercise.

I swept Miss Fernald out of my mind and continued, "And the meaning for you of *The Death of Innocence?*"

"Imagine what it meant to me as a twenty-year-old to have my brother, whom I expected to have as a life companion, snatched from me by a traffic accident. And then I found Jack. And imagine what it means now, at the age of forty-five, to lose him. Imagine what it is like to have my parents, in their seventies, living and my brother dead and my husband dying. Time out of joint. The young dying first."

Irene told me of the blessed relationship she had enjoyed with her brother, Allen, two years her senior. Through her adolescence he had been the protector, the confidant, the mentor every young girl dreams of. But then, in one screeching moment on a street in Boston, Allen was dead. She told me how the police phoned the small house she shared with college roommates, how every detail of that day was frozen forever in her mind.

"I remember everything: the ring of the phone downstairs, my chenille bathrobe with rows of small pink and white tufts, the flopping of my fleece slippers as I went down the steps to the alcove next to the kitchen where the telephone hung on the wall, the wooden banister so smooth to my hand. I remember thinking that the wood had been worn smooth by all the Harvard and Radcliffe undergraduates before me. And then that man's voice, that stranger trying to be kind as he told me that Allen was dead. I sat for hours staring out the beveled glass of the alcove window. I can still see the rainbow-colored mounds of sooty snow in the side yard."

Countless times during therapy we were to return to the dream of the two texts and the meaning of *The Death of Innocence*. The loss of her brother marked her for life. Death exploded her innocence forever. Gone were the myths of childhood: justice, predictability, a benevolent deity, a natural order of things, protecting parents, the safety of home. Alone and unshielded against the capriciousness of existence, Irene struggled to attain safety. Allen might have survived, she believed, if he had had the right emergency medical treatment. Medicine beckoned—it offered the only hope of mastery over death, and at Allen's funeral she suddenly decided to apply to medical school and become a surgeon.

Another decision Irene made in the wake of Allen's death was to have enormous implications for our work in therapy.

"I figured out a way to avoid ever getting hurt again: I would never again have such a loss if I never let anyone matter to me."

"How did that decision play out in your life?"

"For the next ten years I made no attachments, took no chances. I knew a lot of men, but I broke things off quickly—before they got serious and before I felt anything."

"But then something changed. You married. How did that come about?"

"I've known Jack since the fourth grade and somehow had always thought he would be the one. Even when he disappeared from my life and married someone else, I knew he'd be back. My brother knew and respected him. I guess you could say my brother anointed Jack."

"So Allen's approval of Jack permitted you to take the risk of marrying?"

"It wasn't that simple. It took a long, long time, and even then I refused to marry Jack until he promised not to die young on me."

I appreciated Irene's irony and looked up with a grin to gather in her smile in return. But there was no smile. Irene was not being ironic; she was stone serious.

This scenario was to happen again and again throughout our work. I was the designated voice of reason. I often took the bait: I confronted her irrationality; argued; appealed to *her* reason; tried to rouse her precise, scientifically honed mind. Other times I just waited. But the result was always the same: she never budged an inch; she never relinquished her position. And I never got used to her dual nature, her extraordinary lucidity flanked by preposterous irrationality.

Lesson 2: The Wall of Bodies

If Irene's initial dream anticipated the nature of our future relationship, a dream she had in the second year of therapy was the
opposite—a beam directed backward, illuminating the trail we
had already traveled together.

*I am in this office, in this chair. But there is a strange wall in the middle of the
room between us. I can't see you. At first I can't see the wall distinctly; it's irregular, with lots of crevices and protuberances. I see a small patch of fabric, red
plaid; then I recognize a hand; then a foot and a knee. Now I know what it is—
a wall of bodies heaped one upon the other.*

"And the feeling in the dream, Irene?" Almost always my first
question. The feeling in a dream often leads to the center of its
meaning.

"Unpleasant, fearful. My strongest feeling was in the beginning—when I saw the wall and felt lost. Alone—lost—frightened."

"Tell me about the wall."

"When I describe it now, it sounds gruesome—like a heap of
bodies at Auschwitz. And that patch of red plaid—I know that
pattern, it was the pajamas Jack was wearing the night he died. Yet
somehow the wall is not gruesome—it's simply there, something
I'm inspecting and studying. It might have even allayed some of
my fear."

"A wall of bodies between us—what do you make of that,
Irene?"

"No mystery there. No mystery to the whole dream. It's just
what I've been feeling all along. The dream says you can't really

93

see me because of all the dead bodies, all the deaths. You can't imagine. Nothing has ever happened to *you!* You've had no tragedy in your life."

The losses in Irene's life had mounted. First her brother. Then her husband, who died at the end of our first year of therapy. A few months later her father was diagnosed with advanced prostatic cancer, followed shortly by her mother's descent into Alzheimer's disease. And then, when she seemed, to be making progress in therapy, her twenty-year-old godson—the only child of her cousin, a close lifelong friend—drowned in a boating accident. It was in the midst of her bitterness and despair over this last loss that she dreamed of the wall of bodies.

"Keep going, Irene; I'm listening."

"What I mean is, how can you understand me? Your life's unreal—warm, cozy, innocent. Like this office." She pointed to my packed bookshelves behind her and to the scarlet Japanese maple blazing just outside the window. "The only thing missing are some chintz cushions, a fireplace, and a crackling wood fire. Your family surrounds you—all in the same town. An unbroken family circle. What can you *really* know of loss? Do you think you'd handle it any better? Suppose your wife or one of your children was to die right now? How would you do? Even that smug striped shirt of yours—I hate it. Every time you wear it, I wince. I hate what it says!"

"What does it say?"

"It says, 'I've got all my problems solved. Tell me about yours.'"

"You've talked about these feelings before. But they have such force today. Why now? And the dream, why do you dream this dream *now?*"

"I told you I was going to talk to Eric, and yesterday I had dinner with him."

"And?" I prompted her after another of those irritating pauses of hers that implied that I should be able to make the connection between Eric and the dream. She had mentioned this man only once, telling me that his wife had died ten years before and that she had met him at a lecture on bereavement.

"And he confirmed everything I've been saying. He says you're dead wrong about my getting through Jack's death. You don't get through it. You never get over it. Eric's got a new wife and a five-year-old daughter, but the wound still bleeds. He talks to his dead wife every day. He understands me. And I'm convinced now that it's only the people who have been there who *can* understand. There's a silent underground society out there—"

"Underground society?" I interrupted.

"Of people who *really* know—all the survivors, the bereaved. All this time you've been urging me to detach from Jack, to turn toward life, to form a new love—it's all been a mistake. It's a mistake of smugness from those like you who have never lost."

"So only the bereaved can treat the bereaved?"

"Somebody who's been through it."

"I've been hearing that stuff ever since I entered this field!" I burst out at her. "Only alcoholics can treat alcoholics? Or addicts treat addicts? And do you have to have an eating disorder to treat anorexia, or be depressed or manic to treat affective disorders? How about being schizophrenic to treat schizophrenia?"

Irene knew how to press my button. She had an uncanny knack of locating and zeroing in on my major irritants.

"Oh, no, you don't!" she shot back. "I was captain of the varsity debating team at Radcliffe and I know that strategy—reductio ad absurdum! But it's not going to work. Admit it; you know there's truth in what I say."

"No; I disagree. You're totally overlooking the training of therapists! That's what training in my field is all about—to acquire sensitivity, empathy—to be able to enter the world of another, to experience what the patient experiences."

I was irritated all right. And I had learned not to hold back. We worked much better together when I just cut loose with my feelings. Irene could come into my office so depressed she could hardly speak. But once we tangled about something, she inevitably became enlivened. I knew I was assuming Jack's role here. He was the only one ever to stand up to her. Her icy demeanor was daunting to others (her surgery residents referred to her as "the Queen"), but Jack never deferred to her. She told me he took no pains to conceal his feelings, often walking out of the room muttering, "I don't have time for this bullshit."

Not only was I irritated at her insistence that only bereaved therapists can treat bereaved patients but I was also angry at Eric for reinforcing her view that bereavement is never-ending. That idea was part of an ongoing debate between me and Irene. I was taking a well-established, sound position, namely, that the work of mourning consists of gradually detaching oneself from the one who died and redirecting one's energy toward others. Freud first elaborated this understanding of grief in 1915 in *Mourning and Melancholia*, and since then this approach has been supported by much clinical observation and empirical research.

In my own research, completed just before I took on Irene's case, every single widow and widower I studied gradually detached from the dead spouse and then reinvested in something or someone else. And that was true for even those who had had the most loving of marriages. In fact, we found strong evidence that many of the widows who had had the best marriages went through the bereavement and detachment process more easily than those who had had a deeply conflicted one. (The explanation for this paradox lay, it seemed to me, in "regret": for those who had spent their lives married to the wrong person, bereavement was more complicated because they also had to grieve for themselves, for their many squandered years.) Since Irene's marriage appeared to me to have been exceptionally loving and supportive, I had initially predicted a relatively uncomplicated bereavement.

But Irene was highly critical of most traditional attitudes about bereavement. She hated my comments about detachment and dismissed my research out of hand: "We bereaved have learned to give the answers investigators want. We have learned that the world wants us to recover quickly and that it becomes impatient with those who cling too long to losses."

She deeply resented any suggestion that she let go of Jack: two years after his death his personal belongings still lay in his desk drawers, his photos hung throughout the house, his favorite magazines and books were all in place, and she continued long daily conversations with him. I worried that the conversation with Eric would set therapy back months by reinforcing her idea of how wrong I was. Now it would be more difficult than ever to persuade her that eventually she would recover from her grief. As for her foolish belief in a secret silent society of the bereaved who all agreed with her, that was just another of her legion of irrational conceits. No point in dignifying that notion with an answer.

But as always, some of Irene's comments hit home. A story is told about the Swiss sculptor Alberto Giacometti, whose leg was broken in a traffic accident. While lying in the street, waiting for the ambulance, he was heard to say, "Finally, finally, something has happened to me." I know exactly what he meant. Irene had my number all right. Teaching at Stanford for over thirty years, I've lived in the same house, watched my children walk to the same schools, and never had to face darkness. No hard, untimely deaths: my father and mother died old, he seventy, she in her nineties. My sister, seven years older, is healthy. I have lost no close friends, and my four children are nearby and thriving.

For a thinker who has embraced an existential frame of reference, such a benign, shielded life is a liability. Many times I have yearned to venture out of the university's ivory tower into the travails of the real world. For years I imagined spending a sabbatical as a blue-collar worker, perhaps as an ambulance driver in Detroit or a short-order cook in the Bowery or a sandwich maker in a Manhattan deli. But I never did: the siren calls of a colleague's Venetian apartment or a fellowship to Bellagio on Lake Como were irresistible. I've never even had the growth experience of a marital separation and facing adult aloneness. I met Marilyn, my wife, when I was fifteen and decided on the spot that she was the woman for me. (I even bet my best friend $50 that I would marry her—and collected eight years later.) Our marriage has not always been placid—thank God for the Sturm und Drang—but through-out my life she has been a loving friend, always there at my side.

Sometimes I have secretly envied patients living on the edge who have the courage to change their lives radically, who move, leave jobs, change professions, divorce, start all over again. I worry about being a voyeur and wonder if I covertly encourage my patients to take a heroic plunge for me.

All these things I say to Irene. I omit nothing. I tell her she is right about my life—up to a point.

"Yet you're not right when you say I have *no* experience of tragedy. I do whatever I can to bring tragedy closer to me. I keep my death in focus. When I'm with you I often imagine how it would be if my wife were fatally ill, and each time I'm filled with indescribable sadness. I am aware, fully aware, that I'm on the march, that I've moved into another life stage. Taking early retirement from Stanford is an irreversible step. All the signs of aging—my torn knee cartilage, my fading vision, my backaches, my senile plaques, my graying beard and hair, my dreams of my own death—tell me I'm moving toward the end of my life.

"For ten years, Irene, I chose to work with patients dying of cancer, hoping that they would draw me closer to the tragic core of life. That, indeed, happened, and I went back into three years of therapy, seeing Rollo May, whose book *Existence* had been so important to me in my psychiatric training. That therapy was unlike any other personal work I had done before, and I plunged deeply into the experience of my own death."

Irene nodded. I knew that gesture—that characteristic cluster of movements, one sharp chin jerk followed by two or three soft nods, her somatic Morse code signifying that I had made a rea-sonably satisfactory response. I had passed the test—for now.

But I wasn't finished with the dream. "Irene, I think there's more to your dream." I referred to my notes (almost the only notes I take during a session are of dreams because, owing to their evanescence, patients often repress or distort them immediately) and read aloud the first part of her dream: "'I am in this office, in this chair. But there is a strange wall in the middle of the room between us. I can't see you.'

"What impresses me," I continued, "is that last sentence. In the dream it is *you* who can't see *me*. Yet this whole session we've been discussing it the other way around—that it is I who don't see you. Let me ask you something: a few minutes ago when I talked about my aging, you know, my knee surgery, my eyes—"

"Yes, yes, I heard all that," Irene exclaimed, rushing me on.

"You heard it—but as usual, whenever I mention something about my health, your eyes glazed over. Like those couple of weeks after my eye surgery, when I was obviously having a rough time and wore dark glasses, you never asked about the surgery or inquired about how I was doing."

"I don't need to know about your health. I'm the patient here."

"Oh, no, it's much more than that, more than lack of interest, more than your being the patient and me the doctor. You avoid me. You block yourself from learning anything about me. Especially anything that in some way diminishes me. From the very beginning I told you that because of our former social relationship and because of our mutual friends, Earl and Emily, I could not conceal myself from you. Yet you've never once expressed any interest in knowing anything about me. Don't you think that odd?"

"When I started seeing you, I was not going to take the risk of losing someone important to me again. I couldn't go through that. So I had only two choices—"

As she so often did, Irene stopped, as though I should be able to divine the rest of her statement. Although I didn't want to prompt her, it was best, for now, to keep the flow going.

"And those two choices were?"

"Well, not to let you matter to me—but that was impossible. Or not to see you as a real person with a narrative."

"A narrative?"

"Yes, a life narrative—proceeding from a beginning to an end. I want to keep you outside of time."

"Today, as usual, you walked into my office and straight to your chair, without looking at me. You always avoid my eyes. That what you mean by 'outside of time'?"

She nodded. "Looking at you would make you too real."

"And real people have to die."

"Now you've got it."

Lesson 3: Grief Rage

"I just heard, Irene," I began a session one afternoon, "that my brother-in-law died a few hours ago. Suddenly. A coronary. I'm obviously shaken and not at full strength"—I heard my voice quaver—"I'll do my best to stay present with you."

It was hard to say, hard to do, but I felt I had no choice.

Morton, the husband of my only sister, had been a dear friend and an important presence in my life since I was fifteen. I had been staggered by my sister's midday call and immediately booked the next flight to Washington to join her. As I set about canceling my appointments for the next few days, I saw that I had one with Irene in two hours that would still leave me time to catch my flight. Should I keep that appointment?

In our three years together, Irene had never come late for an appointment or missed one, not even during the time of horror when Jack's tumor was ravaging his brain and persona. Despite the nightmare of witnessing her husband's relentless deconstitution, Irene had throughout been faithful to our work. And I had been too. Since our first session, when I promised her, "I will see this through with you," I had committed myself to engaging her as genuinely as I could. My choice, then, on this day of grief, seemed clear: I would meet with her, and I would be honest.

But Irene didn't respond. After we had sat together in silence a couple of minutes, I prodded: "Where do your thoughts go?"

"I was wondering how old he was."

"Seventy. He was just about to retire from his medical practice." I paused and waited. For what? Perhaps just the common

101

decency of a brief condolence. Or even an expression of gratitude for my willingness to see her despite my grief.

Silence. Irene sat unspeaking, her eyes apparently fixed on a small pale coffee stain on the carpet.

"Irene, what's happening in the space between us today?" Without fail I asked this question every session, in accordance with my conviction that nothing took precedence over exploring our relationship.

"Well, he must have been a nice man," she said, her eyes never moving. "Otherwise you wouldn't feel so sad."

"Oh, come on, Irene. The truth. What's going on inside?"

Suddenly she looked up, her eyes blazing. "My husband died at forty-five, and if I can go into the OR every day and operate on my patients and run my office and teach my students, then you sure as hell can come in here and see me!"

It wasn't her words that stunned me but the *sound* of them. That harsh, deep timbre was not Irene. It was not her voice. It was like the preternaturally guttural voice of the young girl in *The Exorcist*. Before I could remark on it, Irene leaned down to pick up her purse.

"I'm leaving!" she said.

My calf muscles tensed—I believe I was preparing myself to tackle her if she bolted for the door. "Oh, no, you're not. Not after that. You're staying right here and talking this out."

"I can't. Can't work, can't stay here with you. Not fit to be with anyone."

"There's only one rule here in this office: that you say exactly what's on your mind. You're doing your job. You've never done it better."

Dropping her purse on the floor, Irene slumped back in her chair. "I told you that after my brother died I always ended my relationships with men the same way."

"How? Tell me again."

"They'd have some mishap, some problem, maybe get sick, and I'd get nasty and cut them out of my life. A quick surgical incision! I cut clean. And I cut sharp."

"Because you'd compare their problem to the immensity of losing Allen? That would make you bitter?"

She nodded her appreciation. "That was most of it, I'm pretty sure. Also that I just didn't want them to matter to me. I didn't want to hear about their puny problems."

"And with me today?"

"Color it red! Rage! I wanted to throw something at you!"

"Because it felt like I was comparing my loss with yours?"

"Yes. And then I thought that when we finish our session, you'll take your loss up your little garden path to your wife, who'll be there waiting with the rest of your tidy, cozy life. That's when it turns red."

My office, only a couple hundred feet from my house, is a comfortable red-tile-roofed cottage enveloped in the lush greens and violets of lupine, wisteria, frangipani, and Spanish lavender. Though Irene loved the serenity of my office, she often made sarcastic comments about my picture-book life.

"It's not just you I feel angry at," she continued. "It's everyone whose life is intact. You've told me about widows who hate being without a role, who hate being the fifth wheel at dinner parties. But it's not the role or being the fifth wheel that matters: it's hating everyone else for having a life; it's envy; it's being filled with bitterness. Do you think I *like* feeling this way?"

"A little while ago when you were preparing to walk out of here, you said you weren't fit to be with anyone."

"Well, am I? Do you want to be with someone who hates you because your wife is alive? Does anyone want that kind of person around? The black ooze—remember? No one wants to be tarred, do they?"

"I stopped you from leaving, didn't I?"

No answer.

"I'm thinking of how dizzy you must feel to be so angry at me and yet so close, so grateful."

She nodded.

"A little louder, Irene. Can't quite hear you."

"Well, I got dizzy thinking about why you told me about your brother-in-law today."

"You seem suspicious."

"Very."

"You have a hunch?"

"More than a hunch. I think you were trying to manipulate me. See how I would react. Giving me a test."

"No wonder you exploded. Maybe it'll help if I tell you exactly what was going on inside of me today after I got the news of Morton's death." I told her how I canceled the rest of my schedule but decided to see her, and why. "I couldn't cancel it—not after your courage in always coming here no matter what. But," I continued, "I still had to face the question of how to be with you and deal with my loss at the same time.

"So what options did I have today, Irene? To shut down and withdraw from you? That would have been worse than canceling. To try to stay close and honest with you and *not* tell you about it? Impossible—a recipe for disaster: I learned long ago that when two people have something big between them and don't talk about it, they don't talk of anything else of importance either. This area here"—I gestured toward the air space between us— "we need to keep it clean and free, and that's my job as well as yours. So that's why I told you what was happening to me straight. Straight as I could—no manipulation, no test, no ulterior motive."

Once again Irene nodded to let me know that I had made a reasonably intelligent response.

Later in the session, just before we ended, Irene apologized for her remark. The following week she told me of describing the incident to a friend who was aghast at her cruelty toward me, and apologized once again.

"No apology was needed," I reassured her, and I meant it, really meant it. In fact, in a curious way I had welcomed her telling me I sure as hell could see her: it was enlivening; it was real; it brought me closer to her. It was the truth about how she felt toward me. Or part of the truth—and I hoped the time would come when I would hear the rest of it.

Irene's rage, which I first encountered in our second month of therapy, was deep and pervasive. Though it flared only occasionally into the open, it always rumbled just below the surface. At first I wasn't much concerned about it. My research had reassured me that such anger was no more worrisome than persistent guilt or regret or denial and would soon dissipate. But in this instance, as often in my work with Irene, the research was misleading. Again and again I have found that "statistically significant" truth (often with the exceptions—the "outliers"—excluded from the calculation for statistical reasons) had little relevance to the truth of my unique encounter with the person of flesh and blood before me.

In a session during our third year, I asked, "What feelings did you take home from our last session? Any thoughts about me during the week?" I pose this type of question often as part of my campaign to focus therapeutic attention on the here-and-now—on the encounter between me and the patient.

She sat in silence for a while, then asked, "Do you think about *me* between sessions?" Although this question from a patient, which most therapists dread, is not uncommon, I somehow hadn't expected it from Irene. Perhaps I hadn't expected her to care, or at least to acknowledge she cared.

"I—I—I often think about your situation," I stuttered. Wrong answer!

She sat for a moment, then stood. "I'm leaving," she said and stomped out, not failing to slam the door behind her.

I saw her through the window, pacing in the garden and smoking a cigarette. I sat and waited. How easy it is for noninteractive therapists, I thought, to deflect that question of hers by such ploys as: "Why do you ask?" or "Why now?" or "What are your fantasies or your wishes about that?" For therapists who are, like me, committed to a more egalitarian, mutually transparent relationship, it's not so easy. Perhaps because the question reveals the limits of therapeutic authenticity: no matter how genuine therapists try to be, how intimate, how honest, there remains an unbridgeable gap, a fundamental inequality between therapist and patient.

I knew that Irene hated my thinking of her as a "situation"—and hated too that she'd allowed me to mean so much to her. I might, of course, have been more sensitive and used a warmer and more personal word than *situation*. But I believe that no appropriate response of mine would have given her what she wanted. She wanted me to be thinking other thoughts—loving, admiring, sensual ones or, perhaps, doting. Yes, *doting*—that's the word.

When she had finished her cigarette, she walked back in with great aplomb and took her seat as though nothing unusual had happened. I continued by appealing to her sense of reality.

"Of course," I pointed out matter-of-factly, "patients think more often about their therapists than therapists think about them. After all, the therapist has many patients, whereas a patient has only one therapist. The same thing was true for me when I was in therapy, and isn't it true for your own surgery patients, and for your students? Don't you loom larger in their minds than they in yours?"

The situation is not really so clear-cut. I didn't talk about the fact that therapists *do* think about patients between sessions—especially about the problematic ones who, in one way or another, vex the therapist. Therapists may ponder their strong emotional reactions to a patient or puzzle about the best technical approach. (A therapist who becomes overly caught up in angry, vindictive, loving, or erotic fantasies about a patient should, of course, seek a discussion with a colleague-friend, a professional consultant, or a personal therapist.)

Of course, I didn't tell Irene that I often thought about her between sessions. She puzzled me. I worried about her. Why was she not getting better? The great majority of widows I had treated began to improve after the first year; every one showed significant improvement by the end of the second year. But not Irene. Her despair and hopelessness continued to deepen. She experienced no joy in her life. After putting her daughter to bed, she wept every evening; she persisted in engaging in lengthy conversations with her dead husband; she rejected all invitations to meet new people and refused even to consider the possibility of another important relationship with a man.

I'm an impatient therapist, and my frustration grew. And so did my concern for Irene: the magnitude of her suffering began to alarm me. I worried about suicide—I am convinced that she would have taken her life if it had not been for her daughter. On two occasions I sent her to colleagues for formal consultation.

Though I was taxed by Irene's major eruptions of grief rage, I found it even more difficult to deal with her milder but more pervasive expressions of rage. Her list of grievances about me was long and growing, and we rarely got through an hour without some expression of anger.

She was angry at me for attempting to help her to detach from Jack and direct her energy elsewhere and for encouraging her to meet other men. And angry at me for not being Jack. As a result of our deep engagement, our intimate exchanges, our fighting, our mutual caring, it was with me that she most approximated the feelings she had had with her husband. And then, at the end of the hour, she hated having to go back to a life with neither me nor Jack. That's what made the ending of every session so tumultuous. She hated the reminder that our relationship had formal boundaries, and no matter how I signaled that we were at the end of our hour, she often exploded: "You call this a real relationship? This is not real! You look at the clock and just kick me out, throw me away!"

Sometimes she sat there at the end of the hour, glaring and refusing to budge. Any appeals to reason—to pointing out the necessity for schedules, to her own scheduling of patients, to suggestions that *she* watch the clock and end the hour, to repeating that my ending the hour was not a signal of rejection—all these fell on deaf ears. Far more often than not, she left my office angry.

She was angry at me for being important to her and angry that I wouldn't do some of the things Jack had done; for example, compliment her on all her good points—her appearance, her resourcefulness, her intelligence. We often had pitched battles about compliments. I felt that a recitation of compliments would infantilize her, but she put so much emphasis on it, was so insistent, that I often complied. I asked her what she wanted me to say and practically repeated her words back, always trying to include some original observation. Yet what seemed like a bizarre charade to me almost without fail raised her spirits. But only temporarily: she had holes in her pockets, and by the next session she insisted that I do it again.

She was angry at my presuming to understand her. If I tried to combat her pessimism by reminding her that she was in the midst of a process that had a beginning and an end and by offering reassurance from some of the results of my research, she responded angrily, "You're depersonalizing me. You're disregarding what's unique in my experience."

Any optimism I expressed about her recovery she invariably turned into an accusation that I wanted her to forget Jack.

Any mention of the possibility of her meeting another man was a minefield. For the most part she was contemptuous of the men she met and angry at me for suggesting she examine her judgmentalism. Any practical suggestion I offered ignited a major eruption. "If I want to date," she said furiously, "I can figure out how to do it! Why pay you good money for dating advice when my friends can give me the same thing?"

She grew angry if I offered concrete suggestions about anything: "Stop trying to 'fix' things!" she said. "That's what my father tried to do my whole life."

She was angry at my impatience with her slow progress and at my failing to acknowledge the efforts she had made to help herself (but never mentioned to me).

Irene wanted me strong and healthy. Any infirmity—a sprained back, a knee injury requiring meniscus surgery, a cold, a case of flu—elicited much annoyance. I knew that she was apprehensive as well, but she kept that well concealed.

Most of all, she was angry at my being alive when Jack was dead.

None of this was easy for me. I have never relished angry confrontations and, in my personal life, generally avoid angry people. Because I am a deliberate thinker and writer, and confrontation tends to slow my thoughts, I have throughout my career declined public debate and discouraged all inquires about my becoming a departmental chairman.

So how did I cope with Irene's anger? For one thing, I leaned on the old therapy adage that one must separate role and person. Often much of a patient's anger toward a therapist is related to his or her *role*, not *person*. "Don't take it personally," young therapists are taught. Or at least, don't take *everything* personally. Make an attempt to discriminate between what belongs to your person and what to your role. It seemed self-evident that much of Irene's anger belonged elsewhere—life, destiny, God, cosmic indifference—but she simply discharged it upon her nearest target: me, her therapist. Irene knew that her anger oppressed me and let me know in many ways. One day, for example, when my secretary called her to reschedule an appointment because I had to see the dentist, Irene replied, "Oh, well, seeing the dentist is probably a pleasure for him compared to seeing me."

But perhaps the main reason I was not ground down by Irene's rage was that I always knew that it masked her profound sadness, despair, and fear. When she expressed anger toward me, I sometimes responded with reflexive irritation and impatience, but more often with compassion. Many of Irene's images or phrases haunted me. One, in particular, set up housekeeping in my mind and never failed to soften my experience of her grief rage. It was in one of her airport dreams (during the first two years after her husband's death, she often wandered through airports in her dreams).

I am dashing through a terminal. Looking for Jack. I don't know the airline. I don't know the flight number. I am desperate . . . scanning the lists of departure flights for some clue—but nothing makes sense—all the destinations are written in nonsense syllables. Then hope appears—I can read one sign over a departure gate: 'Mikado,' it says. I rush to the gate. But too late. The plane has just left, and I wake up crying.

"That destination—Mikado? What are your associations to Mikado?" I asked.

"I don't need associations," she said, flicking away my question. "I know exactly why I dreamed of Mikado. I used to sing the operetta when I was a child. There's a verse in it that will not go away:

> *Though the night may come too soon*
> *we have years and years of afternoon.*

Irene stopped and looked at me, eyes glistening with tears. No point in saying any more. Not for her. Not for me. She was beyond comforting. From that day on, the line "we have years and years of afternoon" reverberated in my mind. She and Jack had never had their share of afternoons, and for that I could forgive her everything.

My third advanced lesson, grief rage, proved of great value in other clinical situations. Where in the past I had generally veered too quickly away from anger, attempting to understand and resolve it as expeditiously as possible, now I was learning how to contain anger, how to seek it out and plunge into it. And the lesson's specific vehicle? That's where the black ooze comes in.

Lesson 4: The Black Ooze

At the time of my brother-in-law's death, when threatening to walk out and asking whether I wanted to be with someone who hated me because my wife was alive, Irene had referred to a *black ooze*. "Remember?" she had asked. "No one wants to be tarred, do they?" It was a metaphor she had invoked in most of our sessions during the first two years of therapy.

What was the black ooze? Over and over, she strained to find the precise words. "It's some black, hideous, acrid substance that seeps out of me and spreads around me in a pool. The black ooze is vile and noisome. It repels and revolts anyone who approaches me. It tars them too, puts them in great danger."

Though the black ooze had many meanings, first and foremost it signified her grief rage. Hence her hating me for having a living spouse. Irene's dilemma was awful: she could remain silent, choking on her own fury, and feel desperately alone. Or she could explode in rage, driving everyone away, and feel desperately alone.

Since the image of the black ooze was deeply etched in her mind, not to be dislodged by reason or rhetoric, I used the metaphor to guide my therapy. To dissolve it I needed not the therapeutic word but the *therapeutic act*.

Hence, I tried to stay close to her in her rage, to face down her anger—as Jack had done. I had to engage her, wrestle with her fury, refuse to let her push me away. Her anger took many shapes—she was forever setting tests and traps for me. One particularly treacherous trap provided an auspicious opportunity for the therapeutic act.

After several months of severe agitation and discouragement, she arrived one day at my office inexplicably calm and content.

"It's wonderful to see you so tranquil," I remarked. "What's happened?"

"I just made a landmark decision," she said. "I've jettisoned all expectations for personal happiness or self-fulfillment. No more yearning for love, for sex, for companionship, for artistic creation. From now on I'm going to devote myself entirely to fulfilling my job description—being a mother and a surgeon." All this she said with an air of great composure and well-being.

During the previous few weeks I had become greatly concerned about the intensity and relentlessness of her despair and wondered how much more she could endure. So despite the odd abruptness of her change, I was so grateful that she had found some way, any way, to diminish her pain that I chose not to inquire further into its source. Instead I took it as a blessed event—not unlike the peace achieved by many Buddhists who, through meditative practice, alleviate suffering by systematically detaching themselves from all personal cravings.

To be honest, I did not expect Irene's transformation to endure, but I hoped that even a temporary respite from her relentless pain might initiate a more positive cycle in her life. If a state of calm permitted her to stop tormenting herself, to make adaptive decisions, to develop new friends, perhaps even to meet a suitable man, then I believed it made little difference how she initially achieved that state of mind: she could simply pull up the ladder and ascend to the next level.

The next day, however, she phoned in a fury: "Do you realize what you've done? What kind of therapist are you? Your caring for me! All pretense! Pretense! The truth is, you're willing to sit back and calmly watch me renounce everything vital in my life—all love, joy, excitement—everything! No, no, it's more than just sitting back; you're willing to be an accomplice to my self-murder!"

Once again she threatened to leave therapy, but I finally persuaded her to return for the next hour.

Over the next couple of days I ruminated about the sequence of events. The more I thought about it, the angrier I became. Once again I had played the balloon-headed Charley Brown trying to kick the football that Lucy invariably pulls away at the last second. By the time our next session rolled around, my anger matched Irene's. That session was less like therapy than a wrestling match. It was the most serious fight we had had. The accusations gushed out of her: "You've given up on me! You want me to compromise by killing vital parts of myself!"

I made no pretense of empathizing or understanding her position, "I'm sick and tired," I told her, "of your minefields. I'm sick and tired of your setting tests for me that more often than not I fail. And of all the tests, this is the dirtiest, most treacherous one.

"We have too much work to do, Irene," I finished, taking a line from her dead husband. "We don't have time for this bullshit."

It was one of our best hours. At its end (after, of course, another skirmish about ending on time and her accusing me of throwing her out of the office) our therapeutic alliance was stronger than ever. Neither in my textbooks nor in my supervision or classroom teaching would I ever dream of advising a student to tangle angrily with a patient; yet such a session invariably moved Irene forward.

It was the metaphor of the black ooze that guided these efforts. By making contact, emotional contact, by wrestling with her (I speak figuratively, though there were times when I felt we were on the brink of a physical struggle), I was proving again and again that the black ooze was a fiction that neither tarred, nor repelled, nor endangered me. Irene clung so strongly to the metaphor that she was convinced each time I approached her rage that I would either abandon her or die.

Finally, in an effort to demonstrate once and for all that her anger would neither destroy me nor drive me away, I laid down a new therapy ground rule: "Whenever you really explode at me, we will automatically schedule an extra appointment that week." This act proved highly effective; in retrospect, I consider it inspired.

The black-ooze metaphor was particularly powerful because it was *overdetermined:* it was a single image that satisfied and expressed several different unconscious dynamics. Grief rage was one important meaning. But there were others; for example, the belief that she was poisonous, contaminated, fatally jinxed. "Anyone," she said to me one session, "who sets foot in the black ooze is signing their own death warrant."

"So you dare not love again because you can offer only a Medusa-love that would destroy anyone who approaches you?"

"All the men I've loved have died—my husband, my father, my brother, my godson, and Sandy, whom I've not yet told you about—a mentally ill boyfriend who twenty years ago committed suicide."

"Coincidence again! You've got to let it go!" I insisted. "It's bad luck, and it has no implications for the future. The dice have no memory."

"Coincidence, coincidence—your favorite term!" she scoffed. "The proper term is *karma*, and it's clearly telling me that I must love no other man."

Her jinxed self-image reminded me of Joe Bfstplk, the character in the *Lil' Abner* comic strip over whose head an ominous black cloud eternally hovers. How was I to undermine Irene's belief in a cursed karma? I ultimately approached it much as I did her rage. More than words were needed: I had to offer a therapeutic act, and that consisted of disregarding her warnings, of repeatedly coming close to her, of moving into the jinxed, toxic space and remaining alive and healthy.

Still another meaning of the black ooze was connected in Irene's mind with a dream she had once had of a beautiful dark-eyed woman who wore a red rose in her hair and reclined on a sofa.

As I approach closer, I realize that the woman is not as she has seemed: her sofa is a bier, her eyes are dark not with beauty but with death, and the crimson rose is no flower but a bloody mortal wound.

"I know I am this woman, and anyone approaching me will, ipso facto, be introduced to death—another reason not to get too close."

The image of the woman with the crimson rose in her hair recalled to my mind the plot of *The Man in the Maze*, an extraordinary futuristic novel by Philip Dick in which a man is sent to a newly discovered world to make contact with an advanced race of beings. Though he employs every imaginable communicational device—geometrical symbols, mathematical invariants, musical themes, hailing, yelling, arm waving—he is sublimely ignored. But his efforts disturbed the tranquillity of the beings, who do not allow his hubris to go unpunished. Just before he departs to return to Earth, they perform a mysterious neurosurgical procedure upon him. Only much later does he understand the nature of his punishment: the surgery makes it impossible for him to contain his existential angst. Not only is he continually buffeted by the dread of sheer contingency and his own inevitable death but he is doomed to isolation, since anyone approaching within hundreds of feet is exposed to the same withering blasts of existential dread.

However much I insisted to Irene that the black ooze was a fiction, the truth is that I was often trapped in it. In my work with Irene, I suffered the fate of those who approached Philip Dick's protagonist too closely: I was buffeted by my own existential verities. Again and again our sessions confronted me with my own death. Though I have always known that death is there waiting, whirring faintly just beneath the membrane of my life, I have generally managed to put it out of mind.

Of course, there are salutary effects of dwelling upon death; I understand that though the *fact* (the physicality) of death destroys us, the *idea* of death may save us. This is old wisdom: it is why, for centuries, monks kept skulls in their cells and why Montaigne advised living in a room with a view of a cemetery. My awareness of death had long served to vitalize my life, helping me to trivialize what is trivial and to value what is truly precious. Yes, I knew these things intellectually, but I knew also that I could not live constantly exposed to the white heat of death terror.

So, in the past, I had generally put thoughts of death on the back burner of consciousness. But my work with Irene would no longer permit that. Again and again my hours with her heightened not only my sensitivity to death and my sense of life's preciousness but also my death anxiety. More times than I can remember, I found myself brooding over the fact that her husband was stricken down at forty-five while I would never see sixty again. I know I am in the dying zone, the time of life when I could be extinguished at any moment.

Whoever said that therapists are overpaid?

Lesson 5: Reason Versus Treason

As our work proceeded into the third year, I grew more and more discouraged. Therapy had hopelessly bogged down. So deeply mired in depression was Irene that I could not budge her. Nor approach her: when I inquired about how close or distant she felt in a session, she responded, "Miles and miles away—I can barely see you."

"Irene, I know you may be tired of hearing this, but we absolutely must consider beginning an antidepressant. We've got to understand and resolve why you're so fixed in your opposition to medication."

"We both know what medication means."

"Oh?"

"It means you're quitting, giving up on our therapy work. I am not looking to be quickly fixed."

"Quickly fixed, Irene? Three years?"

"I mean, making me feel better is no solution. It only postpones dealing with what I've lost."

No matter what arguments I used, I could not dissuade her from these beliefs, but eventually she humored me by allowing me to prescribe antidepressants. The result was the same as on our previous trial two years before. Three different drugs were not only ineffective but resulted in unpleasant side effects: severe somnolence; alien and frightening dreams; loss of all sexuality and sensuality; a frightening sense of nothing mattering, of being removed from herself and her concerns. When I suggested that she consult a psychopharmacologist, she flatly refused. Desperate, I finally laid down an ultimatum: "You must see the consultant

117

and follow his recommendations or I will not continue to work with you."

Irene looked at me unblinkingly. As usual, precise and constrained, she gave nothing extra in speech or movement. "I'll consider it and give you my answer next session," she said.

But at our next meeting she did not respond directly to the ultimatum. Instead she handed me an issue of the *New Yorker*, open to an article by the Russian poet Joseph Brodsky titled "On Grief and Reason."

"In this," she said, "you'll find the key to what's gone wrong in therapy. If not, if you read it and find no answer, then I'll see your consultant."

Patients often ask me to read something of interest to them—some self-help book, an article about a new treatment or theory, a piece of literature that strikes close to their own situation. More than one writer-patient has handed me a long manuscript, saying, "You'll learn a great deal about me by reading this." This proposition has never proved valid: the patient could always have delivered the material verbally in far less time. Nor do they want an honest opinion of the writing from me—I generally loom too important to the patient to have the freedom to offer an objective commentary. Obviously they seek something else—my approval and admiration—and a therapist has far more direct and effective ways of dealing with that need than spending long hours reading a manuscript. I generally search for a gracious way to decline such requests—or at most agree to a quick skim. I value and protect my personal reading time.

Yet I did not feel burdened as I began reading the article Irene had given me. I had great respect not only for her taste but for her clarity of mind, and if she believed this article contained the key to our impasse, I was confident that the time invested would be well spent. Of course, I would have preferred more direct communication, but I was learning to be receptive to Irene's oblique and often poetic mode of discourse—a language she had learned from her mother. Unlike her father, a paragon of lucid rationality who had taught science in a small Midwestern high school, her mother, an artist, had communicated subtly. Irene had learned about her mother's moods indirectly. On good days, for example, her mother might say, "I think I'll put some irises in the blue-and-white vase," or convey her mood by the way she arranged the dolls on Irene's bed each morning.

The article opened with Brodsky's analysis of the first two stanzas of Robert Frost's poem "Come In":

> As I came to the edge of the woods,
> Thrush music—hark!
> Now if it was dusk outside,
> Inside it was dark.
>
> Too dark in the woods for a bird
> By sleight of wing
> To better its perch for the night,
> Though it still could sing.

"Come In" is, I had always thought, a lovely, and simple, nature poem, one I had memorized as an adolescent and recited aloud while bicycle riding through the Old Soldiers' Home in Washington, D.C. But here, in a brilliant line-by-line, word-by-word analysis, Brodsky demonstrated that the poem conveys a darker meaning. For example, in the first stanza, there is something sinister in the thrush's (the poet, the bard himself) coming to the edge of the woods and contemplating the dark interior. And doesn't the second stanza seem far more than a lyrical tune? Indeed, what does the poet mean by saying that it is too dark in the woods for a poet by "sleight of wing" to better his or her perch for the night? Does "sleight of wing" refer to religious ritual, perhaps last rites? Is Frost lamenting that it is too late, that he is slated for damnation? And indeed, later stanzas confirm that view. In short, Brodsky makes a powerful case not only for the poem's being a dark poem indeed but for Frost's being a far darker poet than many have realized.

I was fascinated. This discussion illuminated why this poem, like many of Frost's other deceptively simple works, had so gripped me as a youth. But the connection with Irene? The key to our problems in therapy she had promised? I read on.

Brodsky next turned to an analysis of a long narrative poem, the grim pastoral "Home Burial." The poem, set on a banistered stairway in a small farmhouse, is a conversation, a series of movements, a ballet, between a farmer and his wife. (I immediately thought, of course, of Irene's parents, who had lived on a Midwestern farm, and also of the stairway with banister that Irene had descended almost three decades ago to answer the phone bringing her the news of Allen's death.) The poem begins:

> *He saw her from the bottom of the stairs*
> *Before she saw him. She was starting down,*
> *Looking back over her shoulder at some fear.*

The farmer advances to his wife, asking, "What is it you see/ From up there always?—for I want to know." Although the wife is terrified and refuses to answer, she is confident that he will never see what she sees and allows him to mount the stairs. Coming to the upstairs window, he stares out and discovers what she has been looking at. He is surprised he has never noticed it before.

> *"The little graveyard where my people are!*
> *So small the window frames the whole of it.*
> *Not so much larger than a bedroom, is it?*
> *There are three stones of slate and one of marble,*
> *Broad-shouldered little slabs there in the sunlight*
> *On the sidehill. We haven't to mind those.*
> *But I understand: it is not the stones,*
> *But the child's mound———"*
> > *"Don't, don't, don't,*
> > *don't," she cried.*

With that, the wife slips past him, goes downstairs and turns on him "with such a daunting look," and heads for the front door. Puzzled, he asks, "Can't a man speak of his own child he's lost?"

"Not you!" she answers. Nor perhaps can any man, she adds, reaching for her hat.

The farmer, asking to be allowed into her grief, continues with these unfortunate words:

> *"I do think, though, you overdo it a little.*
> *What was it brought you up to think it the thing*
> *To take your mother-loss of a first child*
> *So inconsolably—in the face of love.*
> *You'd think his memory might be satisfied——"*

When his wife remains aloof, he exclaims, "God, what a woman! And it's come to this, / A man can't speak of his own child that's dead."

His wife responds that he doesn't know how to speak, that he has no feelings. She watched him through her window as he briskly dug their son's grave, "making the gravel leap and leap in air." And after finishing digging, he went into the kitchen. She remembers,

> *"You could sit there with the stains on your shoes*
> *Of the fresh earth from your own baby's grave*
> *And talk about your everyday concerns.*
> *You had stood the spade up against the wall*
> *Outside there in the entry, for I saw it."*

The wife insists that she won't have grief treated in this fashion. Nor let it be lightly dismissed.

> *"No, from the time when one is sick to death,*
> *One is alone, and he dies more alone.*
> *Friends make pretense of following to the grave,*
> *But before one is in it, their minds are turned*

> *And making the best of their way back to life*
> *And living people, and things they understand.*
> *But the world's evil. I won't have grief so*
> *If I can change it. Oh, I won't, I won't!"*

The husband responds patronizingly that he knows she will feel better for having said these things. It's time to end grief, he suggests. "[Your] heart's gone out of it: Why keep it up?"

The poem ends with the wife opening the door to leave. Her husband tries to block her:

> *"Where do you mean to go? First tell me that.*
> *I'll follow and bring you back by force. I will!—"*

Enthralled, I read the piece straight through, and at the end I had to remind myself of the reason I was reading it. What key to Irene's inner life did it hold? I thought first of her initial dream in which she had to read an earlier text before she could read the contemporary one. Obviously, we had more work to do on Irene's loss of her brother. I had already learned that his death had set off, domino fashion, many other losses. Her home was never the same: her mother never recovered from her son's death and remained chronically depressed; her parents' relationship was never again harmonious.

Perhaps the poem was a stark portrayal of what must have gone on in Irene's home after her brother's death, especially the parental clash as her father and mother each dealt with their loss in diametrically opposed ways. This situation is not uncommon after the death of a child: husband and wife grieve in different fashions (characteristically following gender stereotypes: more often than not the female grieves openly and emotively, while the male deals with grief through repression and active diversion). For many couples each of these two patterns actively interferes with the other—that is precisely the reason that so many marriages break up after the loss of a child.

I thought of Irene's connection to other images in Frost's "Home Burial." The changing view of the burial plot's size was a brilliant metaphor: to the farmer it was both the size of the bedroom and so small that it was framed by the window; to the mother it was so large that she could see nothing else. And the windows. Irene was drawn to windows. "I'd like to live out my life in a high-rise apartment staring out the window," she had said once. Or she imagined moving to a large seaside Victorian house where "I'd divide my time there between staring through the window at the ocean and pacing the rooftop widow's walk forever."

The farmer's wife's bitter dismissal of friends who, after visiting the grave briefly, immediately made their way back to their everyday lives had been a familiar theme of Irene's in therapy. Once, to make this point more graphic, Irene had brought in a print of Pieter Brueghel's *Fall of Icarus*. "Look at these peasants," she said, "working away, not bothering to look up at the boy falling from the sky." She had even brought in Auden's poetic description of the painting:

> *In Brueghel's Icarus, for instance: how everything turns away*
> *Quite leisurely from the disaster; the ploughman may*
> *Have heard the splash, the forsaken cry,*
> *But for him it was not an important failure; the sun shone*
> *As it had to on the white legs disappearing into the green*
> *Water; and the expensive delicate ship that must have seen*
> *Something amazing, a boy falling out of the sky,*
> *Had somewhere to get to and sailed calmly on.*

Other aspects of Irene in Frost's "Home Burial"? The mother's clinging to grief and the father's matter-of-factness and impatience with her for not letting it go: that too I had heard her describe in her own family.

But these observations, however graphic and informative, did not sufficiently explain why Irene had placed such importance on my reading the article. "The key to what has gone wrong in therapy": those were her words, her promise. I felt let down. Perhaps I've overestimated her, I thought; for once she has missed the mark.

At our next session Irene entered the office and, as usual, marched past me to her chair without looking at me. She settled in, placed her purse on the floor next to her, then—instead of staring out the window in silence for a few moments as she usually did—she turned immediately to me and asked, "You read the article?"

"Yes, I did, and it's a marvelous piece. Thanks for giving it to me."

"And?" she prodded.

"And it was gripping; I've heard you talk about your parents' life after Allen's death, but the poem brought it home to me with extraordinary intensity. I understand now so much more clearly why you could never return to live with them again and how closely you identified with your mother's way and her struggle with her father and—"

I couldn't continue. The expression of growing disbelief on Irene's face stopped me cold. Her astonished stare was that of a teacher facing some dunderhead of a pupil as she wondered how he could ever have been promoted to her class.

Finally, through clenched teeth, Irene hissed, "The farmer and the wife in that poem are not my mother and my father. *They're us—you and me.*" She paused, caught herself, and a moment later added in a softer voice, "I mean, they may have *characteristics* of my parents, but essentially the farmer and his wife are *you and me in this room.*"

My head reeled. Of course! Of course! Instantaneously, every line of "Home Burial" took on new meaning. I scrambled furiously. Never before or since has my mind worked more quickly.

"So it is *I* who brings the dirty shovel into the house?"

Irene nodded briskly.

"And *I* who enters the kitchen with muddy, grave-stained shoes?"

Irene nodded again. Not uncharitably this time. Perhaps my quick recovery would redeem me yet.

"And *I* who chides you for clinging to grief? Who says you overdo it, who asks, 'Why keep it up when his memory must be satisfied by now?' *I* who digs the grave so briskly that the gravel leaps into the air? *I* whose words continually give offense? And it is *I* who tries to force himself between you and your grief? And certainly *I* who blocks you at the door and tries to force grief medicine down your throat?"

Irene nodded as tears gathered in her eyes and rolled down her cheeks. It was the first time in her three years of despair that she had wept openly in my presence. I handed her a tissue. And took one for myself. She reached out for my hand. We were back together again.

How had we grown so far apart? Looking back, I see that we had a fundamental clash of sensibilities: I an existential rationalist; she a grief-stricken romantic. Perhaps the rift was unavoidable; perhaps our modes of coping with tragedy were intrinsically opposed. How *does* one best face the brutal existential facts of life? I believe that at bottom Irene felt that there were only two, equally unpalatable, strategies: to adopt some form of denial or to live in intolerably anxious awareness. Wasn't Cervantes voicing this dilemma through his immortal Don's question, "Which will you have: wise madness or foolish sanity?"

I have a bias that powerfully affects my therapeutic approach: I have never believed that awareness leads to madness, or denial to sanity. I have long regarded denial as the enemy, and I challenge it whenever possible in my therapy and in my personal life. Not only have I attempted to shed all personal illusions that narrow my vision and foster smallness and dependency but I encourage my patients to do the same. I am persuaded that although honest confrontation with one's existential situation may evoke fear and trembling, it is ultimately healing and enriching. My psychotherapeutic approach is thus epitomized by Thomas Hardy's comment, "If a way to the Better there be, it exacts a full look at the Worst."

And so, from the very beginning of therapy, I spoke to Irene with the voice of reason. I encouraged her to rehearse with me the events surrounding and following her husband's death:

"How will you learn of his death?"

"Will you be with him when he dies?"

"What will you feel?"

"Whom will you call?"

And in the same way, she and I rehearsed his funeral. I told her I would attend the funeral and that if her friends would not linger with her at the graveside, I would be sure to do so. If others were too frightened to hear her macabre thoughts, I would encourage her to speak them to me. I tried to take the terror out of her nightmares.

Whenever she moved into irrational realms, I could be counted on to confront her. Consider, for example, her guilt for enjoying herself with another man. She considered any life enjoyment a betrayal of Jack. If she went with a man to a beach or a restaurant she and Jack had once visited, she felt she was betraying him by violating the specialness of their love. On the other hand, going to a brand-new spot elicited survivor guilt: "Why should I be alive and enjoying new experiences when Jack is dead?" She also felt guilty for not having been a good enough wife. As a result of psychotherapy, she underwent many changes: she became softer, more considerate and affectionate. "How unfair to Jack," she said, "that I should be able to give more of myself to another man than to him."

Again and again I challenged such statements. "Where is Jack now?" I asked. She always answered, "Nowhere—except in memory"—in her memory and in the memory of others. She had no religious beliefs and never posited the persistence of consciousness, or any other form of afterlife. So I pestered her with reason: "If he is not sentient and does not observe your actions, how then can he be hurt by your being with another man?" Besides, I reminded her, Jack had, before he died, explicitly expressed his wishes for her to be happy and to remarry. "Would he want you, and his daughter, to drown in sorrow? So even if his consciousness *did* still exist, he would not feel betrayed; he'd be pleased by your recovery. And either way," I'd wind up, "no matter whether Jack's consciousness survived or did not survive, such concepts as *unfairness* and *betrayal* had no meaning."

At times Irene had vivid dreams of Jack's being alive—a common phenomenon in bereavement—only to awaken with a thud to realize it was but a dream. Other times she would weep bitterly about his being "out there" suffering. Sometimes when she visited the cemetery, she wept at the "awful thought" of his being locked in a cold casket. She dreamed of opening her freezer and finding a miniature Jack, his eyes wide open, staring at her. Methodically and relentlessly, I would remind her of her conviction that he *wasn't* out there, that he no longer existed as a sentient being. And reminded her as well of her wish that he *could* observe her. In my experience, every bereaved spouse suffers from feeling that his or her life is unobserved.

Irene held on to many of Jack's personal effects, often rummaging through the contents of his desk drawers for some memento of him whenever she needed a birthday present for her daughter. So surrounded was she by material reminders of Jack that I worried Irene would become like Miss Havisham in Dickens's *Great Expectations*, a woman so caught up in grief (she had been deserted at the altar) that she lived for years in the cobwebs of loss, never taking off her wedding dress or clearing off the table set for her wedding feast. Hence, throughout therapy I urged Irene to turn away from the past, to rejoin life, to loosen her ties with Jack: "Take down some of your photos of him. Redecorate your home. Buy a new bed. Clean out the desk drawers; throw things away. Travel somewhere new. Do something you've never done before. Stop talking so much to Jack."

But what I called reason, Irene called treason. What I called rejoining life, she called betrayal of love. What I called detachment from the dead, she called abandonment of her love.

I thought I was being the rationalist she needed; she thought I was polluting the purity of her grief. I thought I was leading her back into life; she thought I was forcing her to turn her back on Jack. I thought I was inspiriting her to become the existential hero; she thought I was a smug spectator watching her tragedy from a safe grandstand seat.

I was stunned by her obstinacy. Why can't she get it? I wondered. Why can't she get that Jack is really dead, that his consciousness is extinguished? That it isn't her fault? That she is not jinxed, that she will not cause my death or the death of the next man she loves? That she is not fated to experience tragedy forever? That she is clinging to crooked beliefs because she so fears the alternative: recognizing that she lives in a universe absolutely indifferent to whether she is happy or unhappy.

And she wondered at my obtuseness. Why can't Irv get it? Why doesn't he see that he is defacing my memory of Jack, defiling my grief by tracking in grave mud and leaving the shovel in the kitchen? Why can't he understand that I just want to look out the window at Jack's grave? That it infuriates me when he tries to yank me away from my heart? That there are times when, despite my need for him, I absolutely have to get away from him, squeeze by him on the stairs, breathe fresh air? That I'm drowning, I'm clinging to the wreckage of my life, and he keeps trying to pry my fingers away? Why can't he get it that Jack died because of my poisoned love?

That evening, as I reviewed the session in my mind, another patient whom I had seen decades earlier came into my mind. Throughout adolescence she had been locked in a long, bitter struggle with her nay-saying father. When she left home for the first time, he drove her to college and, in typical fashion, ruined the trip by grousing the entire time about the ugly, garbage-littered stream by the side of the road. She, on the other hand, saw a beautiful rustic, unspoiled creek. Years later, after he died, she chanced to make the trip again and noted that there were *two* streams, one on each side of the road. "But this time I was the driver," she said sadly, "and the stream I saw through the driver's window was just as ugly and polluted as my father had described it."

All the components of this lesson—my impasse with Irene, her insistence that I read Frost's poem, my recollection of my patient's story of the automobile ride—had been deeply instructive. With astonishing clarity, I understood now that it was time for me to listen, to set aside my personal worldview, to stop imposing my style and my views upon my patient. It was time to look out Irene's window.

Lesson 6:
Never Send to Know for Whom the Bell Tolls

One day, in the fourth year of therapy, Irene arrived carrying a large portfolio. She put it on the floor, slowly unbuckled it, and pulled out a big canvas, keeping its back toward me so I couldn't see it.

"Did I tell you I was taking art lessons?" she asked in an uncharacteristically playful manner.

"No. First I've heard of it. But I think that's great."

And I did. I took no umbrage that she mentioned it en passant; every therapist is used to patients' forgetting to mention the good things in their lives. Perhaps it's simply a misunderstanding, a mistaken assumption by patients that since therapy is pathology-oriented, therapists want to hear only about problems. Other patients, however, who are dependent upon therapy choose to conceal positive developments lest their therapists conclude that they no longer need help.

Now, taking a breath, Irene flipped the canvas. Before me gleamed a still life, a simple wooden bowl containing a lemon, an orange, and an avocado. While impressed with her graphic skills, I felt disappointed in her subject matter, so flat and pointless. I would have hoped for something more relevant to our work. But I feigned interest and was convincingly enthusiastic in my praise.

Not as convincing as I had thought, I soon learned. In the next session she announced, "I'm signing up for another six months of art lessons."

"That's wonderful. Same teacher?"

"Yes, same teacher, same class."

"You mean a still-life class?"

"You're hoping not, I think. Obviously there's something you're not sharing."

"Like what?" I began to feel uncomfortable. "What's your hunch?"

"I see I've hit on something." Irene grinned. "Almost never do you fall back on the traditional shrink practice of answering a question with a question."

"Never miss a trick, Irene. Okay, the truth is that I had two very different feelings about the painting." Here I invoked a practice I always teach my students: when two opposing feelings put you in a dilemma, your best recourse is to express both feelings and the dilemma. "First, as I said, I admired it greatly. I have absolutely no artistic talent and am filled with respect for work of such quality." I hesitated, and Irene nudged me:

"But—"

"But—well—uh—I'm so pleased with your finding pleasure in painting that I dread sounding even slightly critical, but I guess I was hoping that you might do something with your art that might be more—uh—how to put it?—*resonant* with our therapy."

"Resonant?"

"One thing I like about our work together is that you invariably respond with substance whenever I ask about what's passing through your mind. Sometimes it's a thought, but even more commonly you describe some mental image. With your extraordinary visual sense, I was hoping you could combine your art and therapy in some synergistic manner. I don't know—possibly I was hoping the painting might be more expressionistic, or cathartic, or illuminating. Maybe you could even work through some painful issues on canvas. But the still life, while technically wonderful, is so—so—serene, so far removed from conflict and pain."

Seeing Irene's eyes rolling up, I added, "You asked for my feelings, and there they are. I'm not defending them. In fact, I suspect

I'm making a mistake by being critical of any activity that provides you an interlude of peace."

"Irv, I don't think you know much about painting. Do you know what the French call a still life?"

I shook my head.

"*Nature morte.*"

"Dead nature."

"Right. To paint a still life is to meditate on death and decay. When I paint fruit, I can't avoid observing how my still-life models are dying and decomposing day after day. When I paint I am very close to our therapy, pointedly aware of Jack's passage from life into dust, very aware of the presence of death and the smell of decay in everything that lives."

"Everything?" I ventured.

She nodded.

"You? Me?"

"Everything," she replied. "Especially me."

At last! I had been scratching for Irene's last statement, or something like it, since the very beginning of our work. It heralded a new phase in therapy, as I recognized from the strong dream she brought in a couple of weeks later.

I am sitting at a table—like an executive board table. There are others there as well, and you are sitting at the head of the table. We are all working on something—perhaps reviewing grant proposals. You ask me to bring some papers to you. It is a small room, and to get to you I have to pass very close to a row of windows that are open and reach all the way to the floor. I could easily fall out the window, and I woke up with a powerful thought in my mind: How could you have exposed me to such great danger?

This general theme—*her being in danger and my failing to protect her*—soon gathered steam. A few nights later she had two companion dreams, one following immediately upon the heels of the other. (Companion dreams may convey the same message. Our friend the dream-writing homunculus often amuses himself by composing several variations on a particularly arresting theme.)

The first:

You are the leader of a group. Something dangerous is about to happen—I'm not sure what, but you are leading the group into the woods to some safer spot. Or you are supposed to be. But the trail you take us on gets rockier, narrower, darker. Then it disappears entirely. You vanish, and we are lost and very scared.

The second:

We—the same group—are all in a hotel room, and again there is some danger. Maybe intruders, maybe a tornado. Again, you are leading us out of danger. You take us up a fire escape that has black metal steps. We climb and climb, but it goes nowhere. It just ends at the ceiling, and we all have to back down.

Other dreams followed. In one she and I take an exam together, and neither of us knows the answers. In another she looks at herself in the mirror and sees red spots of decay on her cheeks. In another she dances with a wiry young man who suddenly leaves her on the dance floor. She turns to a mirror and recoils to see her face covered with sagging red skin pockmarked with hideous boils and blood blisters.

The message of these dreams was crystal-clear: danger and decay are inescapable. And I am no savior—on the contrary, I am unreliable and impotent. Soon a particularly powerful dream added a further component.

You are my travel guide in an isolated site in a foreign country—maybe Greece or Turkey. You are driving an open Jeep, and we are quarreling about what to visit. I want to see some beautiful old classical ruins, and you keep wanting to take me to the modern, tacky, flimsy city. You begin to drive so fast that I get scared. Then the Jeep gets stuck, and we are tottering, swaying back and forth, over some huge pit. I look down and can't see the bottom.

This dream, involving the dichotomy between beautiful ancient ruins and a modern tacky city, reflects, of course, our ongoing "treason versus reason" debate. Which route to take? The old, beautiful ruins (the first text) of her old life? Or the deplorably ugly new life she saw stretching ahead of her? But it also suggested a new aspect of our work together. In the earlier dreams I am inept: I lose the path in the forest; I take Irene up a fire escape that leads to a ceiling with no escape; I do not know the answers to the examination. In this dream, however, not only am I inept and fail to protect her, *I am also dangerous*—I lead Irene to the brink of death.

A couple of nights later she dreamed that she and I embrace and gently kiss. But what starts off sweetly turns to terror when my mouth opens wider and wider and I begin to devour her. "I struggle and struggle," she reported, "but cannot wrench free."

"Never send to know for whom the bell tolls; it tolls for thee." Thus, as John Donne observed nearly four hundred years ago in these now familiar lines, the funeral bell tolls not only for the dead but also for you and me—survivors, yes, but for a limited time. This insight is as old as history. Four thousand years ago in a Babylonian epic, Gilgamesh realized that the death of his friend Enkidu foreshadowed his own: "Enkidu has become dark and cannot hear me. When I die shall I not be like unto Enkidu? Sorrow enters my heart. I am afraid of death."

The death of the other confronts us with our own death. Is this a good thing? Should such a confrontation be encouraged in the psychotherapy of grief? Question: Why scratch where it doesn't itch? Why fan the flame of death anxiety in bereaved individuals already bowed low by loss? Answer: Because the confrontation with one's own death may generate positive personal change.

My first awareness of the therapeutic potential of an encounter with death in the therapy of grief occurred decades ago when a sixty-year-old man described to me his terrible nightmare the night after learning that his wife's cervical cancer had dangerously metastasized and was no longer treatable. In the nightmare he's running through an old deteriorating house—broken windows, crumbling tiles, leaking roof—pursued by a Frankenstein monster. He defends himself: he hits, he kicks, he stabs, he throws the monster off the roof. But—and this is the central message of the dream—*the monster is unstoppable:* it instantly reappears and continues the pursuit. The monster is no stranger to him, having first invaded his dreams when he was a boy of ten, shortly after his father's funeral. It terrorized him for months and eventually vanished, only to reappear fifty years later at the news of his wife's fatal illness. When I asked for his thoughts about the dream, his first words were: "I've got a hundred thousand miles on me as well." I understood then that the death of the other—first of his father and now the impending death of his wife—confronted him with his own. The Frankenstein monster was a personification of death, and the deteriorating house signified his bodily aging and breakdown.

With that interview I believed I had discovered a wonderful new concept with significant implications for the psychotherapy of grief. Soon I began to look for this theme in every bereaved patient, and it was to test this hypothesis that, a few years prior to my seeing Irene, a colleague, Morton Lieberman, and I embarked on our research project in bereavement.

Of the eighty bereaved spouses we studied, a significant proportion—up to one-third—reported a heightened awareness of their own mortality, and that awareness was, in turn, *significantly related to a surge of personal growth*. Although return to a previous level of functioning is generally considered to be the end point of bereavement, our data suggested that some widows and widowers do more than that: as a result of an existential confrontation, they become more mature, more aware, wiser.

Long before psychology existed as an independent discipline, the great writers were the great psychologists, and there are in literature rich examples of death awareness catalyzing personal transformation. Consider Ebenezer Scrooge's existential shock therapy in Dickens's *A Christmas Carol*. Scrooge's astonishing personal change results not from Yuletide cheer but from his being forced to confront his own death. Dickens's messenger (the Ghost of Christmas Yet to Come) uses a powerful existential shock therapy: the ghost takes Scrooge into the future, where he observes his final hours, overhears others lightly dismiss his death, and sees strangers quarreling over his material possessions. Scrooge's transformation occurs immediately after the scene in which he kneels in the churchyard and touches the letters on his own tombstone.

Or consider Tolstoy's Pierre, a lost soul who stumbles aimlessly through the first nine hundred pages of *War and Peace* until he is captured by Napoleon's troops, watches the five men in line ahead of him be executed by firing squad, and then receives a last-minute reprieve. This near death transforms Pierre, who marches through the final three hundred pages with zest, purpose, and a keen appreciation of life's preciousness. Even more remarkable is Tolstoy's Ivan Ilych, the mean-spirited bureaucrat whose agony, as he lies dying from abdominal cancer, is relieved by a stunning insight: *"I am dying so badly because I have lived so badly."* In the few days of life remaining to him, Ivan Ilych undergoes an extraordinary inner change, achieving a degree of generosity, empathy, and integration that he had never before known.

Thus, confrontation with imminent death can propel one into wisdom and a new depth of being. I have run many groups of dying patients who welcomed student observers because they felt that they had much to teach about life. "What a pity," I have heard these patients say, "that we had to wait till now, till our bodies were riddled with cancer, to know how to live." Elsewhere in this book, in the chapter "Travels with Paula," I describe a number of individuals facing terminal cancer who grew in wisdom as they confronted their deaths.

But what about everyday, physically healthy patients in psychotherapy—men and women not facing terminal illness or a firing squad? How can we clinicians expose them to the truth of their existential situation? I try to take advantage of certain urgent situations, often termed "boundary experiences," that offer a window into deeper existential levels. Obviously, facing one's own death is the most powerful boundary experience, but there are many others—serious illness or injury, divorce, career failure, milestones (retirement, children leaving home, midlife, important birthdays), and, of course, the compelling experience of the death of a significant other.

Accordingly, my original strategy in therapy with Irene was to use the leverage of existential confrontation whenever possible. Again and again I attempted to turn her attention from Jack's death to her own life and death. When she spoke, for example, of living only for her daughter, of welcoming death, of spending her remaining life gazing out the window at the family burial plot, I would reflexively say something like: "But aren't you then choosing to squander your life—the only life you'll ever have?"

After Jack's death Irene often had dreams in which some calamity—often a firestorm—engulfs her entire family. She viewed these dreams as reflecting Jack's death and the end of their intact family. "No, no, you're overlooking something," I'd respond. "This dream is not only about Jack and the family—it's also a dream about your own death."

During the first years Irene promptly dismissed such comments: "You don't understand. I've had too much loss, too much trauma, too many deaths stacked up." Respite from pain was her quest, and the idea of death seemed more solution than threat. That is not an uncommon position: many distressed people consider death a magical place of peace. But death is not a state of peace, nor is it a state in which one continues life without pain; it is consciousness extinguished.

Perhaps I was not respectful of her timing. Perhaps I made the error, as I often do, of leaping in ahead of my patient. Or perhaps Irene was simply someone who could not profit from confronting her existential situation. At any rate, finding that I was getting nowhere, I eventually abandoned this tack and sought other ways to help her. Then, months later, when I least expected it, came the episode of the still-life painting, followed by the cascade of images and dreams perfused with death anxiety.

Now the timing was right, and she was receptive to my interpretations. Another dream appeared, one so arresting she could not banish it from her mind.

I am in the screened porch of a flimsy summer cottage and see a large, menacing beast with an enormous mouth waiting a few feet from the front door. I am terrified. I worry something will happen to my daughter. I decide to try to satisfy the beast with a sacrifice and toss a red plaid stuffed animal out of the door. The beast takes the bait but stays there. Its eyes burn. They are fixed on me. I am the prey.

Irene immediately identified the plaid stuffed sacrificial animal: "It's Jack. That's the color of his pajamas the night he died." So strong was the dream that it lingered in her mind for weeks, and she gradually grew to understand that though she had first displaced her anxiety about death onto her daughter, she was really death's prey. "It's *me* the creature is watching so fiercely, and that means there is only one way to read this dream." She hesitated. "The dream is saying that I've unconsciously viewed Jack's death as a sacrifice so that I might continue living." She was shocked at her own thought and even more by the realization that death was out there waiting, not for others, not for her daughter, but for her.

Using this new frame of reference, we gradually reexamined some of Irene's most persistent and painful feelings. We began with guilt, which tormented her, as it does most bereaved spouses. I once treated a widow who had rarely left the bedside of her husband for weeks as he lay unconscious in a hospital. One day, in the few minutes it took her to slip down to the hospital gift shop to purchase a newspaper, her husband died. Guilt for having deserted him plagued her for months. Irene, similarly, had been inexhaustible in her attentiveness to Jack: she had nursed him with extraordinary devotion and rejected all of my urgings to take time off, to give herself some respite by hospitalizing him or engaging a nursing service. Instead, she rented a hospital bed, placed it next to her bed and slept by him until the moment he died. Still, she could not shake the idea that she should have done more: "I should never have left his side. I should have been gentler, more affectionate, more intimate."

"Perhaps guilt is a way of denying death," I urged. "Perhaps the subtext of your 'I should have done more' is that if you had done things differently, *you could have prevented his death*."

Perhaps, too, death denial was the subtext of many of her other irrational beliefs: she was the single cause of the deaths of all those who had loved her; she was jinxed; a black, toxic, deadly aura emanated from her; she was evil, cursed; her love was lethal; she was being punished by someone, by something, for some unforgivable offense. Perhaps *all* these beliefs served to obscure the brutal facts of life. If she were in fact jinxed or responsible for deaths, it would follow that *death is not inevitable*; that it has a human, avoidable cause; that existence is not capricious; that each individual is not thrown, alone, into existence; that there is an overarching, though incomprehensible, cosmic pattern; and that the universe oversees and judges us.

In time Irene was able to converse more openly about existence fear and to reformulate the reasons behind her refusal to make new attachments to others, especially to men. She had claimed that she avoided engagement, including engagement with me, to avoid the pain of another loss. Now she began to apprehend that it was not just the loss of the other she dreaded but all reminders of life's transience.

I introduced Irene to some of Otto Rank's views on the life-phobic individual. In writing that "some individuals refuse the loan of life in order to avoid the debt of death," Rank, an existentially aware disciple of Freud, was describing Irene's dilemma precisely. "Look at the way you refuse life," I chided her, "looking endlessly out the window, avoiding passion, avoiding engagement, immersing yourself in Jack's memorabilia. Don't take an ocean voyage," I advised. "Your strategy would render the trip joyless. Why invest yourself in anything, why make friends, why take an interest in anyone if the voyage is ultimately to end?"

Irene's increased willingness to accept her own limited existence presaged many changes. Whereas she had once spoken of a secret society of people who had lost people they loved, now she proposed a second, overlapping society composed of those enlightened individuals who are, as she put it, "aware of their destination."

Of all her changes, the most welcome was her increased willingness to engage me. I had been important to Irene. I had no doubt about that: there were months when she said she lived only for our visits. And yet, close as we were, I had always thought that she and I met only obliquely, that we had always missed a true "I-thou" encounter. She had tried, as she had put it earlier in therapy, to keep me outside time, to know as little as possible about me, to pretend I had no life narrative with a beginning and an end. Now that changed.

At the beginning of therapy, on a visit to her parents, Irene had come upon an old illustrated Frank Baum Oz book that she had read as a child. On her return she had told me that I had an uncanny physical resemblance to the Wizard of Oz. Now, after three years of therapy, she looked again at the illustration and found the resemblance less striking. I sensed that something important was happening when she mused, "Maybe you're not the wizard. Maybe there is no wizard. Perhaps," she went on, more to herself than to me, "I should simply accept your idea that you and I are just fellow travelers thorough this life, both of us listening to the bell tolling."

And I had no doubt that a new phase of therapy was beginning when she came into my office one afternoon in our fourth year looking straight at me, sat down, looked at me again, and said, "It's strange, Irv, but you seem to have gotten a lot smaller."

Lesson 7: Letting Go

Our final session was unremarkable except for two events. First, Irene had to phone to inquire about its time. Though our meeting time had often changed because of her surgical schedule, she had not once, in five years, forgotten it. Second, I developed a splitting headache just before the session. Since I rarely get headaches, I suspect that this one was in some way related to Jack's brain tumor, which had first made its presence known via a severe headache.

"I've been wondering about something all week," Irene began. "Do you plan to write about any aspect of our work together?"

I had not thought of writing about her, and at that time was immersed in planning a novel. I told her so, adding, "And anyway, I've never written about therapy as current as ours. In *Love's Executioner*, I had usually waited years, sometimes a decade or more, after a particular patient's therapy ended before writing about it. And let me reassure you, if I ever *did* consider writing about you, I'd seek your permission before beginning—"

"No, no, Irv," she broke in, "I'm not worried about your writing. I'm worried about your *not* writing. I *want* my story to be told. There's too much that therapists don't know about treating the bereaved. I want you to tell other therapists not only what *I've* learned but what *you've* learned."

In the weeks following termination, I not only missed Irene but, again and again, found myself musing about writing her story. Soon my interest in other writing projects waned and I began to sketch an outline, at first in a desultory manner, then with increasing commitment.

Several weeks later, Irene and I met for a final check-in session. She had mourned the loss of our relationship. For example, she dreamed we were still meeting; she imagined conversations with me and mistakenly thought she saw my face in a crowd or heard my voice addressing her. But by the time we met, the grief about ending therapy had passed, and she was enjoying life and relating well to herself and to others. She was especially struck by her change in visual perception: everything had become fleshed out again, where for years her surroundings had appeared as a two-dimensional stage set. Moreover, a relationship with a man, Kevin, whom she had met in our last few months of therapy, had not only endured but was flourishing. When I mentioned that I had changed my mind and was now interested in writing about our therapy, she was pleased and agreed to read early drafts as I proceeded.

Several weeks later I sent Irene a draft of the first thirty pages and suggested we meet to discuss them in a San Francisco café. I felt unaccountably tense as I entered and looked about for her. Spotting her before she saw me, I took my time about going up to her. I wanted to savor her from afar—her pastel sweater and slacks, her ease of posture as she sipped a cappuccino and browsed through a San Francisco newspaper. I approached. When she saw me, she stood, and we embraced and kissed on the cheeks much like old dear friends—as, indeed, we were. I ordered a cappuccino also. After my first sip, Irene smiled and reached over with her napkin to dab at the white froth on my mustache. I liked her taking care of me and leaned forward ever so slightly to feel the pressure of her napkin more fully.

"Now," she said, the dabbing done, "that's better. No white mustache—I don't want you aging prematurely." Then, taking my manuscript out of her briefcase, she said, "I like this. It's just what I hoped you'd write."

"And that's what I hoped you'd say. But first, shouldn't we back up and talk about the project as a whole?" I told her that in my revision I would make certain to conceal her identity so that none of her acquaintances might identify her. "How would you feel about being portrayed as a male art dealer?"

She shook her head. "I want it just as I really am. I have nothing to hide, nothing to be ashamed of. We both know I wasn't mentally disturbed: I was a sufferer."

Something had been worrying me about this project, and I decided to get it off my chest. "Irene, let me tell you a story."

I then told her about Mary, a good friend of mine, a psychiatrist of great integrity and compassion, and the patient, Howard, she had treated for ten years. Howard had been horribly abused as a child, and Mary had made a Herculean attempt to reparent him. In the first years of therapy he had been hospitalized at least a dozen times for suicide attempts, substance abuse, and severe anorexia. She had stood by him, done marvelous work, and somehow gotten him through everything, including helping him to graduate from high school, college, and journalism school.

"Her dedication was extraordinary," I said. "Sometimes she met with him seven times a week—and for greatly reduced fees. In fact, I often warned her that she was overly invested and needed to protect her private life more. Her office was in her home, and her husband objected to Howard's intruding on their Sundays and to the amount of Mary's time and energy he consumed. Howard was a wonderful teaching case, and every year Mary interviewed him in front of medical students as part of their basic psychiatry course. For a long time, maybe five years, she labored on a psychotherapy textbook in which her therapy of Howard played an important role. Each chapter was based on some aspect (heavily disguised, of course) of her work with him. And over the years, Howard was grateful to Mary and gave her full permission both to present him to medical students and residents and to write about him.

"Finally the book was finished, about to be published, when Howard (now a journalist stationed abroad, married, with two children) suddenly withdrew his permission. In a short letter he explained only that he wanted to put that part of his life far behind him. Mary asked for explanation, but he refused to give more details and ultimately broke off communication entirely. Mary was distraught—all those years she had devoted to that book—and eventually had no choice but to bury it. Even years later she remained embittered and depressed."

"Irv, Irv, I get your drift," said Irene, patting my hand to still me. "I understand you don't want to go Mary's way. But let me reassure you: I'm not just giving you permission to write my story; I'm *asking* you to write it. I'd be disappointed if you didn't."

"That's putting it strongly."

"I mean it. I meant what I said about too many therapists not having a clue about treating the bereaved. You've learned from our work together, learned a lot, and *I don't want it to end with you.*"

Noting my raised eyebrows, Irene added, "Yes, yes, I have finally gotten it. It's sunk in. You're not going to be around forever."

"Okay," I said, taking out a notepad, "I agree I've learned a great deal from our work, and I've put my version of it into these pages. But I want to be certain *your* voice is heard, Irene. Could you take a crack at summarizing the central points, the parts I mustn't omit?"

Irene demurred: "You know them as well as I do."

"I want your voice. My first choice, as I've said on other occasions, is for us to write together, but since you won't do that, just take a stab at it now. Free-associate—top-of-your-head stuff. Tell me, from your perspective, what was the real center, the core of our work?"

"Engagement," she said at once. "You were always there, leaning forward, getting closer. Just like when I wiped the cappuccino froth from your mustache a minute ago—"

"In your face, you mean?"

"Right! But in a good way. And not in any fancy metaphysical way. I needed just one thing: *for you to stay with me and be willing to expose yourself to the lethal stuff radiating from me.* That was your task."

"Therapists don't generally understand this," she continued. "No one but you could do this. My friends couldn't stay with me. They themselves were too busy grieving for Jack, or distancing themselves from the ooze, or burying the fear of their own deaths, or demanding—and I *do* mean demanding—that I feel okay after the first year.

"That's what you really did best," Irene went on. She spoke quickly, fluently, and stopped only to sip her cappuccino. "You had good staying power. You hung in there close to me. More than just staying close, you kept pushing for more and more, urging me to talk about everything, no matter how macabre. And if I didn't, you were likely to guess—pretty accurately, I'll hand it to you—what I was feeling.

"And your actions were important—words alone wouldn't have done it. That's why one of the best single things you did was to tell me I had to see you an extra session every time I got really enraged with you."

When she paused, I looked up from my notes. "Other useful interventions?"

"Coming to Jack's funeral. Phoning me when you were away on long trips to check on how I was doing. Holding my hand when I needed it. That was precious, especially when Jack was dying. Sometimes I felt like I'd just drift off into oblivion if it weren't for your hand anchoring me to my life. It's funny, most of the time I thought of you as a magus—someone who knows ahead of time exactly what's going to happen. That vision of you began to fade only a few months ago when you started to get smaller. Yet all along I had an opposing, antimagus, feeling—a feeling that you had no script whatsoever, no rules, no planned procedure. It was as if you were improvising on the spot."

"What did that improvising feel like to you?" I asked, scribbling quickly.

"Very scary sometimes. I *wanted* you to be the Oz wizard. I was lost, and I wanted you to know the way home to Kansas. Sometimes I was suspicious of your uncertainty. I wondered if your improvisation was real or whether it was just a pretense at improvisation, just your wizard's way.

"Another thing: you knew how much I insist on figuring out how to fix things for myself. So I thought your improvising with me was a plan—a pretty canny plan—to disarm me.

"Another thought . . . you want me to just ramble like this, Irv?"

"Exactly like this—keep going."

"When you told me about other widows or about your research findings, I knew you were trying to reassure me, and once in a while it helped to realize that I was in the midst of a process, that I would pass through certain states of mind just as other women had done. But generally that kind of comment left me feeling diminished. It was as though you were making me ordinary. I never felt ordinary when we were improvising. Then I was special, unique. We were finding our way together."

"Other helpful things?"

"Again, simple things. You may not even remember, but at the end of one of our very first sessions, as I was walking out the door, you put your hand on my shoulder and said, 'I'll see this through with you.' I never forgot that statement—it was a mighty staff of support."

"I remember, Irene."

"And it helped a lot when sometimes you'd stop trying to fix or to analyze or interpret me and you'd say something simple and straight like, 'Irene, you're going through a nightmare—one of the worst I can imagine.' And the best thing of all was when you'd add—not often enough—that you admired and respected me for my courage in persevering."

Thinking to say something about her courage now, I glanced up and saw her looking at her watch, heard her say, "Oh dear, I've got to go."

So *she* was ending the session. How far the mighty have fallen! For a moment I had an impish impulse to fake a tantrum and accuse her of throwing me out but decided not to be so childish.

"I know what you're thinking, Irv."

"What's that?"

"You probably find the reversal amusing—that it's I, not you, ending the session."

"Right on, Irene. As usual."

"You going to be here for a few minutes? I'm meeting Kevin down the street for lunch and can bring him up here to meet you. I'd like to do that."

While waiting for Irene to return with Kevin, I tried to square her account of therapy with my own. According to her, I had helped most of all by engaging her, by shrinking away from nothing she said or did. And I had helped too by holding her hand, by improvising, by confirming the horror of her ordeal, and by promising to see it through with her.

I bridled at such simplification. Surely my approach to therapy was more complex and sophisticated! But the more I thought about it, the more I came to see that Irene had it quite right.

For sure she was right about "engagement"—the key concept in my psychotherapy. I had decided at the very onset that engagement was the most effective thing I could offer Irene. And that did not simply mean listening well, or encouraging catharsis, or consoling her. It meant rather that I would get as close as I could to her, that I would focus on "the space between us" (a phrase I used in virtually every hour I saw Irene), on the "here-and-now": that is, on the relationship between her and me *here* (in this office) and *now* (in the immediate moment).

Now, it is one thing to focus on the here-and-now with patients who seek therapy because of relationship problems but another matter completely for me to have asked Irene to examine the here-and-now. Think of it: Is it not both absurd and churlish to expect a woman in extremis (a woman whose husband lay dying of a brain tumor, who was also grieving for a mother, a father, a brother, a godson) to turn her attention to the most minute nuances of a relationship with a professional she hardly knows?

Nonetheless, that was just what I did. I began it in the first sessions and never relented. In every session, without fail, I inquired about some aspect of our relationship. "How lonely do you feel in the room with me?" "How far from, how close to me do you feel today?" If she said, as she often did, "I feel miles away," I was sure to address that feeling directly. "At what precise point of our session did you first notice that today?" Or, "What did I say or do to increase the distance?" And most of all, "What can we do to reduce it?"

I tried to honor her responses. If she answered, "The best way for us to be closer is for you to give me the name of a good novel to read," I always responded with a title. If she said that her despair was too overwhelming for words and the most I could do was simply to hold her hand, then I moved my chair closer and held her hand, sometimes for a minute or two, sometimes for ten or fifteen minutes. I was sometimes uncomfortable about the hand-holding, though not because of all the legalistic proscriptions against ever touching a patient: to surrender one's clinical and creative judgment to such concerns is deeply corrupting. Rather, I was uncomfortable because the hand-holding was invariably effective: it made me *feel* like a magus, someone with extraordinary powers I didn't understand. Ultimately, a few months after she had buried her husband, Irene stopped needing and requesting hand-holding.

Throughout our therapy I was dogged about engagement. I refused to be pushed away. To her, "I'm numb; I don't want to talk; I don't know why I'm here today," I responded with some comment such as, "But you *are* here. Some part of you wants to be here, and I want to talk to that part today."

Whenever possible I translated events into their here-and-now equivalents. For example, consider the beginnings and endings of the hour. Frequently Irene entered my office and walked briskly to her chair without even a glance at me. I rarely let that pass. I might say, "Oh, so it's going to be one of *those* sessions," and focus on her reluctance to look at me. Sometimes she responded, "Looking at you makes you real, and that means you'll have to die soon." Or, "If I look at you, that makes me feel helpless and gives you too much power over me." Or, "If I look at you, I might want to kiss you," or, "I'll see your eyes demanding that I get well quickly."

The ending of every session was problematic: she hated my having so much control and balked at leaving my office. Every ending was like a death. During her most difficult periods, she was unable to keep images in her mind and feared that once I was out of sight, I would cease to exist. She also considered endings of sessions as symbols of how little she meant to me, how little I cared for her, how quickly I could dispense with her. My vacations or professional trips invariably posed such major problems that on several occasions, I chose to phone to maintain contact.

Everything became grist for the here-and-now mill: her wishes for me to compliment her; to tell her that I thought about her more than my other patients; to acknowledge that were we not therapist and patient, I would desire her as a woman.

Ordinarily the here-and-now focus in psychotherapy has many advantages. It imparts a sense of immediacy to the therapy session. It provides more accurate data than relying on patients' imperfect and ever-shifting views of the past. Since one's mode of relating in the here-and-now is a social microcosm of one's mode of relating to others, both past and present, one's problems in relating are immediately revealed, in living color, as the relationship with the therapist unfurls. Furthermore, therapy becomes more intense, more electric—no individual or group session focusing on the here-and-now is ever dull. Moreover, the here-and-now provides a laboratory, a safe arena, in which a patient can experiment with new behaviors before trying them in the world outside.

Even more important than all these benefits, the here-and-now approach also accelerated the development of a deep intimacy between us. Irene's outward demeanor—frosty, forbidding, supremely competent and confident—kept others from approach-

ing her. This was precisely what happened when I placed her in a six-month therapy group at the time that her husband was dying. Though Irene quickly won the members' respect and provided considerable help to others, she received little in return. Her air of supreme self-sufficiency told the other group members she needed nothing from them.

Only her husband had cut through her formidable demeanor; only he had challenged her and demanded a deep, intimate encounter. And it was only with him that she could weep and give voice to the young lost girl within her. And with Jack's death she lost that touchstone of intimacy. I knew it was presumptuous, but I wanted to become that touchstone for her.

Was I attempting to replace her husband? That's a crass, shocking question. No, I never thought to do that. But I did aspire to reestablish, for one or two hours a week, an island of intimacy, a place where she could doff her fix-it, supersurgeon state of mind and be openly vulnerable and challenged. Gradually, very gradually, she was able to acknowledge feelings of helplessness and to turn to me for comfort.

When her father died not long after her husband, she felt overwhelmed at the thought of flying home for the funeral. She could not bear the idea of facing her Alzheimer's-stricken mother and seeing her father's open grave next to her brother's tombstone. I agreed and strongly advised her not to go. Instead, I scheduled a session at the exact time of the funeral and asked her to bring pictures of her father, and we spent the hour recalling her memories of him. It was a rich, powerful experience, and later Irene thanked me for it.

Where was the line between intimacy and seduction? Would she become too dependent on me? Would she ever be able to break away? Would the powerful husband-transference prove irresolvable? That thought nagged at me. But I decided to worry about it later.

The here-and-now focus was never difficult to sustain in my work with Irene. She was extraordinarily hardworking and dedicated. Never, not once in all my work with her, did I hear resistant, and expected, comments such as, "This doesn't make sense. . . . It's irrelevant. . . . You are not the issue. . . . You're not my life—I see you only two hours a week; my husband died only two weeks ago—why do you press me about my feelings toward *you?*—This is crazy. . . . All these questions about the way I look at you, or the way I walk into this office—they're too trivial to talk about. Too many big things are going on in my life." On the contrary, Irene immediately grasped what I was trying to do and throughout therapy seemed grateful for all my attempts to engage her.

Irene's remarks about my "improvising" therapy were of great interest to me. Lately I have found myself proclaiming, "The good therapist must create a new therapy for each patient." That is an extreme position, more radical even than Jung's suggestion, many years ago, that we create a new therapy *language* for each patient. But radical positions for these radical times.

The contemporary managed-care movement in health care poses a deadly threat to the field of psychotherapy. Consider its mandates: (1) that therapy be unrealistically brief, focusing exclusively on outward symptoms rather than on the underlying conflicts that breed those symptoms; (2) that therapy be unrealistically inexpensive (which is punishing both to the professionals who have invested the necessary years for in-depth training and to the patients who are forced to consult inadequately trained therapists); (3) that therapists mimic the medical model and go through the charade of formulating precise medical-like goals and conducting weekly evaluations of them; and (4) that therapists employ only empirically validated therapies (EVTs), thus favoring brief, apparently precise cognitive-behavioral modes that demonstrate symptom alleviation.

But of all these wrongheaded and catastrophic assaults on the field of psychotherapy, none is more ominous than the trend toward protocol-driven therapy. Thus, some health plans and HMOs require that the therapist follow a prescribed plan for the course of therapy, at times even a schedule of items to be covered in each of the allowed sessions. The profit-hungry health care executives and their misguided professional advisers assume that successful therapy is a function of information obtained or dispensed rather than the result of the relationship between patient and therapist. This is a grievous error.

Of the eighty bereaved men and women I had studied in my research before seeing Irene, not one was like her. None suffered the same constellation of recent (and cumulative) losses—husband, father, mother, friend, godson. None had been traumatized in just the way she had by the earlier loss of a dearly loved sibling. None had had the interdependent relationship she had had with her husband. None had watched a spouse deconstitute, bit by bit, cruelly devoured by a brain tumor. None had been a physician who understood all too well the nature of her husband's pathology and its prognosis.

No, Irene was unique and required a unique therapy, one she and I had to construct together. And it wasn't that she and I constructed a therapy and then set about employing it—quite the contrary: *the project of constructing a new, unique therapy was the therapy itself.*

I looked at my watch. Where was Irene? I walked to the door of the café and peered out. There she was, a block away, walking hand in hand with a man who must be Kevin. Irene and a man hand in hand. Was it possible? I thought of all the countless hours I had spent trying to reassure her that she was not doomed to being alone, that ultimately there would be another man in her life. God, she had been stubborn! And the opportunities had been legion: early in her bereavement there had been a long queue of attractive and appropriate suitors.

She had rejected each man quickly for one or more of what seemed an endless list of reasons. "I don't dare love again because I can't endure another loss" (that attitude, always at the top of the list, resulted in her rejecting out of hand any man even slightly older than herself or any man not in the best possible physical condition). "I don't want to doom any man by loving him." "I refuse to betray Jack." She compared every man unfavorably to Jack, who was the perfect and predestined mate for her (he had known her family; had been hand-chosen by her brother; and represented a last link with her dead brother, her father, and her dying mother). Furthermore, Irene was convinced that there was no man who could ever understand her, no man who would not, like Frost's farmer, bring the shovel into the kitchen. Except, possibly, a member of the society of the recently bereaved, someone who had an acute awareness of his or her ultimate destination and the preciousness of life.

Picky. Picky. Picky. Perfect health. Athletic. Slim. Younger than she. Recent bereavement. Extraordinary sensibility to art, literature, and existential concerns. I grew impatient with Irene and the impossible standards she set. I thought of all the other widows I had worked with, who would have given anything for any attention whatsoever paid by *any* of the men Irene had summarily rejected. I did my best to keep these sentiments to myself, but she missed nothing, not even my unexpressed thoughts, and grew angry at my wish that she become involved with a man. "You're trying to force me to compromise!" she accused.

Perhaps too she was sensing my growing alarm that she would never let me go. I believed that her attachment to me was a major factor in her refusing to engage a man. God, would I be burdened with her forever? Perhaps that was my penalty for having succeeded in becoming so important to her.

And then Kevin entered her life. From the beginning she knew he was the man she had been seeking. I marveled at her certainty—her prescience. I thought of all those impossible, ridiculous standards she had set. Well, he met every single one of them, and then some. Youth, perfect health, sensitivity—he was even a member of the society of the secretly bereaved. His wife had died a year previously, and he and Irene fully understood and empathized with each other's mourning. Everything clicked immediately, and I was overjoyed for Irene—and for my own liberation. Before she met Kevin, she had entirely regained her high level of functioning in the outside world, but there had remained a deep and almost inexpressible inner sadness and resignation. Now that too had rapidly resolved. Had she improved as a result of meeting Kevin? Or had she been able to be open to him because she had improved? Some of each? I could never be certain.

And now she was bringing Kevin to meet me.

Here they come, through the café entrance. They're walking toward me. Why am I nervous? Look at that man: he's gorgeous—tall, powerful, looks like he does a triathlon every day before breakfast, and that nose . . . unbelievable . . . where do you buy noses like that? Enough, Kevin, let go of her hand. Enough already! There's got to be something not to like about this guy. Oops, I'm going to have to shake hands with him. Why are my hands sweating so? Will he notice? Who cares what he notices?

"Irv," I heard Irene say, "this is Kevin. Kevin, Irv."

I smiled, held out my hand, and greeted him through clenched jaws. Damn you, I thought, you'd better take good care of her. And, goddamnit, you'd better not die.

5

Double Exposure

"So that, Dr. Lash, is why I feel like giving up. There are no men out there. And if they're still unmarried in their forties, then obviously something's wrong—creeps, rejects, diseased—some other woman didn't want them and threw them out. Cleaned them out too. The last three men I've gone out with had no retirement. Zilch. Who can respect them? Could you? I bet you're putting plenty away for your retirement, huh? Oh, don't worry, I know you're not going to answer that. I'm thirty-five. I wake up thinking, the big three-five. Halfway there. The more I think about my ex, the more I realize he murdered me. He murdered ten years of my life—the most important ten years. Ten years—I can't get my mind around it. It's a bad dream, and when he walks out, I wake up, I look around, I'm thirty-five, my life is shot—every decent man has been taken."

[A few seconds of silence]

"Where do your thoughts go, Myrna?"

155

"Thinking about being trapped—thinking about going to Alaska where the man-woman ratio is better. Or to business school—good ratio there."

"Stay here in the room with me, Myrna. What's it been like being here today?"

"What do you mean?"

"Same thing I always mean. Try to talk about what's going on here, between us."

"Frustrating! Another hundred-fifty-dollar pop, and I don't feel better."

"So I failed again today. Took your money and didn't help. Tell me something, Myrna; see if—"

Braking sharply, Myrna swerved to avoid a truck cutting into her lane. She sped up, passed it, screamed, "Asshole!"

She turned off the tape and took a few deep breaths. Several months ago, after their first few sessions, her new shrink, Dr. Ernest Lash, had begun recording their sessions and giving her the tape to listen to the following week as she drove to the next session. Each week she returned the cassette and he recorded the new session over the old one. A good way, he said, to use the commute time from Los Altos to San Francisco. She wasn't so sure. The hours had been frustrating in the first place, and going through them a second time was only more frustrating. The truck, having gained on her, flashed his lights to pass. Pulling over a lane, she cursed the trucker as he gave her the finger. Suppose she had an accident because she was distracted by listening to the tape? Could she sue her shrink? Take his ass into court? That notion brought a smile to her lips. Leaning over, Myrna pressed "rewind" for a few seconds, then the "play" button.

"Stay here in the room with me, Myrna. What's it been like being here today?"

"What do you mean?"

"Same thing I always mean. Try to talk about what's going on here, between us."

"Frustrating! Another hundred-fifty-dollar pop, and I don't feel better."

"So I failed again today. Took your money and didn't help. Tell me something, Myrna; see if you can go back over our hour together and answer this question: What could I have done today?"

"How should I know? That's what you get paid for, isn't it? And paid well too."

"I know you don't know, Myrna, but I want you to dip into your fantasy. How could I have helped you today?"

"You could have introduced me to one of your rich single patients."

"You see 'Dating Bureau' on my T-shirt?"

"You bastard," she muttered, punching the "stop" button. "I pay you one-fifty an hour for this smart-ass shit?" She pressed "rewind" and replayed the exchange.

". . . could I have helped you today?"

"You could have introduced me to one of your rich single patients."

"You see 'Dating Bureau' on my T-shirt?"

"Not funny, Doctor."

"No, you're right. Sorry. What I should have said is that you stay so far away from me—from saying anything about how you feel about me."

"You, you, you. Why always my feelings toward you? *You're* not the issue, Dr. Lash. I'm not going to be dating you—though maybe I'd get more out of that than from what we're doing."

"Let's go over it again, Myrna. You originally came in to see me saying you wanted to do something about your relationships with men. In our very first session, I said I could best help you examine your relationships with others by focusing on our relationship right here in this office. This space here in my office is, or should be, a safe place, where I hope you can talk more freely than elsewhere. And in this safe place we can examine the way we relate to one another. Why is this so hard to understand? So let's look again at your feelings toward me here."

"I already said 'frustrating.'"

"Try to make that more personal, Myrna."

"Frustrating *is* personal."

"Yeah, in a way it's personal, it tells me about your inner state. Things go 'round in a circle in your mind, I know. And they go around in a circle when you're here too. And I get dizzy with you. And I feel *your* frustration. But the word *frustrating* doesn't tell me about *us*. Think of the space here between us. Try to stay there for a minute or two. What's the space like today? What about your comment a couple of minutes ago about getting more out of dating me than being in therapy?"

"Told you already, nothing. The space is empty. Just frustration."

"This—what's going on now, this moment—is precisely what I mean when I say that you shy away from real contact with me."

"I'm confused, lost."

"Our time's about up, Myrna, but try something before we stop—the same exercise I asked you to do a couple of weeks ago. Just for a minute or two, think about something you and I could be doing together. Close your eyes; let some scene, any scene, appear. Describe it as it's happening."

[Silence]

"What do you see?"

"Nothing."

"Force it. *Make* something happen."

"Okay, okay. I see us walking along. Talking. Enjoying ourselves. Some street in San Francisco, maybe Chestnut. I take your hand and lead you into a singles bar. You're reluctant, but you come in with me. I want you to see it . . . see the scene . . . see with your own eyes that there are no suitable men there. It's either singles bars or the Internet match services you mentioned last week. The Internet—that's worse than the bars. Talk about impersonality! I can't believe you're really suggesting that to me. You expect me to form a relationship on the monitor screen, not even seeing the other person . . . not even—"

"Go back to your fantasy. What do you see next?"

"Fade to black—gone."

"So fast! What stopped you from staying with it?"

"Don't know. Felt cold and alone."

"You were with me. You took my hand. What feelings came up?"

"Still felt alone."

"Got to stop, Myrna. One last question. Were the last few minutes different from the first part of the hour?"

"No. It was the same. Frustrated."

"I felt more engaged—less space between us. You didn't feel any of that?"

"Maybe. Not sure. And I still don't see the point of what we're doing."

"Why do I keep feeling that there's something in you that fights against seeing the point? Same time next Thursday?"

Myrna heard chairs being moved, her footsteps crossing the room, the closing of the door. She turned onto I-280. Waste of time and money, she thought. Shrinks. He's just like all the rest. Well, not quite. At least he talks to me. For a moment she imagined his face: he smiling, holding his arms out to her, inviting her to come closer. Truth is, I like Dr. Lash. He's in there with me—at least he seems to care about what happens to me and he's active: he tries to keep things going—he goes halfway, he doesn't leave me sitting in silence like the last two shrinks. She quickly brushed aside these images. He was always nagging her to keep track of her daydreams, especially those occurring on the drive to and from the therapy hour, and she was not about to tell him this corny stuff.

Suddenly she heard his voice on the tape again.

"Hello. This is Ernest Lash returning your call. Sorry to miss you, Desmond. Please try to reach me at 767-1735 between eight and ten this evening or in my office first thing tomorrow morning."

What's going on? she wondered. She suddenly recalled that after leaving his office at the end of the last session and driving a half-block, she had realized he had forgotten to give her the tape and had returned for it. She had double-parked in front of the Victorian house and sprinted up its long stairway to his office on the second floor. Since she was his last hour of the day, she hadn't worried about interrupting another patient. His door was partially open and she had walked right in to find Dr. Lash speaking into a dictating machine. When she had told him why she'd returned, he had removed the cassette from the tape recorder on the table next to the patient's chair and given it to her. "See you next week," he had said. Clearly he'd forgotten to turn off the tape recorder when she'd left his office the first time, and it had been recording for some time before the tape ran out.

Turning the volume all the way up, Myrna heard faint noises: possibly coffee mugs clinking as he cleared them from his desk. Then his voice again as he phoned someone to arrange a tennis appointment. Footsteps, the scrape of a chair. And then something more interesting. Much more interesting.

"This is Dr. Lash dictating notes for countertransference seminar. Notes on Myrna, Thursday, 28 March."

Notes on me? I can't believe it. Straining to hear, clutched with anxiety and curiosity, she leaned forward, closer to the speaker. Suddenly the car swerved and she almost lost control.

She pulled over to the side of the highway, hurriedly ejected the tape, took her Walkman from the glove compartment, inserted the tape, rewound it, put on the headphones, eased back onto the freeway, and turned the volume all the way up.

"This is Dr. Lash dictating notes for countertransference seminar. Notes on Myrna, Thursday, 28 March. Typical, predictable, frustrating hour. She spent most of the session whining as usual about the lack of single available men. I get more and more impatient . . . irritable—lost it for a moment and made an inappropriate remark: 'Do you see "Dating Bureau" on my T-shirt?' Really hostile thing for me to do—very unlike me—can't remember last time I've been so disrespectful to a patient. Am I trying to drive her away? I never say anything supportive or positive to her. I try, but she makes it hard. She gets to me . . . so boring, rasping, crass, narrow. All she ever thinks about is making her two million in stock options and finding a man. Nothing else . . . narrow, narrow, narrow . . . no dreams, no fantasies, no imagination. No depth. Has she ever read a good novel? Ever said something beautiful? Or interesting . . . just one interesting thought? God, I'd love to see her write a poem—or try to write a poem. Now, *that* would be therapeutic change. She drains me. I feel like a big tit. Over and over the same material. Over and over hitting me over the head about my fee. Week after week I end up doing the same thing—I bore myself.

"Today, as usual, I urged her to examine her role in her predicament, how she contributes to her own isolation. It's not such a difficult concept, but I might as well be speaking Aramaic. She just can't get it. Instead she accuses me of not believing that the singles scene is bad for women. And then, as she often does, she threw in a crack about wishing she could date me. But when I try to focus on that, on how she feels toward me or how she makes herself lonely right here in this room with me, things get even worse. She refuses to get it; she will not relate to me, and she will not acknowledge that she doesn't—and insists it's not relevant anyway. She can't be stupid. Wellesley graduate—high-level graphics work—huge salary, hell of a lot bigger than mine—half the software companies in Silicon Valley competing for her—but I feel I'm talking to a dumb person. How many goddamn times do I have to explain why it's important to look at our relationship? And all those cracks about not getting her money's worth—I feel demeaned. She is a vulgar lady. Does everything possible to eliminate any shred of closeness between us. Nothing I do is good enough for her. Presses so many—"

A passing car's honk roused her to the fact that her car was weaving. Myrna's heart pounded. This was dangerous. She switched off the Walkman and drove the few minutes to her turnoff. She pulled into a side street, parked, rewound, and listened:

> ". . . I feel demeaned. She is a vulgar lady. Does everything possible to eliminate any shred of closeness between us. Nothing I do is good enough for her. Presses so many of my buttons that there's got to be something of my mother in this. Every time I ask her about our therapy relationship, she gives me that wary look as though I'm coming on to her. Am I? Not a whisper of it when I check into my feelings. Would I if she weren't my patient? Not a bad-looking woman—I like her hair, gleaming— carries herself well—great-looking chest, popping those buttons—that's definitely a plus. I worry about staring at those breasts but don't think I do—thanks to Alice! In high school once, I was talking to a girl named Alice and hadn't any idea that I was staring at her tits until she put her hand under my chin and tilted my face up and said, 'Yoo-hoo, yoo-hoo, I'm up here!' I never forgot. That Alice did me a big favor.
>
> "Myrna's hands are too big; that's a turnoff. But I do like that great slick, sexy swish of her stockings as she crosses her legs. Yeah, I guess there are some sexual feelings there. If I had run into her when I was still single, would I have hit on her? Probably yes, I'd be attracted to her physically, until she opened her mouth and started whining or demanding. Then I'd want to get away fast. There's no tenderness, no softness to her. She's too self-focused, all sharp angles—elbows, knees, ungiving—"
>
> [A click as the tape came to an end.]

In a daze, Myrna started the car, drove a few minutes, and turned right on Sacramento Street. Only a few blocks now to Dr. Lash's office. She noticed, with surprise, that she was trembling. What to do? What to say to him? Quickly, quickly—only a few minutes until his goddamn clock started ticking off that $150 hour.

One thing for sure, she told herself, there is no way I'm going to give back the tape as I usually do. I've got to hear it again. I'll lie, say I forgot it, left it at home. Then I can rerecord his comments onto another tape and bring back the original next week. Or maybe I'll just say I lost the tape. If he doesn't like it—tough shit!

The more she thought about it, the more sure she was that she would not tell him she'd heard his dictation. Why give away her hand? Maybe she'd tell him some time in the future. Maybe never. The bastard! She pulled up to his office. Four o'clock. Talking time.

"Myrna, come in, please." Ernest always called her Myrna, and she called him Dr. Lash, even though he had often pointed out the asymmetry and invited her to call him by his first name. That day he was, as always, dressed in his navy-blue blazer and white turtleneck sweater. Doesn't he own any other clothes? she wondered. And those scuffed Rockports. Casual is one thing, sloppy another. Hasn't he ever heard of a shoe shine? And that jacket doesn't hide the spare tire around his waist. If I were playing tennis with you, she thought, I'd lob you to death. I'd get those fat little pork chops of yours pumping.

"No problem," he said affably when she confessed to having forgotten the tape. "Bring it next week. I've got a fresh one." He unwrapped a new tape and inserted it into the recorder.

After that, the usual silence. Myrna sighed.

"You look troubled," Ernest commented.

"No, no," Myrna denied. Phony! she thought. What a phony! Pretending to be so concerned. You don't care if I'm troubled. You don't give a shit. I know how you really feel about me.

More silence.

"I feel a great deal of distance between us," Ernest remarked. "Do you feel that way too?"

Myrna shrugged. "I don't know."

"I'm wondering, Myrna, about last week. Did you take home any strong feelings about our session?"

"Nothing out of the ordinary." I have the upper hand, Myrna told herself, and I'm going to make him work for his money today. I want to see him sweat. She drew out a long pause before asking, "Should I have?"

"What?"

"*Should* I have had strong feelings about the last session?"

Surprise showed on Ernest's face. He looked at Myrna. She stared back unflinchingly. "Well," he said, "I wondered whether you might have had any feelings. Maybe some reactions to my comment about my T-shirt and the dating bureau?"

"Did *you* have any feelings about that comment, Dr. Lash?"

Ernest straightened in his chair—he had the oddest feeling about her boldness today. "Yes, I had a lot of feelings about it," he said hesitantly. "And none of them good feelings. I felt I was disrespectful to you. I can imagine you being pretty angry with me."

"Well, I *was* angry."

"And hurt?"

"Yes, hurt too."

"Think of that hurt feeling. Does it take you to some other place? Some other time?"

Oh no, you don't, you worm, Myrna thought. Trying to squirm away. And all these weeks lecturing me on staying in the present. "Can we stay with you, Dr. Lash, here in this office?" she said with her new directness. "I'd like to know *why* you said it— why you were, as you put it, disrespectful."

Ernest took another look at Myrna. A longer one. He pondered his options. Duty to his patient, that came first. Today, finally, Myrna seemed willing to engage him. For months he had been urging, exhorting, begging her to stay in the here-and-now. So encourage her efforts, he told himself. And remain honest.

Honesty above all. A devout skeptic in all other matters, Ernest believed with fundamentalist fervor in the healing power of honesty. His catechism called for honesty—but tempered, selective honesty. And *responsible, caring* honesty: honesty in the service of caring. He would never, for example, reveal to her the harsh, negative—but honest—feelings toward her he had expressed two days earlier when presenting Myrna's case at his countertransference seminar.

That seminar had started a year ago as a biweekly study group of ten therapists who met to deepen their understanding of their personal reactions to their patients. At each meeting one member would discuss a patient by focusing almost entirely on the feelings that patient had evoked in him or her during their therapy hours. Whatever their feelings toward particular patients—irrational, primitive, loving, hateful, sexual, aggressive—the members committed themselves to expressing them candidly and exploring their meaning and roots.

Among the many purposes the seminar served, none was more important than the sense of community it provided. Isolation is the leading occupational hazard of the psychotherapist in private practice, and therapists combat it by membership in organizations: study groups such as this countertransference seminar, advanced training institutes, hospital staff associations, and a variety of local and national professional organizations.

The countertransference seminar loomed large in Ernest's life, and he looked forward to the meetings every other week—not only to the camaraderie but also to the consultation. He had, the previous year, terminated a long supervisory experience with an orthodox psychoanalyst, Marshal Strider, and the seminar was now the only place where he discussed cases with colleagues. Though the group's official focus was upon the inner life of the therapist rather than upon the therapy, the discussion invariably influenced the course of therapy. Merely knowing that you would be presenting a patient inevitably influenced the way you conducted therapy with that patient. And during his session with Myrna today, Ernest imagined the seminar members silently observing him as he pondered her question about why he had been disrespectful to her. He took care to say nothing that he would feel reluctant to report back to the group.

"I'm not sure of all the reasons, Myrna, but I know I was impatient with you last session when I said it. You seemed obstinate. I had a sense of knocking and knocking at your door and your refusing to open it."

"I was doing my best."

"I guess that didn't register. It seemed to me that you knew why it was important to focus on the here-and-now, on the relationship between us, and yet you kept pretending not to know. Lord knows I've tried to spell it out many, many times. Remember in our first session when you talked about your previous therapists? You said they were too distant, too uninvolved, too uncaring? And I told you that I would be engaged with you, and that much of our task here would be to study that engagement? And you said you welcomed that?"

"This is not making sense. You think I'm deliberately opposing you. Tell me, why would I come week after week, on a long drive and blowing one-fifty an hour? One hundred fifty dollars—maybe small change for you but not for me."

"On one level it doesn't make sense, Myrna, yet on another it does. Here's the way I see it. You're unhappy with your life, you're lonely, you feel unloved and unlovable. You come to me for help—at great effort—it *is* a long drive. And expensive too—I *do* hear you, Myrna. But something strange happens here—I think it's fear. I think getting close makes you uncomfortable, and then you back off, close down, find fault with me, ridicule what we're doing. I'm not saying you do it deliberately."

"If you understand me so well, why the T-shirt comment? You still haven't answered that question."

"I was addressing that when I mentioned that I felt impatient."

"That doesn't really feel like an answer."

Ernest took another long look at his patient and thought, Do I really know her? Whence this blast of directness? But it's a welcome, bracing wind—and anything's better than what we've been doing. I'll try to sail with it as far as possible.

"Your point is well taken, Myrna. The T-shirt crack doesn't fit in anywhere. A stupid comment. And a hurtful one. I'm sorry about it. Not sure where it came from. I wish I could recapture what prompted it."

"I remember from the tape—"

"I thought you didn't listen to the tape."

"I didn't say that. I said I forgot to *bring* the tape, but I listened to it at home. The T-shirt comment came right after I said you could introduce me to one of your rich single patients."

"Right, right, I remember. I'm impressed, Myrna. Somehow I had the feeling that our sessions didn't mean enough for you to remember them so well. Let me go back into my feelings in that last hour. One thing I remember for sure—that very comment about introducing you to one of my rich patients really bugged me. Just prior to that, I think I had asked what I could offer you, and that was your answer. I felt put down: your comment hurt me. I should be above that, but I've got my sore spots—and my blind spots too."

"Hurt? Aren't we being a bit touchy? Just a joke."

"Maybe. But maybe more than a joke. Maybe you were giving voice to your sense that I have little of value to offer you—at best, an introduction to another man. So I felt invisible. Devalued. And I guess that's why I lashed out at you."

"Poor thing!" Myrna muttered.

"What?"

"Nothing, nothing—another joke."

"I'm not going to let you drive me away with that kind of comment. In fact, I'm wondering whether we should be meeting more than once a week. For today, though, we have to stop. We're running over. Let's pick up from here next week."

Ernest was glad Myrna's hour was over. But not for the customary reasons: he wasn't bored or irritated by her; he was exhausted. Punch-drunk. Staggering. On the ropes.

But Myrna hadn't finished punching. "You really don't like me, do you?" she remarked as she picked up her purse and started to rise.

"On the contrary," said Ernest, determined to hang in there with his patient, "I felt particularly close to you in this session. It was scary and hard today but good work."

"That's not exactly what I asked you."

"But that's the way I feel. There are times when I feel more distant from you; times when I feel close to you."

"But you really don't like me?"

"Liking isn't a global feeling. Sometimes you do things I don't like; sometimes there are things I like very much about you."

Yeah, yeah. Like my big tits and the swish of my stockings, Myrna thought as she got out her car keys. At the door Ernest, as always, offered his hand. She was repelled. Physical contact with him was the last thing she wanted, but she saw no way to refuse. She took his hand lightly, quickly turned it loose, and left without looking back.

For Myrna, sleep came slowly that night. She lay awake, unable to erase from her mind Dr. Lash's dictated opinion of her. "Whining," "boring," "sharp angles," "narrow," "vulgar"—his phrases whirled around and around in her mind. Awful words—yet none of them as hurtful as his comment that she never said anything interesting or beautiful. His hope that she might write a poem stung, brought tears to her eyes.

A long-forgotten incident drifted into her mind. When she was ten or eleven she had written a great deal of poetry but had kept it secret—especially from her gruff, relentlessly critical father. Before she was born he had been dismissed from his surgical residency program because of alcoholism, and he had lived out the rest of his life as a disillusioned, half-drunk small-town doctor whose office was in his home and who spent every evening in front of the TV, sipping bourbon from an Old Granddad whiskey glass. She had never been able to make him interested in her. Never, not once, had he openly expressed any love for her.

As a child she'd been an inveterate snooper. One day, while her father was making house calls, she had rummaged through the upper compartments and drawers of his walnut rolltop desk and found, under a stack of patients' charts, a packet of yellowed love letters, some from her mother and some from a woman named Christine. Buried under the letters, she was surprised to find some of her poems written on paper that felt strangely damp. She took them back and, on impulse, stole the letters from Christine as well. A few days later, on an overcast autumn afternoon, she poked them, along with all the rest of the poems she'd written, into the center of a mound of dried sycamore leaves and put a match to it. All that afternoon she sat watching the wind have its will with the ashes of her poetry.

From then on a veil of silence fell between her and her father. It was impenetrable. He never acknowledged his violation of her privacy. She never confessed her violation of his. He never mentioned the missing letters, nor did she speak of her missing poems. Though she never wrote another poem, she had wondered ever since why he had kept these pages of her poems and why they were damp. In her daydreams she sometimes imagined him reading them and weeping over their beauty. A few years ago her mother had phoned to tell her that her father had suffered a massive stroke. Though she had rushed to the airport and caught the next plane home, she arrived at the hospital only to find his room empty, the bare mattress covered with a clear plastic sheet. Minutes earlier the orderlies had removed his body.

The first time she met Dr. Lash, she was startled by the antique rolltop desk in his office. It was like her father's, and often during her long silences she caught herself gazing at it. She never told Dr. Lash about the desk and its secrets, or about her poems, or about the long silence between herself and her father.

Ernest also slept poorly that night. Again and again he reviewed his presentation of Myrna to the countertransference study group, which had met a couple of days earlier in a member's group therapy room on Couch Row, as upper Sacramento Street was often called. Though the seminar had started out leaderless, the discussions had grown so intense and so personally threatening that a few months ago they had hired a consultant, Dr. Fritz Werner, an elderly psychoanalyst who had contributed many astute papers to the psychoanalytic literature on countertransference. Ernest's account of Myrna had provoked a particularly animated discussion. Though praising him for his willingness to expose himself so candidly to the group, Dr. Werner had also been sharply critical of the therapy, especially the T-shirt comment.

"Why so impatient?" Dr. Werner asked as he scraped the bowl of his pipe, filled it with acrid-smelling Balkan Sobranie, tamped it down, and lit it. When first invited he had stipulated that his pipe be part of the deal.

"So she repeats herself?" he continued. "So she whines? So she makes impossible requests of you? So she's critical of you and doesn't behave like a good, grateful patient? My God, young man, you've only seen her for four months! What's that—a total of fifteen or sixteen sessions? Why, I'm currently seeing a patient who for the *entire first year*—that's four times a week, *two hundred hours*—simply repeated herself. Over and over, the same lament, the same yearning for different parents, different friends, a different face, different body—the same endless pining for what could never be. Eventually she got fed up with listening to herself, fed up with her own repetitive cycle. She *herself* realized she was squandering not only her analytic hours but her entire life. You can't fling the truth in your patient's face: the only real truth is the truth we discover for ourselves.

"*Evenly suspended attention*, young man," he said firmly. "That's what you need to give the patient. Evenly suspended attention; words as true now as when Freud first uttered them. That's what is required of us—to attend to the patient's words without preformulations, without bias, without personal reactions limiting our vision. It's the heart and soul of the entire analytic enterprise. Remove that and the entire process goes bankrupt."

At that point the seminar had exploded, everyone speaking at once. Dr. Werner's criticism of Ernest had, like a lightning rod, drawn to itself the tension that had been building for months. The participants, all eager to improve their skills, had been irritated by what they perceived as the arrogant elitism of their elderly consultant. They were the muddied, shit-splattered troops working in the trenches. Every day they faced the highly compromised clinical conditions imposed by the HMO juggernaut, and they were incensed by Dr. Werner's all too apparent indifference to the realities of their practice. One of those lucky ones who had been untouched by the managed-care debacle, he accepted no insurance; he simply continued his practice of seeing wealthy analytic patients four times a week and could afford to be leisurely, to let the patient's resistance wear itself down. The seminar members bristled at his uncompromising endorsement of the hard psychoanalytic line. And his certainty and smugness, his unquestioning acceptance of institutionalized dogma: this too they resented with the gall and the envy anxious skeptics have always felt toward cheerful believers.

"How can you say Ernest has seen her for *only* fourteen sessions?" one asked. "I'm lucky to have an HMO give me *eight* visits. And only if I can coax out of my patient one of the magic words—*suicide*, *revenge*, *arson*, or *homicide*—do I have a chance of begging a few more sessions from some clinically untrained case manager whose own job depends on turning down as many such requests as possible."

And another: "I'm not as sure as you are, Dr. Werner, that Ernest did the wrong thing. Maybe the T-shirt crack wasn't a blunder. Maybe that's just what this patient needed to hear. We've talked here about the therapy hour being a microcosm of a patient's life. So if she bores and frustrates Ernest, she's undoubtedly doing the same to everyone else around her. Maybe he's doing her a favor by letting her know. Maybe he doesn't *have* two hundred hours to let her get impatient with herself."

And another: "Sometimes this fine-tuned analytic procedure is just too much, Dr. Werner, just too precious, too out of touch with reality. This business of the patient's empathic unconscious *always* picking up the therapist's feelings—I just don't buy it. My patients are generally in crisis. They come in once a week, not four times a week like yours, and are too busy choking on their own stuff to tune in to the nuances of my mood. This unconscious picking up the therapist's feelings—my patients don't have the time, don't have the desire."

Dr. Werner couldn't let that remark pass. "I know that this seminar is on countertransference, not on therapy technique, but you cannot keep them separate. Once a week, seven times a week—it matters not. The handling of countertransference *always* influences therapy. At some level the therapist's feelings about the patient are invariably transmitted. *I've never seen it fail!*" he said, waving his pipe for emphasis. "And this is why we *must* understand, and work through, and reduce our neurotic responses to patients.

"But here, in this—this T-shirt instance," Dr. Werner continued, "we're not even considering *nuances;* we're not dealing with the patient's *subtle* perceptions of the therapist's feelings. Dr. Lash insulted the patient openly—no nuanced guesswork required here. I can't shirk my responsibility to label that an egregious therapeutic error—an error that threatens the foundations of the therapeutic alliance. Don't let the California ethos of 'anything goes, everything is permitted' contaminate your therapy. Anarchy and therapy are not mutually compatible. What is your first step in therapy? You've got to establish a safe frame. How in the world, after this incident, can Dr. Lash's patient free-associate? How can she trust the therapist to consider her words with evenly suspended attention?"

"Is evenly suspended attention possible for any therapist?" asked Ron, a heavily bearded and intense therapist, and one of Ernest's closest friends; they had been linked since medical school by their mutual iconoclasm. "It wasn't for Freud. Look at his cases—Dora, the rat man, Little Hans. He *always* entered into his patients' lives. I don't believe it's humanly possible to maintain a position of neutrality—that's what Donald Spence's new book argues. You never *really* apprehend the patient's real experience."

"That doesn't mean you give up trying to listen without letting your personal feelings contaminate the scene," said Dr. Werner. "The more neutral you are, the closer you approximate the patient's original meaning."

"Original meaning? Discovery of another's original meaning is an illusion," Ron shot back. "Look at the leaky communicational pathway. First, some of the patients' feelings are transformed into their own images and then into their favorite vocabulary—"

"Why do you say 'some'?" asked Dr. Werner.

"Because many of their feelings are ineffable. But let me finish. I was talking about the patients transforming images into words: even that process is not pure—the choice of words is heavily influenced by the individual's imagined relationship with the audience. And that's just the transmitting part. Then the reverse has to take place: if therapists are to grasp the meaning of the patients' words, they must retranslate the words into their own private images and then into their own feelings. By the end of the process, what kind of match is possible? What's the chance that one person can really understand the other's experience? Or to put it another way, that two different people will hear another person in the same manner?"

"It's like that word game 'Telephone' we played as kids," Ernest chipped in. "One person whispers a phrase into another's ear, and that person whispers to another, and so on around the circle. By the time the phrase returns to the sender, it bears little relationship to the original."

"Which means that *listening is not recording*," Ron said, coming down hard on each word. "*Listening is a creative process*. That's why the analytic pretense that psychoanalysis is a science always rankles me. It cannot be a science, since science demands accurate measuring of reliable external data. In therapy that's not possible, because listening is creative—the therapist's mind distorts as it measures."

"We all know we err," Ernest gleefully charged in, "unless we're silly enough to believe in *immaculate perception*." Since reading that phrase somewhere a few weeks before, he had been itching to use it in conversation.

Dr. Werner, never one to shrink from a debate, was unfazed by his students' barrage and responded confidently, "Don't be blinded by the false goal of absolute identity between speaker's thoughts and listener's perceptions. The best we can hope for is mere approximation. But tell me," he asked, "is there anyone here, even my iconoclastic Katzenjammer duo"—nodding toward Ron and Ernest—"who doubts that a well-integrated individual is more likely to apprehend accurately a speaker's intent than, let us say, a paranoid individual who reads portents of personal danger into every communication? Personally, I believe we're selling ourselves short with this breast-beating lament about our inability to really know the other or to reconstruct the other's past. This humility has led you, Dr. Lash, into the dubious practice of focusing exclusively on the here-and-now."

"How so?" Ernest asked coolly.

"Because you, of all our participants, are most skeptical about accurate recall and the entire process of reconstructing a patient's past. And I think you carry it so far that you confuse your patient. Yes, the past is undoubtedly elusive and undoubtedly shifts according to a patient's mood, and undoubtedly our theoretical beliefs influence what one recalls, but I still believe that underneath it all there is a valid subtext, a true answer to the question, 'Did my brother hit me when I was three?'"

"A valid subtext is an antiquated illusion," Ernest retorted. "There is no valid answer to that question. Its context—whether he hit you purposefully or playfully, or gave you a mere tap or a knockout punch—is lost forever."

"Right," Ron cut in. "Or whether he hit you in self-defense—in response to your hitting him a moment before? Or in defense

of your sister? Or because he had just been punished by your
mother for something you did?"

"There is no valid subtext," Ernest repeated. "It's all interpretation. As Nietzsche knew a century ago."

"Aren't we straying from the intent of this conference?" interrupted Barbara, one of the group's two woman members. "Last
time I looked, it was called a countertransference seminar." She
turned to Dr. Werner. "I'd like to make a process comment.
Ernest does exactly what we're supposed to do in this seminar—
report on his innermost feelings about his patient—and then gets
blasted for it. How come?"

"Right, right!" said Dr. Werner. The gleam in his blue-gray
eyes showed that he relished the uprising, the spectacle of grown
siblings suspending their rivalry and uniting in a joint patricidal
campaign. In fact, he loved it. By God, he was thinking, just imagine! Freud's primal horde alive and rampaging right here on
Sacramento Street! For a moment he considered offering this
interpretation to the group but thought better of it. The children
weren't ready for it yet. Maybe later.

Instead he responded, "But keep in mind, I was *not* critical of
Dr. Lash's *feelings* about Ms. Myrna. What therapist who has ever
lived has not had such thoughts about an irritating patient? No, I
do not criticize his thought. I criticize only his incontinence, his
inability to keep his feelings to himself."

That triggered another round of protests. Some defended
Ernest's decision to express his feelings openly. Others criticized
Dr. Werner for not building a trusting environment in the seminar. They wanted to feel safe there. They most definitely did not
want to dodge broadsides about their therapeutic technique,
especially when the critique was based on a traditional analytic
approach inappropriate to their current clinical setting.

Finally Ernest himself suggested that the discussion was no
longer productive and urged the group to return to the topic of
his countertransference. A few members then spoke of similar

patients who had drained and bored them, but Barbara's comment most piqued Ernest's interest.

"This is not like any other resistant patient," she said. "You say she gets to you like no one else and that you've never been so disrespectful to a patient before."

"It's true, and I'm not sure why," Ernest responded. "Several things about her tick me off. I get infuriated at her persistent reminders of the money she's paying me. She is constantly turning this process into a commercial transaction."

"It's not a commercial transaction?" interposed Dr. Werner. "Since when? You give her a service, and in return she gives you a check. Looks like commerce to me."

"Well, parishioners tithe, but that doesn't make a church service an act of commerce," said Ernest.

"Oh, yes, it does!" insisted Dr. Werner. "The circumstances are just more refined and concealed. Read the genteel fine print at the end of a prayer book: no tithing, eventually no service."

"Typical analytic reductionism, everything reduced to its basest level," said Ernest. "I'm not buying it. Therapy is *not* commerce, nor am I a merchant. That's not why I'm in the field. If money were uppermost, I'd have gone into something else—law, investment banking, even one of the rich medical specialties like ophthalmology or radiology. I see therapy as something else—call it an act of *caritas*. I signed up for a life of service. For which I also, incidentally, happen to get paid. But this patient keeps slapping me in the face with the money."

"You give and give," Dr. Werner purred in his most professional sonorous voice, appearing to relent. "But she gives nothing back."

Ernest nodded. "Right! She gives nothing back."

"You give and give," repeated Dr. Werner. "You give her your *best stuff* and she keeps saying, 'Give me something worthwhile.'"

"That's exactly the way it feels," said Ernest more softly.

This exchange happened so smoothly that none of the seminar members, perhaps not even Dr. Werner himself, was conscious of his switch into his seductive professional voice—or, it seemed, of Ernest's eagerness to snuggle into the warmth of the therapeutic comforter.

"You said there's something of your mother in it," remarked Barbara.

"I never got much good stuff from her either."

"Does her ghost influence your feelings toward Myrna?"

"It was different with my mother. I was the one who kept pulling away. I was embarrassed by her. I didn't like thinking I was born of her. When I was young—maybe eight, nine—I felt suffocated when my mother got too close to me. I remember telling my analyst that my mother 'sucked up all the oxygen in the room.' That phrase became a slogan, a major motif, of my analysis: my analyst referred to it again and again. I used to look at my mother and think, I have to love her as my mother, but if she were a stranger I'd dislike everything about her."

"So," said Dr. Werner, "now we know something important about your countertransference. Although you invite your patient to come closer, you unintentionally give her a simultaneous 'don't get too close' message. She'll intrude too far, suck up all the oxygen. And without a doubt she's perceiving this second message and accommodating you. Again, let me repeat, we can't hide these feeling from patients. I'll say it once again: we can't hide these feeling from patients. It's the lesson for today. I cannot emphasize the point too strongly. No experienced therapist can possibly doubt the existence of unconscious empathy."

"Lot of ambivalence too," said Barbara, "in your sexual feelings toward her. I'm struck by your response to her breasts—both longing and repulsion. You like those blouse buttons popping, but they bring up unpleasant memories of Mother."

"Yes," added Tom, another of Ernest's close friends, "and then you get self-conscious, start to question whether you may have unwittingly been staring at her breasts. Happens to me often."

"And your sexual attraction to her coupled with a wish to get away? What do you make of it?" asked Barbara.

"Some dark primitive *vagina dentate* fantasy in me, no doubt," replied Ernest. "But still there's something in this patient that particularly ignites that fear."

Just before drifting off to sleep, Ernest wondered again whether he should stop seeing Myrna. Maybe she needs a female therapist, he thought. Maybe my negative feelings are too deep, too entrenched. But when he had raised that question in the seminar group, everyone, including Dr. Werner, said, "No, stay the course." Myrna's major problems, they felt, were with men and could best be addressed with a male therapist. Too bad, Ernest thought: he really wanted out.

Yet, he wondered, what about that strange session today? Although as obnoxious as ever in most ways, including her reference to his fee, Myrna had at least acknowledged his presence in the room. She had challenged him, asked him whether he liked her, taken him to task about the sarcastic T-shirt comment. Exhausting—but at least something different, something real, was happening.

On her drive to the next session, Myrna listened again to Dr. Lash's hateful dictation and then to the tape of the last session. Not bad, she thought—she liked the way she had held her own in the last session. She enjoyed making the sucker work for his money. How delicious that he was unsettled by her barbs about his fee: I'll make sure, she resolved, to zap him with a money-jab each session. The long drive zipped by.

"Yesterday at work," Myrna began the hour, "I was sitting in the lavatory and overheard some girls at the sink talking about me."

"Oh? What did you hear?" Ernest was always intrigued by the drama of overhearing oneself being discussed.

"Things I didn't like. That I'm obsessed with earning money. That I talk about nothing else, have no other interests. That I'm boring and hard to be with."

"Oh, terrible! How painful that must have been."

"Yeah, I felt betrayed by someone I thought cared for me. Kicked in the stomach."

"Betrayed? What sort of relationship had you had with them?"

"Well, they'd pretended to like me, to care about me, be my friends."

"How about others in your office? How do they feel about you?"

"If you don't mind, Dr. Lash, I've been thinking about what you've been saying about staying *here* in *this* office. You know, focusing on our relationship. I'd like to try that."

"Absolutely." A look of astonishment crossed Ernest's face. He couldn't believe his ears.

"So let me ask you," said Myrna, crossing her legs with a loud swish of her stockings, "do *you* feel that way about me?"

"What way?" stalled Ernest.

"What I just said. Do you find me narrow? Boring? Hard to be with?"

"I never feel just one way about you, or anyone. It varies."

"Well, let's say *in general*," said Myrna, who was clearly not about to be deterred.

Ernest felt his mouth go dry. He tried to swallow surreptitiously. "Well, let me put it this way. When you avoid me, when you talk in a repetitious way about certain things—for example, your stock options or your ongoing conflict with your CEO at work—that's when I feel less in touch with you. *Less engaged* is the better term."

"*Less engaged?* Isn't that shrink code for *boring?*"

"Uh, no—I mean, boring in a social situation doesn't really pertain to the therapy situation. The patient—I mean *you*—isn't here to entertain me. I'm focusing on how my patient interacts with me and others so that—"

"But surely," she interrupted, "you find some patients boring."

"Well," said Ernest, pulling out Kleenex from the box on his side table and squeezing it between his palms, "I'm examining my feelings all the time, and if I'm—uh—less engaged—"

"Bored, you mean?"

"Well, in a way. If I feel—uh—*distant* from a patient, I don't think of that as a *judgment*. I think of that feeling as *data*, and I try to find out what's happening between us."

Ernest's attempt to dry his palms had not escaped Myrna. Good, she thought. A $150-an-hour sweat. "And today? Am I boring you today?"

"Now? I can absolutely say that you are not boring or hard to be with today. I feel engaged. A little threatened. Trying to stay open and not defensive. Now, you tell me what you're experiencing."

"Well, it's okay today."

"'Okay'? Could you be a little more vague?"

"What?"

"Sorry, Myrna. A poor attempt at humor. I'm trying to say that I feel like you're evasive and holding back what you're experiencing."

The hour was up, and as she rose to leave, Myrna said, "I can tell you one other thing I'm experiencing."

"Yes?"

"I'm a little worried that I'm pushing you too hard. Making you work too much."

"So? What's wrong with my working too hard?"

"I don't want you raising my rates."

"See you next week, Myrna."

Ernest spent the evening reading but felt fatigued and preoccupied. Though he had seen eight patients that day, he spent more time thinking about Myrna than about the other seven combined.

That evening Myrna felt full of energy. After surfing Internet dating services and then lurking in a singles chat room, she phoned and had a long, satisfying conversation with her sister, to whom she hadn't spoken for months.

When she finally fell asleep, Myrna dreamed that she was holding a suitcase and staring out the window. A bizarre taxicab drives up—a jolly, bouncy, cartoon cab. On its door is written

"The Freud Taxi Company." Moments later, she watches the letters change to "The Fraud Taxi Company."

Despite her wounded feelings and her distrust of Ernest, therapy had become more interesting for Myrna; even during her working hours she found herself anticipating the upcoming session.

The ploy about having overheard a conversation in the lavatory had worked well, she thought, and she intended to continue inventing devices that would allow her to use some part of the overheard dictation each hour. Next week it would be his label of "whining."

"My sister told me on the phone the other day," she said disingenuously, "that my parents often called me 'Miss Whiner' when I was small. That hits home somehow. You said I should try to use this safe place here in your office to explore things I can't talk about elsewhere."

Ernest nodded vigorously.

"So I was wondering whether you think I whine a lot."

"What do you mean by 'whine,' Myrna?"

"Well, you know—complain, speak in a whiny voice, talk in a way that makes people want to get away from me. Do I?"

"What do *you* think, Myrna?"

"I don't think so. And your opinion?"

Unable to procrastinate indefinitely, or to lie, or to tell the truth, Ernest squirmed. "If by 'whine' you mean you tend to complain about your situation repetitively and unproductively—then, yes, I've heard you do that."

"An example, please."

"I promise to answer that," said Ernest, deciding it was time for a process comment, "but let me say something first, Myrna. I'm struck by the change in you these last weeks. It's been so fast. You aware of it?"

"Change how?"

"How? In almost every way. Look at what you're doing— you're direct, focused, challenging. Like you say, you're keeping it in the room; you're talking about what's taking place between us."

"And that's good?"

"It's great, Myrna. I'm delighted to see it. To be honest, there were times in the past when I felt you hardly noticed I was in the room with you. When I say it's great, I mean you're moving in the right direction. But still you seem so—what should I say? So one-sided, so—well, *acerbic*, as though you're continually angry with me. Am I off base?"

"I don't feel angry with you, just frustrated with my whole life. But you said you'd give me examples of my whining."

Suddenly this woman who had been too slow for him was becoming almost too fast. Ernest had to concentrate all his attention on their discourse.

"Not so fast. I'm not buying into that word, Myrna. I feel you're trying to brand me with it. I said 'repetitious,' and I'll give you an example of *that:* your feelings about your CEO. How he's not efficient, how he should make the company leaner, how he should fire incompetent workers, how his softheartedness is going to cost you big money in your stock options—that's the kind of thing I mean. You've discussed this over and over again, hour after hour. Just like your comments about the dating scene—you know what I mean. During those hours I've ended up feeling less engaged with you and less helpful as well."

"But those are the things that preoccupy me—you tell me to share what I'm thinking."

"You're absolutely right, Myrna. I know it's a dilemma, but it's not *what* you say but *how* you say it. But I don't want to detract from my earlier point. The mere fact that we're talking so openly supports what I said a little while ago—that you're different, working better and harder in therapy.

"It's time to stop for today, but let's try to pick up from here next week. Oh, yes, here's the bill for last month."

"Hmmm," said Myrna, uncrossing her legs, not neglecting to swish them vigorously, and scanning the proffered bill before dropping it into her purse. "How disappointing!"

"What do you mean?"

"Still one-fifty an hour. No discounts for being a better patient?"

The following week, as she listened yet again to Ernest's counter-transference dictation on the way to her therapy hour, Myrna decided to steer the discussion to his comments about her physical appearance and sexual attractiveness. It wasn't difficult.

"Last week," she began, "you said we should continue where we left off."

"All right. Where shall we start?"

"At the end of the session last week, you were talking about my whining about the singles scene—"

"Whoa! You keep quoting me as though I said you were whining. That was *not* my word—repeat, *not* my word. I said something about your *circular* or *repetitious* comments."

Myrna, of course, knew better. *Whining* was precisely his term: she had heard him use it on the tape. But, eager to proceed, she'd let him have his little lie.

"You were saying you were bored by my talking about the singles scene. How am I supposed to deal with it if I don't talk about it?"

"Certainly you've got to talk about the major concerns in your life. As I said, it's *how* you talk about them."

"What does 'how' mean?"

"Well, you didn't seem to be speaking to me. I felt out of the loop. Time and again, you'd tell me the exact same things—the unfair ratio, the meat-market scene, the ten-second visual check-out in singles bars, the impersonality of Internet matching services. And each time you'd say it as though you were telling me for the first time, as though you'd never thought of asking yourself whether you'd ever said this before or how I might regard your repeating it so often."

Silence. Myrna stared at the floor.

"What do you feel about what I just said?"

"I'm digesting it. Tastes a little bitter. Sorry I wasn't more considerate."

"Myrna, I'm not judging you. It's good that the issue has come up, and it's good that I gave you feedback. That's how we learn."

"Hard to think of others when you're feeling trapped, feeling you're spinning in a vicious circle."

"You're going to stay in the vicious circle as long as you keep thinking it's always someone else's fault. Your incompetent CEO, say, or the dating scene being a jungle, or the people in marketing being jerks. I'm not saying these things aren't true; I'm saying"—Ernest gave it all he had, emphasizing each word forcefully—"*I can't help you with them*. The only way I can help you break the vicious circle is to focus on whatever it is in *you* that might initiate or aggravate these happenings."

"I go into a singles event, and there are ten women for each guy," Myrna spoke more hesitantly, the steam going out of her words, "and you want me to focus on *my* responsibility for that?"

"Wait! Stop action, Myrna! Here we are again, back in that space. Listen to me. I do not disagree—the dating situation is rough. Hear me: *I do not disagree*. But our job is to help you make changes in yourself that might make the situation better. Look, I'll put it straight. You're an intelligent and attractive woman, very attractive. If you weren't tied up by disturbing feelings—like resentment and anger, fear and competitiveness—then you'd have no trouble meeting a suitable man."

Myrna felt shaken by Dr. Lash's bluntness. Although she knew she should stay and respond to his point, she persisted in her agenda. "You've never said anything before about my being attractive."

"You don't consider yourself attractive?"

"Sometimes, sometimes not. But I don't get much affirmation from men. I could use some direct feedback from you."

Ernest paused. How much to say? Knowing he'd have to repeat his words to the countertransference seminar in a few weeks gave him pause. "I have a hunch that if men aren't responding to you, it's not because of your physical appearance."

"If you were single, would *you* respond to my physical appearance?"

"Same question; I've already answered that. Just a minute ago I said you were an attractive woman. So, tell me, what are you *really* asking now?"

"No, I'm asking a *different* question. You say I'm attractive, but you haven't said whether *you* would respond to my attractiveness."

"Respond?"

"Dr. Lash, you're *hedging*. I think you know what I mean. If you had met me not as a patient but in some singles situation, then what? Would you check me out in ten seconds and then walk away? Or flirt with me, or maybe try for a one-night stand, planning to walk away afterward?"

"Can we take a look at what's going on between us today? You're really putting me on the spot. How come? What's your payoff for that? What's going on inside, Myrna?"

"But aren't I doing what you've said I should be doing, Dr. Lash? Talking about our relationship, about the here-and-now?"

"I agree. No question, things have changed here—and for the better. I feel better about the way we're working, and I hope you do too."

Silence. Myrna refused to meet Ernest's gaze.

"I hope you do too," Ernest tried again.

Myrna nodded, ever so slightly.

"You see? Your nod, that microscopic, that embryonic nod! Three millimeters at best. That's what I mean. I could hardly see it. It's as though you want to give me as little as possible. That's what puzzles me. It seems to me that you're primarily *asking*, not talking, about our relationship."

"But you said—and said it more than once—that the first stage of change was getting feedback."

"Getting and *assimilating* feedback. Right. But in our last few hours you've just been collecting feedback—more of a question-and-answer format. I mean, I give you feedback, and you then proceed to another question."

"Rather than?"

"Rather than a lot of things. For example, rather than turning inward to consider and discuss and digest the meaning of the feedback. How it felt, whether or not it rang true, what it stirred up inside, how you felt about my saying it to you."

"Well, okay. To be honest, I'm really *surprised* to hear you say you find me attractive. You don't act that way toward me."

"I do think you're attractive, but here, in this office, I'm more interested in a deeper meeting with you: with your essence, with your—I know it sounds corny—but with your soul."

"Maybe I shouldn't persist"—Myrna felt the energy going out of her question—"but my physical appearance is important to me, and I'm still curious about how you experience me—what features about my appearance are attractive to you, and that other question about what might have happened if we had met socially rather than professionally?"

I'm being crucified, Ernest whimpered to himself. His worst nightmare about the here-and-now had come to pass. He had played out all his options. He had always feared that one day he would be cornered like this. The typical therapist would, of course, not answer the question but would reflect it back to her and explore all its implications: Why do you ask this question? And why now? And what were your underlying fantasies? How would you want me to respond?

But this option was not available for Ernest. Having based his therapeutic approach squarely on authentic engagement, he couldn't abandon it now and turn back to convention. Nothing to do now but hold on to his integrity and dive into the cold pool of truth.

"Physically, you're attractive in every way—pretty face, wonderful glossy hair, terrific figure—"

"By 'figure,' you mean my breasts?" interrupted Myrna, arching her back ever so slightly.

"Well, yes, everything—your carriage—grooming—slim—everything."

"Sometimes it seems you stare at my breasts—or at my blouse buttons." Myrna felt a flush of pity and added, "A lot of men do."

"If I do, I'm not aware of it," said Ernest. Too flustered to do what he knew he should—encourage her to express in depth her feelings about her appearance, including her breasts—he tried to scramble back to safe ground. "But, as I said, I do think of you as an attractive woman."

"Does that mean you might come on to me—I mean in this hypothetical situation?"

"Well, I'm not in the singles world—been in a relationship for a while—but if I project myself back to that era, I'd say you'd pass all my physical checkpoints. But some of the other things we've been discussing would give me pause."

"Such as?"

"Such as what's happening right here, right now, Myrna. Listen hard to what I'm going to say. You're collecting and hoarding. You're accumulating information from me, but *you're not giving anything back!* I believe you're trying to relate to me differently now, but I'm not experiencing it as engagement. I don't feel yet that you're relating to me as a person—it's more like you regard me as a data bank from which you make withdrawals."

"You mean I'm not relating because of my whining?"

"No, that's not what I said. Now, Myrna, our time is up today, and we've got to stop, but when you play the tape of this session I'd like you to listen carefully to what I just said to you a minute ago about how you're relating to me. I think it's the most important thing I've ever said to you."

After the session Myrna wasted no time putting in the cassette and following Ernest's instructions. Starting with *"I'd say you'd pass all my physical checkpoints,"* she listened intently.

> "But some of the other things we've been discussing would give me pause. . . . Listen hard to what I'm going to say. You're collect- ing and hoarding. You're accumulating information . . . *but you're*

not giving anything back! . . . I don't feel yet that you're relating to me as a person—it's more like you regard me as a data bank from which you make withdrawals. . . . When you play the tape of this session I'd like you to listen carefully to what I just said to you. . . . I think it's the most important thing I've ever said to you."

Switching cassettes, Myrna listened to the countertransference dictation again. Certain phrases struck home:

"She will not relate to me, and she will not acknowledge that she doesn't—and insists it's not relevant anyway. . . . How many goddamn times do I have to explain why it's important to look at our relationship? . . . Does everything possible to eliminate any shred of closeness between us. Nothing I do is good enough for her. . . . No tenderness . . . too self-focused . . . ungiving."

Perhaps Dr. Lash is right, she thought. I really never have thought about him, his life, his experience. But I can change that. Today. Right now as I drive home.

But she couldn't stay focused for more than a minute or two. To still her mind, she turned to a useful mind-quieting technique she had learned a few years before at a Big Sur meditation weekend (which in most other ways had been a rip-off). Keeping one part of her mind on the highway, with the rest she imagined a broom sweeping out every stray thought that popped in. That done, she concentrated only on her breathing, on the inhalation of cool air and on the exhalation of the air slightly heated in the nest of her lungs.

Good. Her mind quieter now, she allowed Dr. Lash's face to appear, first smiling and attentive, then frowning and turning away. Over the past several weeks, ever since she had overheard his dictation, her feelings toward him had gyrated wildly. One thing I've got to say for him, she thought; he's persistent. I've had the poor guy on the ropes for weeks now. Making him sweat. Belting him again and again with his own words. Yet he's taking his licks. Hanging in there. Doesn't throw in the towel. And no weasel in him: no slinking, no crooked twists and turns, no trying to lie his way out as I'd have done. Oh, maybe a little fibbing, like denying he said "whining." But maybe he was just trying to spare me pain.

Myrna came out of her reverie just in time to take the Highway 380 turnoff and then effortlessly slipped back into fantasy. Wonder what Dr. Lash's doing now? Dictating? Making notes of our session? Storing them in one of the desk compartments? Or maybe he's just sitting at his desk thinking of me this very minute. That desk. Daddy's desk. Is Daddy thinking of me now? Maybe he's still somewhere, maybe watching me now. No, Daddy is dust. Bare shiny skull. Heap of dust. And all his thoughts about me—dust too. And his memories, his loves, his hates, his discouragement—all dust. No, less than dust—they are just electromagnetic blips long vanished without a trace. I know Daddy must have loved me—told everyone else he did—told Aunt Eileen, Aunt Maria, Uncle Joe—but he couldn't say it to me. If only I could have heard his words.

Pulling off the highway, Myrna parked at a lookout with a view stretching over the valley from San Jose all the way to San Francisco. She glanced upward through her windshield. What a sky today, she mused. A big sky. The words—what words to describe it? *Sweeping—majestic—cloud-layered. Pellucid cloud ribbons.* No, *diaphanous.* Better—I love that word. *Diaphanous—* diaphanous cloud ribbons. Or maybe *a screen of fluted clouds— clouds like white-butter-sand rippled by gentle wind waves?* Nice. Nice. I like that.

She reached for a pen and jotted down the lines on the back of a pink dry-cleaning receipt she found in the glove compartment. Starting her car, she prepared to drive on, then turned off the ignition and thought some more.

But suppose Daddy had said the words? "Myrna, I love you— Myrna, you fill me with pride—love you—love you—Myrna, you are the best—the best daughter a man ever had." What then? Still dust. Words decay even faster than brains.

And so what if he never said them? Did anyone ever say them to *him?* His parents? Never. The stories I heard of them—that bourbon-guzzling father who died sallow and silent, and his mother encoring twice with marriages to other alcoholics. And I? Did I ever say those words to him? Have I ever said them to anyone?

Myrna shivered, yanking herself out of her reverie. How unlike her it was—these thoughts. The language, the search for beautiful words. And the memories of her father? That too was strange: she rarely visited him in her mind. And where was her resolve to concentrate on Dr. Lash?

She tried again. For a moment she imagined him sitting at his rolltop desk, but then another image from the past superimposed itself. Late at night. She should have been long asleep. Tiptoeing down the hall. A crack of light streaming from under her parents' door. Soft, intimate voices. Her name murmured. "Myrna." They would be lying under the thick, downy comforter. Pillow talk. Talk about her. She flattened on the floor, scrunching her cheek against the icy beet-red linoleum, straining to see under the door, to hear her parents' secret words about her.

And now, she thought, glancing at her Walkman, I've captured the secret; I own the words. Those words at the end of the session—what were they again? She slipped in the cassette, rewound for a few seconds, and listened:

". . . Myrna. Listen hard to what I'm going to say. You're collecting and hoarding. You're accumulating information from me, but *you're not giving anything back!* I believe you're trying to relate to me differently now but I'm not experiencing it as engagement. I don't feel yet that you're relating to me as a person—it's more like you regard me as a data bank from which you make withdrawals."

Making withdrawals from a "data bank." She nodded. Maybe he's right.

She started her car, eased back onto the 101 south freeway.

Myrna sat in silence at the beginning of the next session. Impatient as always, Ernest tried to prod her: "Where have your thoughts been these last few minutes?"

"I think I've been wondering how you'll begin the session."

"What would be your preference, Myrna? If a genie granted your wish, how would you like me to start? What's the perfect statement or question?"

"You might say, 'Hello, Myrna; I'm really glad to see you.'"

"Hello, Myrna; I'm really glad to see you today," Ernest immediately repeated, concealing his astonishment at Myrna's response. In past meetings with her, such clever opening gambits had invariably flopped, and he had thrown out his question now with little hope of success. What a marvel that she had become so audacious! And that he was really glad to see her—that was even more of a marvel.

"Thank you. That was nice of you, even though you didn't do it perfectly."

"Huh?"

"You stuck in an extra word," Myrna said. "The word *today*."

"The implications being . . . ?"

"Remember Dr. Lash, how you always used to say to me, 'A question ain't a question if you know the answer.'"

"You're right, but humor me. Remember, Myrna, sometimes a therapist has special conversational privileges."

"Well, it seems clear to me that 'today' implies you often *haven't* been glad to see me."

Is it only recently, Ernest thought, that I considered Myrna an interpersonal retard?

"Go on," he said, smiling. "Why would I not want to see you?"

She hesitated. This was not the direction she wanted the hour to take.

"Try. Try to speak to that question, Myrna. Why do you think I'm not always glad to see you? Just free-associate; say anything that comes to your mind."

Silence. She felt words stirring, welling up. She tried to pick and choose, to contain them, but there were too many words, all pouring quickly into her mind.

"Why are you not glad to see me?" she erupted. "Why? I know why. Because I'm indelicate and vulgar and have bad taste"—I don't want to do this, she thought, but couldn't stop, compelled to burst the boil, to cleanse the space between them— "and because I'm rigid and narrow and never say anything beautiful or poetic!" Enough, enough! she told herself, trying to clamp her teeth shut, to lock her jaws. But the words now welled up into a force she could not resist, and she vomited them out: "And I'm not soft, and men want to get away from me—too many sharp angles, elbows, knees—and I'm too ungrateful, and I pollute our relationship by talking about the bill, and—and—" She stopped for a moment and then finished with a whimsical note: "And my tits are too big." Exhausted, she sank back in her chair. Everything had been said.

Ernest was stunned. Now it was he who sat speechless. Those words—*his* words. Where had they come from? He looked at Myrna, who was bent over, holding her head in her hands. How to respond? His head swam; he had an impish impulse to say, "Your tits aren't too big." But thank God, he didn't. Bantering was not called for. He knew that he needed to take Myrna's words with the greatest possible seriousness and respect. He snatched at the life vest that in the stormiest of seas, therapists always have available: *process commentary*, that is, to comment on the process, the relationship implications, of the patient's utterance rather than on its content.

"Lot of emotion in your words, Myrna," he said quietly. "Sounds like you've wanted to say them for a long time."

"I guess so." Myrna took a couple of deep breaths. "The words had a life of their own. They *wanted* to come out."

"A bushel of anger there toward me—maybe toward both of us."

"Both? At you and at myself? Probably true. But getting less. Maybe that's why I could say those things today."

"Feels good that you trust me more."

"I had really wanted to talk about other things today."

"Such as?" Ernest leaped at the idea—anything to change direction.

As Myrna paused to catch her breath, he reflected on her uncanny intuition, her chilling burst of words. Amazing that she had grasped so much of him! How had she known? Only one possibility: unconscious empathy. Just as Dr. Werner had said. So Werner was right all the time, he thought. Why didn't I allow myself to learn from him? What a jerk, a twerp, I've been. How did Werner put it? That I'm an iconoclastic Katzenjammer Kid? Well, maybe it's time to let go of some of my juvenile questioning and debunking of elders—not *everything* they say is bullshit. Never again will I doubt the power of unconscious empathy. Perhaps it was this type of experience that prompted Freud to take seriously the idea of telepathic communication.

"Where are your thoughts going, Myrna?" he finally said.

"So much to say. Not sure where to start. Here's a dream I had last night." She held up a spiral tablet. "See, I wrote it down—that's a first."

"You *are* taking our work more seriously."

"Gotta get my one-fifty's worth. Oops!" She covered her mouth with her hands. "Didn't mean that—sorry—please press delete key."

"Delete key pressed. You caught yourself—that's great. Perhaps you were flustered by my paying you a compliment."

Myrna nodded but hurried on and read her dream from her notepad:

I go to have my nose reconstructed. They remove the bandages. My nose is okay, but the skin has puckered or pulled up and my mouth is locked open and is a huge gaping hole taking half my face. My tonsils are visible—huge, swollen, inflamed. Crimson. Then a doctor with a nimbus comes by. I am suddenly able to close my mouth. He asks me questions, but I won't answer. I don't want to open my mouth and show him the big gaping hole.

"Nimbus?" Ernest asked when she stopped.

"You know, uh—radiance, holy light, halo."

"Oh, right. Yes, nimbus. So, Myrna, what are your thoughts about the dream?"

"I think I know what *you'll* say about it."

"Stay with *your* experience. Try to free-associate. What comes to you immediately as you think about the dream?"

"The big hole in my face."

"What comes to mind as you think of it?"

"Cavernous, abyssal, abysmal, inky black. More?"

"Keep going."

"Gigantic, vast, stupendous, monstrous, Tartarean."

"Tartarean?"

"You know, hell—or the abyss below Hades where the Titans were confined."

"Oh, right. Interesting word. Hmm—but back to the dream. You're saying there's something you don't want doctors to see, and I guess I'm the doctor?"

"Hard to quarrel with that. Don't want you to see the big gaping hole, that emptiness."

"And if you open your mouth I'll see it. So you guard yourself, guard your words. You still see the dream, Myrna? Still vivid?"

She nodded.

"Keep looking at it—what part of it draws your attention now?"

"The tonsils—lot of energy there."

"Look at them. What do you see? What comes to mind?"

"They're hot, scalding."

"Keep going."

"Bursting, turgid, livid, distended, tumescent, turgescent—"

"'Tumescent, turgescent'? And that other one—'Tartarean.' These words, Myrna?"

"I've been browsing in a thesaurus this week."

"Hmm, I'd like to hear more about that, but right now let's stay with the dream. These tonsils; they're visible if you open your mouth. Just like the emptiness. And they're about to burst. What'll come out?"

"Pus, ugliness, something odious, hideous, loathsome, disgusting, execrable, abhorrent, rancid—"

"More thesaurus browsing?"

Myrna nodded.

"So the dream suggests that you're seeing a doctor—me—and our work is uncovering some things you don't want seen, or you don't want me to see it—a vast emptiness, and tonsils ready to burst and spew something vile. Somehow the scalding red tonsils make me think of just a few minutes ago when all those words burst out of you."

She nodded again.

"I'm moved by your bringing in this dream," Ernest said. "It's a sign of trust in me and what we're doing together. It's good work—real, good work." He paused. "Now can we talk thesaurus?"

Myrna described the fiery end of her poetry career as a child and her growing wish to write a poem. "This morning when I wrote down my dream, I knew you'd ask about the hole and the tonsils, so I searched for interesting words."

"Sounds like you wanted something from me."

"Interest, I guess. I didn't want to be boring anymore."

"Your word, not mine. I never said that."

"Still, I'm convinced you feel that way about me."

"I want to come back to that, but first let's look at something else in the dream—the halo around the doctor."

"The nimbus—yes, it was curious. I guess I've got you in the good-guy category now."

"So you think better of me and maybe want to be closer to me, but the dilemma is that if we get close, I might discover shameful things about you: maybe a void inside, maybe something else— explosive rage, self-loathing." He looked at his watch. "I'm sorry we have to stop. The time has sped by. Again, good hard work today. It's been good being with you."

The hard work continued, solid therapy hours following one upon the other. Week after week, Ernest and Myrna reached new levels of trust. She had never before risked so much of herself; he felt privileged to be a witness to her transformation. It was for such experiences that Ernest had become a psychotherapist. Fourteen weeks after he'd last presented Myrna to the countertransference seminar, he sat at his desk, microphone in hand, and prepared another presentation.

"This is Dr. Lash dictating notes for countertransference seminar. In the past fourteen weeks, both my patient and the therapy process have undergone astounding change. It's as if I can divide therapy into two stages: before and after my ill-advised T-shirt comment.

"Only a few minutes ago Myrna left my office, and I was aware of feeling surprised that the hour had passed so quickly. And sorry to see her go. Amazing. She used to bore me. Now she's a vivacious and engaging person. Haven't heard a whine in weeks. We banter a lot—she's so sharp that it's hard for me to keep up with her. She's open, introspective, produces interesting dreams, even dabbles in interesting words. No more monologues: she is very conscious of me in the room, and our process has become harmoniously interactive. I look forward to seeing her as much as any other patient—perhaps more.

"The sixty-four-dollar question is: How did the T-shirt comment launch this transformation? How to reconstruct and interpret the events of the last fourteen weeks?

"Dr. Werner was certain that the T-shirt comment was an egregious error, that it would result in a rupture of the therapeutic alliance. He was dead wrong about that. My thoughtless, insensitive crack turned out to be the pivotal incident of therapy!

"But he was right—oh, so right—about the patient's ability to tune in to the therapist's countertransference. She intuited virtually every single countertransferential feeling I described at the last presentation. And with uncanny accuracy. It's enough to make a Kleinian out of me. She missed nothing. She nailed me on everything. There is not one comment I shared with the group the last time I presented her that I haven't had to acknowledge explicitly to her. Perhaps there is some validity to parapsychology after all. So what if the research has failed to replicate positive findings? A remarkable incident like this simply demonstrates the irrelevance of empirical research.

"Why is she better? What else could it be but the wake-up call of the T-shirt comment? This case has demonstrated to me that there is a place for cruel honesty, for what Synanon used to call 'hard love.' But the therapist has to back it up, has to stay present, stay honest with the patient. It requires a relationship that has to be well established, that will enable therapist and patient to weather the ensuing storm. And in these litigious days it requires courage. The last time I presented Myrna, someone—I think Barbara—labeled the T-shirt comment 'shock therapy.' I agree: that's exactly what it was. It changed Myrna radically, and in the post-shock period I grew to like her better. I admired the way she hung in there and kept insisting on straight feedback. She has a lot of guts. She must have sensed my growing admiration for her. People love themselves if they see a loving image of themselves reflected in the eyes of someone they really care about."

As Ernest dictated his seminar notes, Myrna drove home, also contemplating the last several therapy sessions. "Good solid work," Dr. Lash had called it, and so it was. She was proud of herself. Over the past few weeks she had opened herself up as never before. She had taken great risks; she had aired and discussed every aspect of her relationship with Dr. Lash. Save one, of course: she had never revealed having listened to his dictation.

Why not? At first it was simply to luxuriate in the pleasure of tormenting him with his own words. To be honest, she had enjoyed clubbing him with her secret knowledge. There were times—especially when he seemed so full of himself, so smug and certain of his superior knowledge—when she amused herself by imagining his face when she finally told him the truth.

But things had changed. In the past several weeks, as she grew closer to him, most of the fun had gone out of it. The secret had become a burden, an irritating burr she wanted to remove, and she had even rehearsed confessing it. More than once she had entered his office and taken a deep breath, intending to tell all. But she never had—partly out of embarrassment at having concealed it for so long, partly out of genuine caring. Dr. Lash had played it straight: he had denied none of the things she had confronted him with—almost nothing. He had been devoted to her welfare. Why embarrass the poor man now? Why cause him pain? That was the caring part. But there was still another reason. She liked being a magus, liked the excitement of secret knowledge.

Her penchant for secrets expressed itself in an entirely unpredictable fashion. Thesaurus in hand, she devoted her evenings to writing poetry that teemed with themes of trickery, secrecy, rolltop desks, hidden compartments. The Internet offered the perfect outlet, and she shipped out many poems to the singlepoet.com chat room.

> *Upward I gaze*
> *at sealed edges of honeycombed compartments*
> *swollen with nectared mysteries.*
> *When I am big*
> *I shall have my own chambers,*
> *fill them with grown-up secrecy.*

The secret she had never revealed to her father loomed larger. As never before, she felt his presence. His slim, bent frame, his medical instruments, his desk with its secrets held a particular fascination for her, which she tried to express in verse.

> *Stoop-shouldered presence absent now and forever*
> *cobwebbed stethoscope*
> *ruby crackled-leather chair*
> *rolltop desk cubicles brimming with the mystery and scent*

of dear dead patients
chattering in the dark
until silenced by morning sunspears
piercing the dust
illuminating the wooden desk, which,
like a meadow that once bore dancing feet
and now greens idly
yet remembers still the crease of peopled times.

Myrna hadn't shared these poems with Dr. Lash. She had plenty to talk about in her therapy sessions, and the poetry seemed irrelevant. Besides, her poems might have invited questions about the theme of secrecy, and they might have led directly to the secret of the dictation tape. Sometimes she worried that her withholding would create a wedge between them. But she assured herself that she could overcome that.

Nor did she need Dr. Lash's approval of her poetry. She found plenty of affirmation elsewhere. The singlepoet.com Internet chat room was crowded with single male poets.

Life had become exciting. No more overtime at her Silicon Valley office. Nightly, Myrna rushed home to open her e-mail box, which bulged with praise for her poetry and her refreshing directness. Perhaps she had been too hasty to dismiss e-mail relationships as impersonal. Perhaps the opposite was true. Perhaps electronic friendships—because they did not depend on skin-deep physical attributes—were more genuine and complex.

The electronic suitors who praised her poetry never failed to include their personal profiles and phone numbers. Her self-esteem surged. She read and reread her fan mail. She collected: praise, profiles, phone numbers, information. Dimly, she remembered Dr. Lash's admonition about making withdrawals from data banks. But she liked collecting. She developed a meticulous suitor-rating scale, which weighed earning potential, stock options, corporate influence, and quality of verse as well as personal characteristics such as openness, generosity, and expressivity. Several of the singlepoet chat room suitors asked for a face-to-face meeting—for an afternoon espresso at a Silicon Valley café, for a walk, lunch, dinner.

Not yet—she wanted more data. But soon.

6

The Hungarian Cat Curse

ut tell me, Halston, why do you want to stop therapy? It seems to me we're only just beginning. We've met only, what—three times?" Ernest Lash skimmed though the pages of his appointment book. "Yes, that's right. This is our fourth meeting."

Waiting patiently for a response, Ernest gazed at his patient's gray paramecium-patterned tie and his six-button gray vest and tried to remember when he had last seen a patient who wore a formal three-piece business suit or a paisley tie.

"Please don't take it wrong, Doctor," Halston said. "It's not you; it's that there are too many unexpected things going on. It's hard taking time off to come here in the middle of the day—harder than I expected ... causes more stress ... a paradox because, after all, the point of seeing you was to reduce stress.

. . . And the money for therapy, I cannot deny it's a factor . . . feeling a financial pinch now. There's child support . . . three thousand a month alimony . . . oldest son commences Princeton in the fall . . . thirty thousand a year . . . you know how it is. I considered just outright canceling today, but I thought it was the proper thing, that I owed it to you, to come to a final session."

One of his mother's Yiddish expressions suddenly crept out of a deep cortical crevice, and Ernest whispered it to himself: *"Geh Gesunter Heit"* (Go in good health), similar to the blessing said after a sneeze. But *Geh Gesunter Heit,* as his mother mockingly used the phrase, was more insult than blessing and meant, "Go away and stay away," or "God willing, it will be a long time before I ever see *you* again."

Yes, it's true, Ernest acknowledged to himself, I wouldn't mind if Halston went away and stayed away. I cannot get interested in this man. Ernest took a good look at his patient—a partial profile because Halston never met his gaze. Long, mournful face, slate-black skin—he was from Trinidad, the great-great-grandchild of fugitive slaves. If Halston had ever had any sort of sparkle, it had long been extinguished. He was lusterless, a compilation of shades of gray: graying hair, perfectly manicured gray-streaked goatee, flint eyes, gray suit, dark socks. And gray buttoned-down mind. No, no trace of color or animation enlivened Halston's mind or body.

Geh Gesunter Heit; go away and stay away. Isn't that what Ernest was hoping for? "A final session," Halston had said. Hmm, thought Ernest, has a nice ring to it. I could live with that. He was swamped now, heavily overscheduled. Megan, a former patient whom he hadn't seen in years, was back. She had attempted suicide two weeks ago and was making extraordinary demands on his time. To keep her safe and out of the hospital, he needed to see her at least three hours a week.

Hey, wake up! he prodded himself. You're a therapist. This man came to you for help, and you made a commitment to him. You don't like him much? He doesn't entertain you? He's boring, distant? Has a broomstick up his ass? Great; that's good data. Use it! If you feel that way toward him, then so do most people. Remember his reason for coming for therapy in the first place—a deep sense of estrangement.

It was obvious that Halston was stressed because of cultural dislocation. From the age of nine he had lived in Great Britain and had only recently arrived in the United States and California as the managing officer of a British bank. But Ernest believed that cultural dislocation was only part of the story—there was something profoundly remote about this man.

Okay, okay, Ernest took his own counsel, I won't say, I won't even think, *"Geh Gesunter Heit."* He went back to work, choosing his words carefully so as to engage Halston. "Well, I can certainly understand that you want to reduce stress in your life, not to increase it by more time and money pressures. Makes sense. But you know, one thing about your decision puzzles me."

"Yes, and that is—?"

"Well, I was pretty explicit about the time required and the fees before we started meeting. There have been no real surprises there. Right?"

Halston nodded. "I cannot take issue with that. Doctor, you're entirely correct."

"So it seems only logical to think there's more to it than money and time pressures. Something about you and me? Is it possible you'd feel more comfortable seeing a black therapist?"

"No, Doctor; off the mark. Wrong tree, as you Americans say. The racial difference is not an issue. Remember, I spent several years at Eton and six more at the London School of Economics. Very few blacks there. I'd feel no different, I assure you, consulting a black therapist."

Ernest decided to give it one final shot so that he need never accuse himself of having failed to fulfill his professional obligations.

"Well, Halston, let me put it another way. I understand the reasons you gave. They make sense. Can't be faulted. Let's assume those are sufficient reasons to stop. I can honor that decision. But before we call it a day, I wonder if you'd consider one other question."

Halston looked up warily and, with a slight nod, gestured for Ernest to continue.

"My question is, Could there be any additional reasons? I've known many patients—every therapist has—who've shied away from therapy for reasons that weren't quite so rational. If that is true for you, would you be willing to give voice to any of those reasons?"

He paused. Halston closed his eyes. Ernest could almost hear the gray cylinders of cognition creaking into motion. Would Halston take a chance? Even-money bet, Ernest thought. He watched Halston open his mouth, just a crack, as though to speak, but no words issued forth.

"I'm not talking about anything big, Halston. But even a smidgen, a hint, of other reasons?"

"Perhaps," Halston ventured, "I belong neither in therapy nor in California."

Patient and therapist sat looking at each other: Ernest at Halston's perfectly buffed fingernails and six-button gray vest; Halston, it seemed, at his therapist's untidy mustache and white turtleneck sweater.

Ernest decided to hazard a guess.

"California too loose? Prefer London formality?"

Bingo! Halston's nod was almost animated.

"How about in this room?"

"Yes, here too."

"For example?"

"No offense, Doctor, but I'm accustomed to more professionalism when I see a physician."

"Professionalism?" Ernest felt energized. Finally, something was happening.

"I prefer to consult a physician who offers a discrete diagnosis and prescribes a treatment."

"And your experience here?"

"I mean no offense, Dr. Lash."

"None will be taken, Halston. Your only task here is to speak your mind freely."

"Things are just—how to put it?—too informal here, too—too familiar. Your wish that we address one another by first names, for example."

"You see this informality as a denial of our professional relationship?"

"Precisely. Makes me uneasy. Makes me feel we're fumbling about as though we were somehow going to stumble upon the answer together."

Ernest played it loose. Nothing to lose. Halston was most likely gone anyway. Might as well, Ernest thought, give him something he can use in his next therapy.

"I understand your preference for more formal roles," he said, "and I appreciate your willingness to express your feelings about working with me. Let me try to do the same and share with you my experience in working with you."

Ernest had Halston's full attention. Few patients are indifferent to the prospect of obtaining feedback from their therapist.

"One of my major feelings is a certain frustration—I think it has to do with your being a trifle stingy."

"Stingy?"

"Stingy—word-stingy. You don't give me much. Whenever I ask you a question, you send me back a terse telegram. That is, you give me as few words, as few descriptive details, as few personal revelations as possible. And it is for this very reason that I have tried to establish a more intimate relationship between us. My approach to therapy depends on my patients' sharing their deepest feelings. In my experience, formal roles slow down that process, and that's my reason—my sole reason—for shucking them. And that's also why I often ask you to look at your feelings toward me."

"Everything you say is eminently reasonable—I'm sure you know what you're doing. But I can't help it—the California touchy-feely culture sets my teeth on edge. That's the way I am."

"One question about that. Are you satisfied with the way you are?"

"Satisfied?" Halston looked baffled.

"Well, when you say that's the way you are, I believe you're saying too that that's the way you *choose* to be. So I'm asking, are you satisfied with that choice? With keeping such distance, remaining so impersonal?"

"I'm not sure it's a choice, Doctor. That," he repeated, "is the way I am—my innermost constitution."

Ernest considered two alternatives. He could either attempt to persuade Halston of his own responsibility for his remoteness or launch one final major investigation of a specific crucial episode of Halston's withholding. He chose the latter.

"Well, let me go back once again to the very beginning, to the night you entered the emergency room. Let me tell you my side of it. At about four in the morning, I received a call from the emergency room physician describing a patient in a state of great panic touched off by a nightmare. I told the physician to start you on medication for the panic and arranged to meet with you two hours later, at six. When we met you could recall neither the nightmare nor any of the events of the previous evening. In other words, I had no content, nothing to go on."

"That's the way it was; everything about that evening remains a blackout."

"And so I've tried to work around it, and I agree with you—we've made little headway. But in our three hours together, I've been struck by your general remoteness from others, from me, possibly from yourself. I believe this remoteness, and your discomfort about my challenging it, is the major factor motivating your wish to terminate.

"Let me share a second observation: I'm struck by your lack of curiosity about yourself. I feel that I have to supply the curiosity for both of us—that I alone must carry the entire burden of our work."

"I'm not deliberately concealing anything from you, Doctor. Why would I do that intentionally? That is just the way I am," Halston repeated in his wooden way.

"Let's try one last time, Halston. Humor me. I want you to review again the events of the day preceding the evening of the nightmare. Let's go over it with a fine-tooth comb."

"As I told you, a normal day at the bank, and that night a horrible nightmare, which I've forgotten—the drive to the emergency room—"

"No, no, we've done that. Let's try another approach. Get your date book out. Let's see," Ernest checked his calendar, "our first meeting was May 9. Go over your appointments the day before. Start with the morning of May 8."

Halston took out his week-at-a-glance date book, turned to May 8, and squinted. "Mill Valley," he said, "now why on earth was I in Mill Valley? Oh, right—my sister. I remember now. I wasn't in the bank that morning after all. I was investigating Mill Valley."

"What do you mean, 'investigating'?"

"My sister lives in Miami, and her firm is transferring her to the Bay area. She's considering a house in Mill Valley, and I offered to reconnoiter the town for her—you know, morning traffic patterns, parking, shopping, the best residential areas."

"Good. Excellent start. Now take me through the rest of the day."

"Everything is strangely hazy—it's almost eerie. I can't recall anything."

"You live in San Francisco—do you remember driving to Mill Valley across the Golden Gate Bridge? What time?"

"Early, I think. Before the traffic. Maybe seven."

"Then what? Had you eaten breakfast at home? Or in Mill Valley? Try to picture it. Let your mind wander freely back to that morning. Close your eyes, if it helps."

Halston closed his eyes. After three or four minutes of silence, Ernest wondered whether he had fallen asleep and in a soft voice prodded, "Halston? Halston? Don't move, stay where you are, but try to think aloud. What are you seeing in your mind?"

"Doctor"—Halston slowly opened his eyes—"did I ever tell you about Artemis?"

"Artemis? The Greek goddess? No, not a word."

"Doctor," said Halston, blinking his eyes and shaking his head as if to clear it, "I'm a little shaken. I've just now had the oddest experience. As though a rent suddenly appeared in my mind, letting all the uncanny events of that day pour through. I don't want you to think I've been deliberately withholding this from you."

"Rest assured, Halston. I'm with you. You started to talk about Artemis."

"Well, I'm just sorting things out—I'd better start from the beginning of that accursed day—the day before I wound up in the emergency room. . . . "

Ernest loved stories and sat back, full of anticipation. He had the strongest feeling that this man, with whom he had spent three puzzling hours, was now going to reveal the key to a mystery.

"Well, Doctor, you know I've been single for almost three years and a little cautious—more than a little—about another—er—liaison. I informed you that I was greatly injured, emotionally and financially, by my ex-wife?"

Ernest nodded. A glance at the clock. Damnit, only fifteen minutes left. He would have to move Halston along if he was to hear this story. "And this Artemis?"

"Well, yes, back to the point, thank you. It's funny, but it was your question about breakfast that morning that triggered something. It's coming clearly now—stopping to breakfast at a café in the center of Mill Valley, sitting down at a large, empty table for four. Then the café got crowded, and a woman inquired if she could share my table. I looked up at her, and I confess I liked what I saw."

"How so?"

"Extraordinary-looking woman. Beautiful. Perfect features, fetching smile. My age, I guess, around forty, but a lithe body, like a teenager. A body, as American films put it, to die for."

Ernest gazed at Halston, a different, animated Halston, and felt himself warming to him.

"Tell me."

"A 'ten.' Like Bo Derek. Small waist and a most impressive bosom. Many of my Brit friends prefer androgynous women, but I hereby plead guilty to large-breast fetishism—and, no, Doctor, I don't want to change that."

Ernest smiled reassuringly. Changing Halston's—or his own—adoration of breasts was not on his agenda.

"And?"

"Well, I started to converse with her. Her name was strange—Artemis—and she looked . . . what shall I say? Well . . . different, New Age type. Not a customer who would appear at my bank. Imagine, she spread *avocado* on her morning bagel and then took out of her string purse plastic packets of condiments and sprinkled it with sea salt and pumpkin seeds. And her costume was straight from King's Road—flowered peasant blouse, long flowery purple skirt, cord belt, lots of gold chains and beads. A flower child grown up, so she seemed.

"But," he continued, his story flowing out all the more forcefully for having been dammed, "in actuality she was down-to-earth, well educated, and most lucid. We struck up an immediate friendship and conversed for hours, until the waitress came to set the table for lunch. I was fascinated by her and invited her to lunch with me. This despite the fact that I had a business luncheon scheduled. And I don't have to tell you, Doctor, that this was very unlike me. In fact, most of this was unlike me. Eerie."

"What do you mean, Halston?"

"I feel strange saying this because I view this office as a bastion of rationality, but there was something very strange about Artemis—*alien* is not too strong a term—it's as though I were under a spell. Let me go on. When she told me she couldn't have lunch with me because she had a prior commitment, I asked, 'What about dinner tonight?'—again without even checking my date book. 'Sure,' she said and asked me to dine at her home. She lived alone, she said, and had planned to cook a mushroom ragout with some chanterelles she had picked the day before from the Mount Tamalpais forest."

"And you did?"

"Did I? Most assuredly I did. And it was one of the premier evenings of my life—at least, up to a momentous point." He paused, shaking his head as he had when his memory had first returned to him, then went on, "It was extraordinary being with her. Everything flowed naturally. Legendary dinner—what a marvelous cook. And I'd brought some first-class California wine, a Stag's Leap cabernet. And then after dessert, a first-rate British trifle—the first I've seen in this country—she brought out some marijuana. I hesitated but decided, 'When in California, live as the natives,' and I took the first puff of my life." A befuddled look on his face, Halston paused.

"And?" Ernest prodded.

"And then, after we cleared the dishes, I began to feel a warm, pleasant glow." Another pause, another headshake.

"And?"

"That was when the most extraordinary thing happened—she asked me if I wanted to go to bed with her. Just like that, all matter-of-fact, She was so natural, so graceful, so—so—I don't know—adult. None of that typical American 'Will she or won't she?' melodrama I detest."

Good Lord! Ernest thought. What a woman; what an evening! Lucky man! Then, glancing again at the clock, he hurried Halston along. "You said it was one of the great evenings of your life—but only up to some momentous point?"

"Yes; the sex was sheer ecstasy. Extraordinary. Unlike any I've ever even imagined."

"How so extraordinary?"

"It's all still a bit of a haze, but I remember her licking me like a kitten, every square centimeter, head to toe, until every pore on my body was gaping open, begging for more, tingling with delight, receptive to her touch, her tongue, drinking in her scent and warmth." He stopped. "I'm a bit embarrassed expressing all this, Doctor."

"Halston, you're doing exactly what you should be doing here. Try to continue."

"Well, the pleasure just kept spiraling up. It was unworldly, I tell you. The head of my—my—what do you say?—organ—lit up, hotter and hotter, until I had an absolutely incandescent orgasm. And then I think I passed out."

Ernest was amazed. Was this the same boring, constricted man with whom he had spent those tedious hours?

"Then what happened, Halston?"

"Ah, that was the turning point; that's when everything changed. The next thing I knew I was somewhere else. Now I realize it must have been a dream, but at the time it was so real I could touch and feel and smell everything in it. It's faded away, but I can recall being chased through a forest by a menacing giant cat—a house cat the size of a lynx but all black, with a white mask around its red, gleaming eyes, a thick, powerful tail, huge fangs, and razor claws. It was chasing the bloody hell out of me! Far away I saw a naked woman standing in a pond. Looked like Artemis, so I jumped in and waded toward her for help. Closer up I saw that it wasn't Artemis at all but a robot with enormous breasts out of which streamed jets of milk. Then, even closer, I saw that it wasn't milk but some kind of glowing radioactive liquid. And then I realized, with horror, that I was standing thigh-deep in the corrosive stuff, which was starting to eat away at my feet and legs. I waded frantically toward land again, but there—still hissing and waiting for me—was that damned cat, now bigger—big as a lion. That's when I bolted out of bed and ran for my life. I put on my clothes running down the stairs and was still shoe-less when I started the car. I couldn't breathe, and I called my physician on the car phone. He instructed me to go to the emergency room—and that's when I was referred to you."

"And Artemis?"

"Artemis? Nada. I wouldn't go near her again. She's poison. Even now, just talking about her is starting to bring back some of that panic back. I think that's why I buried all of this so deeply in my mind." Halston quickly checked his pulse. "See, I'm racing right now—twenty-eight in fifteen seconds—approximately one hundred twelve."

"But how did she feel about your suddenly running out?"

"I don't know. Or care. She slept right through everything."

"So she went to sleep next to you and woke up with you gone, and she has no idea why."

"And it's going to remain that way! I tell you, Doctor—that dream was from another world, another reality—from hell."

"Halston, we've got to stop. We're running way late, but it's clear there's much to work on. Most obviously, your feelings toward women—you make love to a woman, then encounter this cat that personifies danger and punishment, and then desert her with no word of explanation. And then the breasts that promise nurturance but instead squirt poison. Tell me, where are you in your wishes to stop therapy?"

"It is obvious even to me, Doctor, that there is much to explore. Same time available next week?"

"Yes. And—good work today. I'm pleased, Halston, honored, that you trusted me enough to remember and reveal to me this whole remarkable and frightening incident."

Two hours later, on his walk to Jasmine, a Clement Street Vietnamese restaurant where he often lunched, Ernest had time to think about his session with Halston. On the whole, he was satisfied with the way he had handled Halston's inclination to terminate. Even though he was overscheduled, he would not have liked himself if he had just let his patient walk out. Halston was struggling to break through to something important, and Ernest knew that his concerned, methodical, but not overly aggressive tactics had saved the day.

It was remarkable how, Ernest thought, as he grew more experienced, fewer and fewer patients terminated prematurely. How threatened he had been, as a young therapist, by termination, taking everything personally and regarding every patient who quit as a personal defeat, a mark of ineffectiveness, a public disgrace. And he was grateful to Marshal, his former supervisor, for teaching him that such a reaction ensures ineffectiveness. Whenever therapists have too much ego riding on a patient's decision, whenever they *need* a patient to stay in therapy, that's when they lose their effectiveness: they begin to wheedle, to be seductive, to give patients exactly what they wish—*anything* to get them to return the following week.

Ernest was glad too that he had supported and complimented Halston rather than voicing any doubts about the authenticity of the dramatic recall of the Artemis evening. Ernest wasn't sure how to evaluate what he had just heard. He knew, of course, of sudden returns of repressed memories, but he had had little personal experience with such phenomena in his clinical work. Though relatively common in post-traumatic stress disorder, to say nothing of Hollywood portrayals of therapy, it was rare in Ernest's quotidian psychotherapy.

But all of Ernest's self-congratulatory impulses passed quickly, as did all of his benevolent thoughts about Halston. What really captured his attention was Artemis. The more he thought about it, the more horrified he was by Halston's behavior toward her. What kind of monster would make love, fantastic love, to a woman and then abandon her with no explanation, no note, no phone call? It was beyond belief.

Ernest's heart went out to Artemis. He knew exactly how she must have felt. Once, fifteen years ago, he had arranged a weekend rendezvous with Myrna, an old girlfriend, at a New York hotel. They had spent a lovely night together, or so Ernest believed. In the morning he had left for a brief appointment and returned with a huge, grateful bouquet of flowers. But no Myrna. She had left without a trace. Packed her bags and absconded—no note, and no response to his later phone calls or letters. No explanation, ever. He had been devastated. Psychotherapy had never entirely erased his pain, and even now, all these years later, the memory still stung. Above all, Ernest hated not knowing. Poor Artemis: she had given so much to Halston, taken such risks, and in the end been so shabbily treated.

Over the next few days Ernest thought occasionally about Halston but dwelled often upon Artemis. In his fantasy she became a goddess—beautiful, giving, nurturing but badly wounded. Artemis was a woman to revere, honor, treasure: the idea of debasing such a woman seemed hardly human to him. How tormented she must be by not knowing what had happened! How many times must she have relived that night, trying to understand what she had said, what she had done, to drive Halston away. And Ernest knew he was in a privileged position to help her. Aside from Halston, I am, he thought, the only one who knows the truth of that night.

Ernest had often been awash in grandiose fantasies of rescuing distressed damsels. He knew that about himself. How could he not know? Again and again his analyst, Olive Smith, and his supervisor, Marshal Strider, had rubbed his nose in it. Rescue fantasies played a role both in his personal relationships, where he often overlooked warning signals of obvious incompatibility, and in his psychotherapy, where his countertransference sometimes ran wild and he became overinvested in curing his female patients.

Naturally, as Ernest pondered the rescue of Artemis, the voices of his analyst and supervisor came to mind. Ernest listened and accepted their critique—but only to a point. Deep inside he believed that his overinvestment made him a better therapist, a better human being. *Of course* women should be rescued. That was an evolutionary truism, a species-survival strategy built into our genes. How horrified he'd been long ago when, in his comparative anatomy course, he had found that the cat he was dissecting had been pregnant and was carrying five tiny, marble-sized fetuses in her uterus. Likewise he abhorred caviar, possible only through the slaughter and plundering of pregnant sturgeon. Most horrifying had been the Nazi extermination policy, that had carried the terror to women housing the "seeds of Sarah."

And so Ernest never questioned his decision to persuade Halston to redress his transgression. "Consider what she must have felt," he repeatedly asked his patient in subsequent sessions—to which Halston would irritably reply, "Doctor, *I'm* the patient, not her." Or Ernest would urge on Halston the wisdom of the eighth and ninth steps of the twelve-step recovery program: *Make a list of all persons we have harmed, and make direct amends to such persons whenever possible.* But all his arguments, no matter how skillfully put, failed to budge Halston, who seemed unimaginably self-absorbed and callous. Once he chided Ernest for his softheaded-ness. "Aren't you overromanticizing this one-night stand? This is her mode of life. I'm not the first man she's accosted, and probably not the last. I assure you, Doctor, this lady can take care of herself."

Ernest wondered whether Halston had dug in his heels out of sheer spite. Perhaps he had sensed his therapist's overinvolvement with Artemis and was retaliating by rejecting, automatically, all of Ernest's advice. But in any event, Ernest gradually realized both that Halston would *never* make amends to Artemis and that he, Ernest, would have to assume that burden. Curiously, despite his heavy schedule, he did not mind accepting the task. It seemed like a moral imperative, and he began to view it not as a millstone but as his ministry. Curiously too, Ernest, generally self-analytic to a fault, subjecting every whim, every decision, to a searching and tedious scrutiny, never once questioned his motives. He did real-ize, however, that he was undertaking an unorthodox and illegiti-mate mission—what other therapist had ever taken it upon him-self to make personal amends for his patient's misdeeds?

Despite his realization that secrecy and delicacy were required, Ernest's first steps were clumsy and transparent: "Hal-ston, one last time. Let's go over your meeting with Artemis and the type of connection you made with her."

"Not again? As I've said, I was in a café when—"

"No, try to paint the scene vividly and precisely. Describe the café. The time? Its location?"

"It was in Mill Valley, about eight A.M., in one of those quaint California innovations—combination bookstore and café."

"Its name?" Ernest urged when Halston paused. "Describe everything about your meeting."

"Doctor, I don't understand. Why these questions?"

"Humor me on this, Halston. Painting the scene as vividly as possible will help you to recall all the feelings you experienced."

In response to Halston's protests that he had no interest in recalling the feelings, Ernest reminded him that the development of empathy was a first step in improving his relationships with women. Hence, recalling his experiences and what Artemis may have experienced would be a valuable exercise. A lame rationale, Ernest knew, but plausible.

As Halston dutifully recounted all the details of that eventful day, Ernest listened hard but learned only a few new particulars. The café was the Book Depot, and Artemis was a lover of literature—that, Ernest felt, might be useful information. She had told Halston that she was in the midst of rereading the great German novelists—Mann, Kleist, Böll—and that very day had purchased a copy of the new translation of Musil's *The Man Without Qualities*.

Because of Halston's increasing suspiciousness, Ernest eased off—lest at any moment his patient might say, "Look, you want her address and phone number?"

Which, of course, was precisely what Ernest did want. Would save him a lot of time. But he now had enough to begin.

Bright and early one morning a few days later, Ernest drove to Mill Valley, parked, and walked into the Book Depot. He looked around the long, narrow bookstore, once a train depot, and then checked the cheery café attached to it and the dozen outdoor tables warming in the morning sun. Finding no woman resembling Halston's description of Artemis, he went to the counter and ordered an extra-seedy bagel from the waitress, whose nose and lips were lavishly beringed.

"Bagel with what?" she asked.

Ernest scanned the menu board. No avocado. Was Halston fabricating? Finally he decided to put himself at an advantage by requesting a double order of cucumbers and sprouts with his herb-and-chive cream cheese.

As he settled himself at a table, he saw her enter. Flowered bulging blouse, long plum-colored skirt—his favorite hue—beads, chains, and all: it had to be Artemis. More beautiful than he had imagined. Halston hadn't mentioned, perhaps had not even noticed, her lustrous golden hair, which she wore Middle European style, swept into a coil and held firm with a tortoiseshell clasp at the back of her head. Ernest melted: all his lovely Viennese aunts, the first objects of his pubescent erotic drive, had worn their hair in that very fashion. He took her in quickly as she ordered and paid at the counter. What a woman—lovely in all ways, penetrating turquoise-blue eyes, heavy lips, finely dimpled chin, about five feet four inches tall in her flat sandals, a stirring, rippling, perfectly proportioned body.

Now came the part that always flummoxed Ernest: How to begin a conversation with a woman? He took out Mann's *The Holy Sinner*, which he had bought the day before, and laid it open on the table, the title clearly visible. Perhaps it would provide the opening gambit in a conversation—if, that is, she chose a table nearby. Ernest glanced nervously around the half-empty café. Plenty of free tables. He nodded when she passed, and Artemis nodded in response as she made her way to an empty table. But then, mirabile dictu—a couple of seconds later she backed up.

"Oh, *The Holy Sinner*," she, incredibly, remarked. "What a surprise!"

A bite! A bite! But Ernest wasn't sure how to reel his catch in. "I—er—I beg your pardon," he stammered. He was in shock—the shock of a resignedly unsuccessful fisherman who is astounded by a tug on his line. He had used the book lure countless times through the years and not even once had had a nibble.

"That book," she explained. "Why, I read *The Holy Sinner* years ago, but I've never seen anyone else reading it."

"Oh, I love it, and go back to it every few years. I love some of Mann's shorter works too and am just starting to reread all of him. This one is the first."

"I just reread *The Transposed Head*," Artemis said. "What's next on your list?"

"I'm doing them in the order I treasure them. Next'll be the *Joseph and His Brothers* tetralogy. And then, perhaps, *Felix Krull*. But," he half rose, "won't you sit down?"

"And last?" asked Artemis, setting her bagel and coffee on the table and sitting down across from him.

"*The Magic Mountain,*" Ernest responded, not missing a beat, revealing neither his sheer astonishment at hooking this catch nor his uncertainty about how to reel it in. "It just hasn't aged well— Settembrini's endless conversations strike me now as tedious. Also, at the bottom of the list is *Doctor Faustus*. The musicological concerns are just too technical and, I'm afraid, boring."

"I agree with you entirely," said Artemis, reaching into her shoulder bag and extracting a ripe black avocado and several plastic bags of seeds, "though I never cease to be fascinated with the Nietzsche-Leverkühn connection."

"Oh, I'm sorry, I haven't introduced myself—lost in our conversation. I'm Ernest Lash."

"I'm Artemis," she said as she peeled her avocado, spread half of it on her bagel, and topped it with sprinkles of various seeds.

"Artemis; a lovely name. You know, it's warming up outside. How about grabbing a table and joining your twin out there?" Ernest had industriously done his homework.

"My twin?" Artemis pondered as they moved to a table in the sun. "My twin? Oh, Apollo! The golden sunlight of brother Apollo. You are an unusual man—all my life I've lived with my name, and you're the first person who has ever said that to me."

"But you know," Ernest continued, "I must confess I may put aside Mann for a while so as to get to the new Wilkins translation of Musil's *Man Without Qualities*."

"What a coincidence." Artemis's eyes opened wide. "I'm reading that book right now." Reaching into her shoulder bag again, she pulled out a book. "It's glorious."

From then on Artemis never took her eyes off Ernest. Indeed, her gaze was so fixed on his lips that every few minutes Ernest self-consciously brushed his mustache to dislodge any errant crumbs.

"I love living in Marin, but sometimes it's not easy to have a serious conversation here," she said, offering him a slice of avocado. "The last time I talked about this book I was with someone who'd never heard of Musil."

"Well, everyone's not up to Musil." What a pity, Ernest thought, that a soul like Artemis had had to put up for any time at all with the tight-assed Halston's company.

For the next three hours they meandered happily through the work of Heinrich Böll, Günter Grass, and Heinrich von Kleist. Ernest looked at his watch. Almost noon! What an extraordinary woman, he thought. Though he had cleared his morning schedule, he had five consecutive sessions starting at one o'clock. Time was running out, and he turned to the real business of the day.

"I'm going to have to leave soon," he said, "very much against my will, but my patients await me. I cannot tell you how much I've enjoyed our talk. It's really brought me out of myself. I needed it at this point in my life."

"How come?"

"It's been a bad time." Ernest sighed, hoping his words, which he had rehearsed several times the night before, would seem spontaneous. "About two weeks ago I visited an old girlfriend of mine. Hadn't seen her for a couple of years, and we had a lovely twenty-four hours together. Or so I thought. In the morning, I awoke and she was gone. Vanished. Not a trace of her. I've been in a bad way since. A very bad way!"

"That's dreadful." Artemis was more concerned than Ernest had ever hoped for. "She was important to you? You were hoping to reconnect with her?"

"Well, no." Ernest thought of Halston and how she must have felt about him. "That's not quite it. She was—well, what should I say?—more of a playmate, a sexual friend. So I'm not in grief about losing her. The real pain is not knowing. Was it something I did that caused her to run? Did I hurt her in some manner? Something I said? Was I an inconsiderate lover? Was I in some fundamental way unacceptable? You know what I mean. Stirs up a lot of bad stuff."

"I'm with you on that one," she said, shaking her head sympathetically. "Been through that myself—and not too long ago."

"Really? It's amazing how much we seem to have in common. Shouldn't we try to heal one another? Continue this conversation some other time—say, at dinner tonight?"

"Yes, but not a restaurant. I'm in a cooking mood. Yesterday I picked some beautiful chanterelles, which I'm going to make into a Hungarian mushroom ragout. Join me?"

Never had therapy hours ticked by so slowly. Ernest could think of nothing but Artemis. He was enchanted with her. Again and again he prodded himself: Concentrate! Focus! Earn your fee! Sweep this woman from your mind. But Artemis refused to be swept. She had set up housekeeping in his frontal cortex, and there she stayed. There was something eerie and alluring about Artemis that brought to mind the immortal, irresistible African queen he remembered from Rider Haggard's novel *She*.

It did not escape Ernest that he was thinking more about Artemis's charms than about alleviating her distress. Ernest, mind your priorities, he rebuked himself. What are you doing? This whole project is deeply suspect even without any sexual adventures. You're already treading on thin ice—milking Halston for data about how to find Artemis, turning yourself into an uninvited traveling therapist paying a house call on an attractive female stranger. You're being grandiose, he cautioned himself, and unethical and unprofessional. Careful, careful, careful!

"Your honor," he imagined his supervisor's voice booming from the witness stand, "Dr. Lash is a fine and ethical clinician except when he occasionally lapses into thinking with his small head."

No, no, no! Ernest protested. I'm doing nothing unethical. I intend an act of integrity, an act of charity. Halston, my patient, wantonly inflicted a grievous wound on another person, and it is inconceivable that he will ever be willing to make reparation. I, and only I, can redress the injury and do it quickly and efficiently.

Artemis's Hansel-and-Gretel house—small, high-gabled, dripping with gingerbread lacework and surrounded by a dense row of topped junipers—would have better suited Germany's Black Forest than Marin County. Greeting him at the door with a glass of fresh-squeezed pomegranate juice, Artemis apologized for not having alcohol in the house—"Drug-free zone here," she said, then added, "except for ganja, the holy herb."

As soon as he sat down on the sofa, a faux–Louis XVI *canapé* covered with petit point and supported by dainty gray-white legs, Ernest returned to the subject of abandonment. But although he used all his practiced skills to draw her out, he soon had to recognize that he had overestimated Artemis's distress.

Yes, she acknowledged, she had been through the same kind of experience as Ernest, and it had not been easy. But it was less painful than she had suggested: she was, she confessed, only being polite. It was only to help Ernest to talk about his difficulties that she had mentioned she'd recently been deserted by a man. Though he had bailed out with no explanation to her, she had not been much troubled by the event. The relationship hadn't been meaningful, and she was certain that it was far more his problem than hers. Ernest looked at her in amazement: this woman was more centered than he could ever hope to be. Relaxing, he officially went off duty as a therapist and turned to enjoying the rest of the evening.

Halston's enthusiastic account had prepared Ernest for the events to come. But it soon became clear that Halston had understated, and probably underappreciated, everything. The conversation with Artemis was delightful, the chanterelle ragout a small miracle, and the rest of the evening a much larger miracle.

Suspecting that Halston's experience might have been drug induced, Ernest refused the after-dinner marijuana that Artemis offered. But even without it, something unusual, almost surreal, seemed to be working in him. During dinner a warm, wonderful flush began to sweep over him from head to toe. Pleasant feelings from the past flooded his mind, each entering from a different portal. The smell of his mother's baking *kichel* on Sunday mornings; the warmth in the first few seconds after wetting his bed; his first kiss; his first pistol-shot orgasm while masturbating in the bathtub and imagining undressing Aunt Harriet; eating hot-fudge ice-cream cakes at the Georgia Avenue Hot Shoppe; the weightlessness during roller-coaster rides at Glen Echo Amusement Park; moving his queen, protected by a sly bishop, and saying *"Shah mott"* (Checkmate) to his father. His sense of *heimlichkeit*—warm and wet at-homeness—was so strong, so enveloping, that he momentarily lost track of where he was.

"Do you want to go upstairs to the bedroom?" Artemis's soft voice snapped him out of his reverie. Where had he gone? Could there have been something in the mushrooms, he wondered? Do I want to go to the bedroom? I would follow this woman anywhere. I desire her like no other woman I have ever known. Maybe it is neither the grass nor the mushrooms but some unusual pheromone. My olfactory bulb, behind my back, consorting with her musk aroma?

Once in bed Artemis began licking. Every inch of his skin tingled, glowed, until his whole body felt red-hot. Each stroke of her tongue sent him higher and higher until he exploded—not with the sharp crack of a young pistol shot but with the roar of a mighty howitzer. In a brief moment of lucidity, he suddenly noticed Artemis dozing by his side. He had been so transported by his pleasure that he had all but forgotten her, had failed to attend to her pleasure. Reaching out to touch her face, he felt her cheeks wet with streaming tears. Then he fell into the deepest sleep he had ever known.

Some time later the sound of scratching awakened him. At first he could see nothing in the pitch-black room. But he knew that something was wrong, terribly wrong. Gradually, as the black receded, a ghostly green light eerily illuminated the room. His heart pounding, Ernest slid out of bed, pulled on his trousers, and ran to the windows to find out what was scratching. But all he could see, staring back at him, was the reflection of his own face.

He turned to rouse Artemis—but she had vanished. The scratching and scraping grew louder. Then an unearthly *yeeeoooowwww*, like a thousand cats in heat. The room started to vibrate, softly at first, then with increasing intensity. Ever louder, ever coarser grew the scratching. He heard the sound of pebbles striking the ground, then larger stones, then a small avalanche. The noise seemed to come from behind the bedroom wall. Approaching it gingerly, Ernest saw cracks appear in the wall; plaster flaked, falling into a heap on the carpet. Soon he could see drywall; under that, moments later, the wooden laths of the house skeleton lay bare. Crash! A gigantic paw bristling with claws broke through.

Ernest had seen enough. Too much! Grabbing his shirt, he headed for the stairs. But there were no stairs, no walls, no house. Before him lay a black starlit expanse. He began to run and soon found himself in a forest of towering conifers. Hearing a thundering roar, he looked back to see behind him a monstrous cat with fire-red eyes—like a lion but black and white and much larger. Bear-sized. Saber-toothed-tiger-sized. He ran faster, he practically flew, but ever louder and closer grew the thump of the beast's padded paws pounding the pine-needle floor of the forest. Seeing a lake, he headed toward it. Cats hate water, Ernest thought, and waded in. He heard, from far off in the misty center of the lake, the sound of water streaming. Then he saw her: Artemis, standing stock-still in the middle of the lake. One hand was raised high like that of the Statue of Liberty while the other hand cupped one of her enormous breasts, out of which, as she pointed it toward him, gushed a mighty stream of water or milk. No, he saw as he approached closer, it was not milk but a fluorescent green liquid. Nor was the figure Artemis; it was a metal robot. And the lake was not water but acid, eating away at his feet and legs. He opened his mouth and with all his strength tried to scream: "Momma! Momma! Help me, Momma!" But no words came.

The next thing Ernest knew, he was in his car, half dressed, pressing hard on the accelerator and zooming down Marin Drive away from Artemis's Black Forest house. He tried to focus on what had happened to him, but fear overwhelmed him. How many times had he preached to patients and students that a crisis represents not only danger but opportunity? How many times had he preached that anxiety is a trail that leads to insight and wisdom? That of all dreams, the nightmare is the most instructive? Yet, upon reaching his Russian Hill apartment, Ernest dashed in the door and headed not to his writing pad to record the dream but to his medicine cabinet and a professional sample pack of two-milligram tablets of Ativan, a heavy-duty antianxiety drug. But that night the drug brought neither relief nor sleep. In the morning he canceled his entire day's schedule and managed to squeeze his more urgent patients into slots the following evening.

He spent the early morning on the phone talking through his experience with good friends, and some twenty-four hours later the terrible cramping, anxious oppression in his chest began to lessen. The process of talking to his friends, the sheer confessional act, was helpful even though none of them seemed able to grasp what had happened. Even Paul, his closest and oldest chum, who had been his confidant since residency training, was off the mark: he tried to persuade Ernest that the nightmare was a blessing, a cautionary tale warning Ernest to be more circumspect about honoring professional boundaries.

Ernest defended himself vigorously: "Remember, Paul, Artemis is no friend of my patient. And I did not intentionally use my patient to supply me with women. And throughout, my intentions were high-minded. My purpose in seeking her out was not carnal but simply to repair the damage my patient had done. I did not visit her for a sexual assignation—it just seemed impossible to stop that from happening."

"Prosecuting attorneys wouldn't see it that way, Ernest," Paul responded somberly. "They'd make mincemeat out of you."

Ernest's former supervisor, Marshal, offered him a fragment of the cautionary lecture he routinely delivered to his Sea Scout troop: "Even if you're doing no wrong, don't get into any situation where a snapshot of you would suggest the *semblance* of doing wrong."

Ernest was sorry he had phoned Marshal. The snapshot homily did not impress him; on the contrary, he thought it outrageous to advise children to behave circumspectly simply to avoid misrepresentation in the media.

In the end Ernest paid little heed to his friends' advice. They were all pusillanimous, preoccupied with issues of appearance and potential malpractice litigation. From the inside perspective, the one that counted, Ernest was entirely persuaded that he had acted with integrity.

After twenty-four hours' recuperation, Ernest took up his practice again and, four days later, met with Halston, who announced that he had decided after all to terminate therapy. Ernest knew he had failed Halston, who had undoubtedly sensed Ernest's disapproval of him. Ernest's guilt about his poor therapy was brief, however, because shortly after saying goobye to Halston he had a stunning revelation: in the last seventy-two hours, ever since his phone conversations with Paul and Marshal, he had entirely forgotten the existence of Artemis! That breakfast with her, everything afterward! Not once had he thought of her! My God, he thought, I have acted in precisely the same repugnant manner as Halston, deserting her without a word of explanation and never bothering to phone or see her.

For the rest of that day and the next, Ernest encountered the same strange phenomenon: again and again he tried to think about Artemis but could not keep his focus; within a few moments his mind would wander to inconsequential topics. Late the next evening he decided to phone her, and it was only with the greatest effort—Ernest visualized himself curling eighty pounds—that he succeeded in dialing her number.

"Ernest! Is that really you?"

"Of course it's me. I'm very late, days late. But it's me." Ernest paused. He had expected anger and was thrown off by her pleasant tone. "You seem surprised," he added.

"Very surprised. I never thought to hear your voice again."

"I must see you. Things seem unreal, but the sound of your voice is waking me up. We have much to do: I a lot of apologizing and explaining and you a lot of forgiving."

"Of course I'll see you. But on one condition. No explaining or forgiving—they're not needed."

"Dinner tomorrow? Eight?"

"Fine. I'll cook."

"No." Ernest remembered his suspicions about the chanterelle stew. "My turn. Leave dinner to me."

He arrived at Artemis's home laden with takeout dishes from the Nanking, a hole-in-the-wall on Kearny with San Francisco's worst decor and best Cantonese food. By nature a feeder, he eagerly laid the various packages out on the table, identifying each for Artemis. He was crestfallen when she told him she was a vegan and would have to pass on many of the dishes, including the superb Rolling Lettuce Chicken and Five Mushroom Beef. Thank God, Ernest chanted silently, for the rice, the steamed pea sprouts, and the vegetarian dumplings!

"I have some things to say to you, and I'm not known for reserve," he said as they sat down at her table. "My friends all say I'm a compulsive revealer, so I warn you, here goes—"

"Remember my conditions." Artemis put her hand upon Ernest's arm. "No apologies, no explaining needed."

"Not sure I can honor the conditions, Artemis. As I told you the other night, I take my work as a healer very seriously. It's me, it's my life, and I can't switch it on and off. So I'm absolutely mortified at the damage I've inflicted on you. I acted inhumanly. For us to make such love—beautiful love, love that I've never imagined possible—and then for me to desert you without a word, it's indefensible—I can't put it any other way—I acted inhumanly. My thoughtlessness must have devastated you. You must have wondered again and again what kind of man I am and why I treated you so vilely."

"I've told you before, I don't worry about such things. Naturally I was disappointed, but I understood fully. Ernest," she added gravely, "I *know* why you left me that night."

"You know, do you?" Ernest said playfully, finding her naïveté charming. "I don't believe you know as much as you think you do about that night."

"I'm certain," she said emphatically, "I know far more than you think I do."

"Artemis, you couldn't even imagine what happened to me that night. How could you? I left you because of a dream—a horrible and very private vision. What can you know of it?"

"I know it all, Ernest. I know about the cat and about the poisonous water and about the statue standing in the middle of the lake."

"You're making my blood run cold, Artemis!" Ernest exclaimed. "That was *my* dream. Dreams are a private domain, each person's most private, sovereign sanctuary. How could you know my dream?"

Artemis sat silent, head bowed.

"And so many other questions, Artemis. The depth of my feelings that evening—that magical glow, that irresistible desire. Not to take anything away from you and your charm, but that desire was of an unnatural intensity. Could it have been chemical? Maybe the chanterelles?"

Artemis bowed her head lower.

"And then when we were in bed, I touched your cheek. Why were you weeping? I felt wonderful; I thought it was mutual. Why the tears? Why pain for you?"

"I wasn't crying for me, Ernest, but for *you*. And not because of what had happened between us—that was wonderful for me too. No, I wept because of what was about to happen to you."

"*About* to happen? Am I going mad? This is getting worse and worse. Artemis, tell me the truth!"

"I don't think the truth will satisfy you, Ernest."

"Try me. Trust me."

Artemis stood up, left the room briefly, and returned with a vellum folder from which she extracted a sheaf of paper, yellowed and old. "The truth? The truth is here," she said, holding it out,

IRVIN D. YALOM

"in this letter my grandmother wrote a long time ago to my mother, Magda. It's dated June 13, 1931. Shall I read it to you, Ernest?"

He nodded. And, by the light of three candles as the redolent food waited in its containers, Ernest listened to Artemis's grandmother's story, the story behind his dream.

To Magda, my dear daughter, on her seventeenth birthday, in the hope that this message is neither too late nor too early.

It is time for you to know the answers to the important questions in your life. Where have we come from? Why have you been uprooted so many times? Who and where is your father? Why have I sent you away and not kept you with me? The family history, which I write here, is something you must know and must pass on to your daughters.

I grew up in Ujepest, a few miles outside Budapest. My father, Janos, your grandfather, worked as a machinist in a large plant that assembled buses. When I was seventeen I moved to Budapest. I had several reasons. For one thing, Budapest offered better jobs for a young woman. But the main reason, and I am ashamed to tell you this about your own family, is that my father was like an animal, preying on his own child. He made repeated advances to me when I was too young to defend myself and finally despoiled me when I was thirteen. My mother knew about this but pretended not to know and refused to defend me. In Budapest I moved in with my Uncle Laszlo, my father's brother, and Aunt Juliska, who arranged a position for me to assist her in the house where she worked as a cook. I learned to cook and to bake and, a few years later, took Aunt Juliska's place when she became sick with consumption. When Aunt Juliska died the next year, Uncle Laszlo behaved like my father and demanded that I take Aunt Juliska's place beside him in bed. I couldn't endure that and so moved out on my own. Everywhere men were predatory—like animals. Everyone, the other servants, the delivery boy, the butcher, made lewd comments and leered and tried to touch me whenever I passed. Even the master tried to put his hand under my skirts.

228

I moved to 23 Vaci Ut in the center of Budapest near the Danube, and there, for the next ten years, I lived alone. Men leered and groped me wherever I went, and I protected myself by pulling my world in around me, making it smaller and smaller. I stayed unmarried and lived my small, happy life with my cat, Cica. And then a monster, Mr. Kovacs, moved into the upstairs flat and with him his cat, Merges. Merges means "rageful" in Hungarian [Artemis drew the name out with a Magyar intonation—*Mare*-gesh], and that beast was well named. He was a vicious, hideous, black-and-white cat direct from hell and he terrorized my poor Cica. Over and over Cica returned home cut and bleeding. She lost an eye to infection; one of her ears was half torn off.

And Kovacs terrorized me. I barricaded my doors at night against him and closed the shutters because he wandered around the outside of the house peering in through every crack. Every time we met in the hall, he tried to force himself on me, so I made sure to avoid crossing paths with him. But I was helpless; I couldn't complain to anyone—Kovacs was a police sergeant. A vulgar, rapacious man. I'll tell you what kind of man he was. Once I put aside my pride and pleaded with him to keep Merges inside for only an hour a day so Cica could go out in safety. "Nothing wrong with Merges," he sneered. "My cat and I are alike; we both want the same thing—sweet Hungarian pussy." Yes, he would agree to keep Merges at home—for a price. And the price was me!

Things were bad, but every time Cica entered heat they got even worse. Not only did Kovacs do his usual prowling around my windows and knocking on my door but Merges went berserk: all night long screeching, yowling, scratching at the wall of my house, and flinging himself against my windows.

As if Merges and Kovacs were not pestilence enough, Budapest at that time was infested by huge Danube river rats, which swarmed through my neighborhood, pillaged the potato and carrot bins in the cellar, and slaughtered the backyard chickens. One day my landlord helped me set a trap-cage for the rats in the cellar, and that very night I heard ungodly squeals. Descend-

ing the stairs by candlelight, I was full of fear. What would I do
with the rat or rats I had caught? Then, by the flickering candle, I
saw the cage and, peering out from its bars, the largest, most horrible rat I had ever seen or, in my worst dreams, imagined. I flew
back up the stairs and decided to call for help later, when my landlord awoke. But an hour later, as dawn broke, I ventured back
down and took another look. It was no rat. It was worse—it was
Merges! As soon as he saw me he hissed and spat and tried to claw
me through the bars of the cage. God, what a monster! I knew just
what to do, and it was with great pleasure that I threw an entire
pitcher of water on him. He kept on hissing, and I picked up my
skirts and pranced with joy three times around the cage.

But then what? What should I do with Merges, who now was
howling an ungodly song? Something within me made the decision without my knowing it. For the first time in my life, I would
take a stand. For me! For women everywhere! I would fight back.
I put an old blanket over the cage, lifted it by the handle, walked
out of the house—the streets still empty, no one up yet—and
marched to the train station. I bought a ticket for Esztergom,
about an hour away, but then, deciding it was not far enough, I
rode all the way to Szeged, about two hundred kilometers away.
When I got off the train I walked a few blocks, then stopped, took
the cover off the cage, and prepared to release Merges.

As I looked at him, his eyes slashed at me—sharp, like a razor,
and I shuddered. There was something about his wild look, so
hateful, so relentless, that I knew then, with an eerie certainty, that
Cica and I would never be free of him. Animals have been known
to return home from across a continent. No matter how far I took
Merges, he would return. He would track us from the ends of the
earth. I picked up the cage and walked a few squares farther until I
came to the Danube. I walked to the center of the bridge, waited
until there was no one in sight, and threw the cage into the water.
It floated for an instant, then began to sink. As it sank lower in the
water, Merges never stopped looking at me and hissing. Finally
the Danube stilled him, and I waited until I saw no more bubbles,
until he had reached his riverbed grave, until I was safe forever
from the hellcat. Then I boarded a train for home.

On the ride back, I thought of Kovacs, of his retaliation, and I was terrified. When I returned, his windows were still shuttered. He was then working nights, had slept through Merges's exodus, and would never, never know of my act of defiance. For the first time in my life I felt free.

But not for long. That night, an hour or two after I fell asleep, I heard Merges's yowling outside. It was, of course, a dream, but a dream so vivid, so tangible, that it was more real than my life awake. I heard Merges clawing and scraping a hole in the wall of my bedroom. Staring at the splintering wall, I saw his paw thrust into the room. More scraping, plaster falling all over my room. Then Merges burst into my bedroom. A big cat to start with, he had grown to now double, maybe triple his old size. Soaking wet, the dirty water of the Danube still dripping off him, he spoke to me.

The beast's words are frozen in my mind. "I am old, you murdering bitch," he hissed, "and I have already lived eight of my lives. I have a single life left, and I swear here and now to dedicate it to revenge. I will dwell in the dream dimension, and I will haunt you and your female descendants forever. You separated me forever from Cica, the bewitching Cica, the great passion of my life, and now I will make certain that you will forever be separated from any man who ever shows an interest in you. I'll visit them when they are with you"—here he hissed most terribly—"and drive them from you in such terror that they will never return—they will forget your very existence."

At first I felt exultant. Stupid cat! Cats are, after all, simpleminded, pinheaded animals. Merges had no real understanding of me. His brilliant revenge—that I would no longer be able to be with a man twice! Not revenge but a blessing, a blessing exceeded only by my being forbidden to be with a man even once. Never again to touch or even see a man—that would be paradise.

But I soon found that Merges was not simpleminded—far from it. He could read thoughts; I am sure of it. He sat on his haunches, stroking his whiskers, staring at me with his enormous red eyes for a very long time. Then he proclaimed, this time in a strangely human voice, sounding like a judge or a prophet, "What you feel toward men will be changed forever. Now you shall know desire. You shall be like a cat, and when your heat comes each month, your desire will be irresistible. But it will never be fulfilled. You will please men but never be pleased, and each man you please will leave you, never to return or even to remember you. You shall bear a child, and she and her child and her child's child shall know what I and Kovacs feel. This shall be for all time."

"For all time?" I asked. "Such a long sentence?"

"For all time," he replied. "What greater offense than separating me forever from the love of my life?"

Suddenly overcome, I began to tremble and beg for you, my unborn daughter. "Please punish me, Merges. I deserve it for what I did to you. I deserve a loveless life. But for my children and my children's children, I beg you." And I bowed low before him and pressed my forehead to the ground.

"There is only one exit for your children. None for you."

"What is the exit?" I asked.

"Redress the wrong," said Merges, now licking—with a tongue larger than my hand—his monstrous paws and cleaning his hideous face.

"Redress the wrong? How? What should they do?" I moved toward him, pleading.

But Merges hissed and brandished his unsheathed claws. As I stepped back, he faded away. The last thing I saw of him were those terrible claws.

This, Magda, was my curse. Our curse. It drove me to ruin. I grew wild with desire and ran after men. I lost my position. No one would hire me. My landlord evicted me. I had no way to survive except to sell my body. And thanks to Merges I had no return trade. Men who had once been with me would never approach me again; they retained no memory of me but only of some vague terror connected with our meeting. Before long everyone in Budapest despised me. No doctor would believe me. Even the famous psychiatrist Sándor Ferenczi could not help. He spoke of my fevered imagination. I swore that I spoke truly. He requested proof, some witness, some sign. But how could I give proof? No man I had loved could remember me or the dream. I told Ferenczi he would have his proof if he would only spend an evening with me and see for himself. I had sought him out because of the rumor that he practiced "kissing therapy," but he would have no part of my invitation. Finally, in desperation, I emigrated to New York, hoping against hope that Merges would not cross the water.

The rest you know. A year later I conceived you. I never knew who your father was. Now you know why. And now you know why I could never keep you with me and why I sent you away to school. Knowing this, Magda, you must decide what you will do when you graduate. You may, of course, always come to me in New York. Whatever you decide, I shall continue to send you money each month. In other ways, I cannot help you. I cannot help myself.

Your Mother, Klara

Artemis folded the letter carefully, placed it back in the vellum folder, and then looked up at Ernest. "Now you know my grandmother. And me."

Ernest was both fascinated by the extraordinary story he had just heard and distracted by the intoxicating aroma of the pungent Chinese spices drifting over to him. Throughout the reading he had furtively eyed the steam drifting up from the cooling containers, yet, though he was famished, he maintained good form and resisted the food. Now enough was enough. He passed the pea sprouts to Artemis and dug his chopsticks into the Five Mushroom Beef.

"What about your mother, Artemis?" asked Ernest, chomping contentedly on a slightly crisp but marvelously succulent shitake mushroom.

"She went into a convent but was ejected after a few years for nocturnal roaming. Then she entered my grandmother's profession. She sent me away to school, and when I was fifteen she took her own life. It was my grandmother who gave me this letter; she lived twenty years after my mother's death."

"Merges's recipe for lifting the curse—redress the wrong—did you ever find out what that meant?"

"My grandmother and mother puzzled about it for years but never solved the mystery. My grandmother consulted another doctor, Dr. Brill, a famous New York psychiatrist, but he regarded her as out of touch with reality. Hysterical psychosis was his diagnosis, and he advised her to take the Weir rest cure—one to two years of total rest in a sanitarium. Given my grandmother's finances and the nature of Merges's curse, it is obvious that it was Dr. Brill who was out of touch with reality."

As Artemis began to put away the dishes, Ernest stopped her. "We can do that later."

"Perhaps, Ernest," Artemis said, her voice tight and strained, "now that dinner is over, you might like to come upstairs." After a pause, she added, "You know now that I cannot keep myself from asking this."

"Excuse me," Ernest said, rising and heading for the front door.

"Good-bye, then," Artemis called after him. "I know. I understand completely. No excuses necessary. And no guilt, please."

"What do you know, Artemis?" asked Ernest, looking back from the open door. "Where am I going?"

"You're going far away as fast as you can. And who can blame you? I know why you go. And I understand, Ernest."

"You see, Artemis, as I told you before, you don't know as much as you think you do. I'm going just twenty feet to my car, from which I intend to fetch my overnight bag."

When he returned, she was upstairs bathing. He cleared the dinner table, packed up the remaining food, and then, bag in hand, ascended the stairs.

The next hour in the bedroom proved one thing: it wasn't the chanterelle stew. All was as before. The warm, lush lust, the cat-licking, the sensuous tongue, the Fourth of July fireworks slowly building up to their pyrotechnic climax, the incandescent roman candles, the roar of the howitzer. For a few moments Ernest was visited by extraordinary flashbacks: all the past orgasms of his life swooooshing through him, years of jerking spasms into palms and towels and sinks and then watching a procession of the large-breasted lovers, lovely vessels of consolation, into whom he had drained the cares of his life. Gratitude! Gratitude! And then blackness as he fell into the sleep of the dead.

Ernest was awakened by Merges's howling. Again he felt the room shake; again the scratching and scraping at the wall of the house. Fear flickered, but he got quickly out of bed and—shaking his head vigorously and inhaling deeply—calmly opened the window wide, leaned out, and called, "This way, this way, Merges. Save your claws. The window is open."

Sudden silence. Then Merges bounded in, ripping and shredding the thin linen curtains. Hissing, his head raised, his red eyes blazing, his glistening claws unsheathed, he circled Ernest.

"I've been expecting you, Merges. Won't you please sit down?" Ernest settled into a massive redwood burl chair next to the night table, beyond which all was darkness. The bed, Artemis, and the rest of the room had vanished.

Merges stopped hissing. He looked up at Ernest, spittle dripping from his fangs, his muscles tensed.

Ernest reached into his overnight bag. "Won't you have something to eat, Merges?" he said, opening some of the dinner containers he had carried upstairs.

Merges peered cautiously into the first container. "Five Mushroom Beef! I hate mushrooms. That's why she always makes them. That chanterelle ragout!" He uttered these last words in a high-pitched, mocking singsong, then repeated them: "Chanterelle ragout! Chanterelle ragout!"

"Here, here," Ernest said in the soothing drone he used sometimes in therapy sessions. "Let me pick out the beef pieces for you. Oh, my God, I am so sorry! I could have gotten the whole baked cod. Or the Peking Duck. Even the Hunan Meatballs. Perhaps the Pork Shue Mai. Or the Beggar's Chicken. Or the Ming's Beef. Or the—"

"All right, all right," Merges snarled. He swiped at the chunks of beef and devoured them in a single gulp.

Ernest droned on: "Or I could have gotten the Seafood Delight, the salted shrimp, the whole roasted crab, the—"

"You could have, you could have, you could have, but you didn't, did you? And even if you had, then so what? Is that what you think? That some stale scraps would redress the wrong? That I would settle for leftovers? That I am nothing but brute appetite?"

Merges and Ernest stared silently at each other for a moment. Then Merges nodded toward the container with the Rolling Chicken and Cilantro in Lettuce Cups. "And what's in there?"

"It's called Rolling Chicken. Delicious. Here, let me pick out the chicken for you."

"No, leave it be," said Merges, batting the container out of Ernest's hand. "I like the green stuff. I come from a family of Bavarian grass eaters. Hard to find good grass that's not soaked in dog piss." Merges gobbled down the cilantro and chicken, then licked the lettuce cups clean. "Not bad. So you could've gotten roast crab?"

"I only wish I had, but as it was, I got too much meat. Turns out Artemis is a vegan."

"Vegan?"

"A vegetarian who eats no animal products at all—not even dairy products."

"So she's stupid as well as a murdering bitch. And I remind *you* again that you're stupid too if you think you'll redress the wrong by courting my stomach."

"No, Merges, I don't think that. But I fully understand why you'd be suspicious of me or anyone who approaches you in a friendly fashion. You haven't been treated well in your life."

"*Lives*—not life. I've had eight of them, and every one, without exception, has ended the same way—in unspeakable cruelty and murder. Look at the last one! Artemis murdered me! Threw me into a cage and nonchalantly tossed it into the river and watched me sink slowly until the filthy water of the Danube covered my nostrils. The last thing I saw in that life was her triumphant leer as my final breath bubbled out of me. And do you know what my crime was?"

Ernest shook his head.

"My crime was that I was being a cat."

"Merges, you're not any ordinary cat. You are an unusually intelligent cat. I hope I may speak frankly to you."

Merges, who was licking the sides of the empty Rolling Chicken container, growled assent.

"Two things I must say. First, of course, you realize it was not Artemis who drowned you. It was her grandmother, Klara, now long dead. Secondly—"

"She smells the same to me—Artemis is Klara in a later life. Didn't you know that?"

Ernest was thrown off guard. Needing time to ponder that notion, he merely continued, "Secondly, Klara did not hate cats. In fact, she loved a cat. She was no murderer: it was in an effort to save the life of Cica, her own dear cat, that she acted against you."

No answer. Ernest could hear Merges breathing. Am I, he wondered, being too confrontational, not showing enough empathy? "But," he said gently, "perhaps this is all beside the point. I think we should stick to what you said a minute ago—that your only crime was being a cat."

"Right! I did what I did because I am a cat. Cats protect their turf, they attack other, threatening cats, and the best of the cats—those bursting with catness—let nothing, *nothing*, stand in their way when they whiff the sweet muskiness of a cat in heat. I was doing nothing more than fulfilling my catness."

Merges's comment gave Ernest pause. Wasn't Merges being true to Ernest's favorite of Nietzsche's maxims: "Become he who you are?" Wasn't Merges right? Wasn't he simply fulfilling his own feline potential?

"There was once a famous philosopher," Ernest began, "that is, a wise man or a thinker—"

"I know what a philosopher is," the cat broke in crossly. "In one of my first lives, I lived in Freiburg and made nighttime visits to Martin Heidegger's home."

"You knew Heidegger?" said Ernest, amazed.

"No, no. Heidegger's cat, Xanthippe. She was something! Hot! Cica, hot as she was, was nothing compared to Xanthippe. It was many lives ago, but I remember well that army of heavy-weight Teutonic bullies I had to battle to get to her. Tomcats came all the way from Marburg when Xanthippe entered heat. Ah, those were the days!"

"Well, let me finish my point, Merges." Ernest tried not to allow himself to be distracted. "The famous philosopher I'm thinking of—he was German too—often said that one must become who one is, must fulfill one's ordained destiny or poten-tial. Isn't that exactly what you were doing? You *were* fulfilling your basic catness. Where is the crime in that?"

At Ernest's first words, Merges had opened his mouth to protest but slowly closed it again when he realized that Ernest was agreeing with him. He began grooming himself with wide swipes of his tongue.

"There is, however," Ernest continued, "a problematic para-dox here—a fundamental conflict of interest—in that Klara was doing exactly what you were doing: becoming herself. She was a nurturer and protector and cared for nothing in the world more than her cat. She wanted only to protect Cica and keep her safe. Thus, Klara's actions were all in the service of fulfilling her own basic loving nature."

"Hmmpf!" scoffed Merges. "Do you know that Klara refused to mate with my master, Kovacs, who was a very strong man? Just because Klara hated men, she assumed that Cica did too. Hence, there is no paradox. Klara acted not for Cica but in the service of her illusion about what Cica wanted. Believe me, when Cica was in heat, she was hot for me! Klara was unspeakably cruel to keep us apart."

"But Klara feared for her cat's life. Cica had suffered many grievous wounds."

"Wounds? Wounds? Mere scratches. Toms intimidate and subdue the lady. Toms claw the hell out of other toms. That's how we woo. That is catdom. We are being cats. Who is Klara, who are you, to judge and condemn catness?"

Ernest backed off. Nothing there, he decided. He tried another tack. "Merges, a few minutes ago you said that Artemis and Klara were the same, and that was why you continued to haunt Klara."

"My nose does not lie."

"When in one of your early lives you died, did you remain dead for a while before entering another life?"

"Only for an instant. Then I was reborn into another life. Don't ask me how. There are some things even cats don't know."

"Well, even so, you're certain that you're in one life, then cease to be, and then enter another. Correct?"

"Yes, yes, get on with it!" Merges growled. Like all ninth-lifers, he had little patience with picayune semantic discussions.

"But since for some years Artemis and her grandmother, Klara, were both alive at the same time and spoke to each other many times, how can Artemis and Klara be the same person in different lives? It's not possible. I don't mean to question your nose, but perhaps you were sensing the genetic connection between the two women."

Merges silently considered Ernest's comment as he continued to groom himself, licking a massive paw and scrubbing his face with its dampness.

"I was just thinking, Merges, is it possible you didn't know that we humans have only one life?"

"How can you be so sure?"

"Well, that's what we believe. And isn't that the important thing?"

"Perhaps you have many lives and don't know it."

"You say you remember your other lives. We don't. If we have new lives and don't remember the old ones, then it still means that this life—this existing me, the consciousness that is here right now—is going to perish."

"The point! The point!" the beast growled. "Get on with it. God, how you talk and talk and talk."

"The point is that your revenge was wonderfully effective. It was good revenge. It ruined the rest of Klara's one and only life.

She lived in great misery. And her crime was only to take one of your nine lives. Her sole life for one of your nine lives. Seems to me the debt has been paid many times over. Your revenge is complete. The slate is clean. The wrong redressed." Exultant at his persuasive formulation, Ernest leaned back in his chair.

"No," hissed Merges, glowering and thumping the floor with his powerful tail. "No, it is not complete! Not complete! The wrong has *not* been redressed! Revenge will go on and on! Besides, I like the way this life goes."

Ernest didn't allow himself to flinch. He rested a moment or two, caught his second wind, and began again from another perspective.

"You say you like the way your life goes now. Will you tell me about your life? What is your typical day like?"

Ernest's unruffled manner seemed to relax Merges, who stopped glowering, sat back on his haunches, and responded calmly. "My day? Uneventful. I don't remember much of my life."

"What do you do all day?"

"I wait. I wait until I am called by a dream."

"And between dreams?"

"I told you. I wait."

"That's it?"

"I wait."

"And that's your life, Merges? And are you satisfied?"

Merges nodded. "When you consider the alternative," he said as he gracefully rolled over and set to work grooming his belly.

"The alternative? You mean not living?"

"The ninth life is the last."

"And you want this last life to go on and on forever."

"Wouldn't you? Wouldn't anyone?"

"Merges, I'm struck by an inconsistency in what you're saying."

"Cats are highly logical beings. Sometimes that is not appreciated because of our ability to make lightning-quick decisions."

"Here's the inconsistency. You say you want your ninth life to go on and on, but in fact you're not living your ninth life. You're merely existing in some state of suspended animation."

"Not living my ninth life?"

"You said it yourself: you're waiting. I'll tell you what comes to my mind. A famous psychologist once said that some people so fear the debt of death that they refuse the loan of life."

"Meaning what? Talk plainly," said Merges, who had stopped grooming his belly and now sat on his haunches.

"Meaning that you seem so fearful of death that you refrain from entering into life. It's as though you fear using up life. Remember what you taught me just a few minutes ago about essential catness? Tell me, Merges, where now is the territory you defend? Where are the toms you battle? Where are the lustful, howling females you subdue? And why," Ernest asked, emphasizing each word, *"do you allow your precious Merges sperm seeds to rot unused?"*

As Ernest spoke, Merges's head bowed low. Then, somewhat mournfully, he asked, "And you have only one life? How far are you into it?"

"About halfway through."

"How can you stand it?"

Suddenly Ernest felt a sharp pang of sadness. He reached for one of the napkins from the Chinese dinner and dabbed at his eyes.

"I'm sorry," said Merges, unexpectedly gently, "to have caused pain."

"Not at all. I was prepared. This turn in our conversation was inevitable," Ernest said. "You ask how I can stand it? Well, first of all, by not thinking about it. And more, sometimes I even forget about it. And at my age that's not too hard."

"At your age? What does that mean?"

"We humans go through life in stages. As very young children, we think about death a great deal; some of us even obsess about it. It's not hard to discover death. We simply look around and see dead things: leaves and lilies and flies and beetles. Pets die. We eat dead animals. Sometimes we're privy to the death of a person. And before long we realize that death will come to everyone—to our grandma, to our mother and father, even to ourselves. We brood about this in private. Our parents and teachers, thinking it's bad for children to think about death, keep silent about it or give us fairy tales about a heaven and angels, eternal reunion, immortal souls." Ernest stopped, hoping Merges was following his words.

"And then?" Merges was following all right.

"We comply. We push it out of our minds, or we openly defy death with great feats of daredevilry. And then, just before we become adults, we brood a great deal about it again. Although some cannot bear it and refuse to go on living, most of us blot out our awareness of death by immersing ourselves in the tasks of adulthood—building a career and family, personal growth, acquiring possessions, exercising power, winning the race. That's where I am now in life. After that stage, we enter the later era of life, where awareness of death emerges again, and now death is distinctly menacing—in fact, imminent. At that point, we have the choice of thinking about it a great deal and making the most of the life we still have or pretending in various ways that death is not coming at all."

"So what about you, yourself? Do you pretend to yourself that death will not come?"

"No, I can't really do that. Since in my work as a psychiatrist I talk to many people who are terribly troubled about life and death, I have to face the truth all the time."

"Let me ask you again, then"—Merges's voice, now soft and weary, had lost all its menace—"how you stand it? How can you take pleasure from any part of life, any activity at all, with death looming ahead and only one life?"

"I'd turn that question upside down, Merges. Perhaps death makes life more vital, more precious. The fact of death bestows a special poignancy, a bittersweet quality, to life's activities. Yes, it may be true that living in the dream dimension confers immortality upon you, but your life seems to me to be soaked in ennui. When I asked you, a while back, to describe your life, you answered with the single phrase 'I wait.' Is that life? Is waiting living? You still have one life left, Merges. Why not live it to the fullest?"

"I cannot! I cannot!" Merges said, bowing his head deeper. "The thought of no longer existing, of not being among the living, of life going on without me, is—is—simply too terrible."

"So the point of the curse is not perpetual revenge, is it? You use the curse to avoid coming to the end of your last life."

"It is simply too terrible to just end. To not be."

"I have learned in my work," said Ernest reaching over and patting Merges's great paw, "that those who most fear death are the ones who approach it with too much unlived life inside them. It's best to use all of life. Leave death nothing but the dregs, nothing but a burned-out castle."

"No, no," moaned Merges, shaking his head. "It is simply too terrible."

"Why so terrible? Let's analyze it. Precisely what is so fearful about death? You've already experienced it more than once. You said that each time your life ended, there was a brief interval before the next life began."

"Yes, that's right."

"What do you remember of those brief moments?"

"Absolutely nothing."

"But isn't that the point, Merges? Much of what you fear about death is how you imagine it might feel to be dead and yet to know that you can no longer be among the living. But when you're dead, you have no consciousness. Death is the extinguishing of consciousness."

"Is that supposed to be reassuring?" Merges growled.

"You asked me how I can stand it? That's one of my answers. I've also always gotten comfort from the maxim of another philosopher, who lived a long, long time ago: 'Where death is, I am not; where I am, death is not.'"

"Is that any different from 'When you're dead, you're dead'?"

"A big difference. In death there is no 'you.' 'You' and 'dead' cannot coexist."

"Heavy, heavy stuff," Merges said, his voice barely audible, his head almost touching the floor.

"Let me tell you about another perspective that helps me, Merges, something I learned from a Russian writer—"

"Those Russians—this isn't going to be cheery."

"Listen. Years, centuries, millennia passed before I was born. Right?"

"No denying that." Merges nodded wearily.

"And millennia will pass after I'm dead. Right?"

Merges nodded again.

"Thus, I picture my life as a brilliant spark between two vast and identical pools of darkness: the darkness existing before my birth and the darkness following my death."

That seemed to strike home. Merges was listening hard, his ears pricked up.

"And doesn't it astound you, Merges, how much we dread the latter darkness and how indifferent we are to the first?"

Suddenly Merges stood and opened his mouth in an enormous yawn, his fangs gleaming faintly in the moonlight streaming through the window. "Guess I've got to be shuffling along," he said and trudged toward the window with a heavy, uncatlike gait.

"Wait, Merges, there's more!"

"Enough for today. A lot to ponder, even for a cat. Next time, Ernest, the roast crab. And more of that green-grass chicken."

"Next time? What do you mean, Merges, next time? Haven't I redressed the wrong?"

"Maybe yes, maybe no. I told you, too much to think about all at once. I'm out of here!"

Ernest plopped back into his chair. He was spent, his patience exhausted. Never before had he had a more nerve-wracking and fatiguing session. And now to see it all go for naught! Watching Merges trudge off, Ernest muttered to himself, "Go! Go!" And then added, *"Geh Gesunter Heit"*—that mocking Yiddish phrase of his mother's.

At the words, Merges stopped dead in his tracks and turned back. "I heard that. I can read minds."

Uh-oh, thought Ernest. But he held his head high and faced the oncoming Merges.

"Yes, I heard you. I heard your, *'Geh Gesunter Heit.'* And I know what that means—didn't you know that I speak good German? You blessed me. Even though you didn't imagine I would hear, you wished me to go in good health. And I am moved by your blessing. Very moved. I know what I've put you through. I know how much you want to liberate this woman—not only for her sake but also for yours. And yet even after your tremendous effort, and after your not knowing whether you were successful in redressing the wrong, even then you still had the grace and the loving-kindness to wish for my good health. That may be the most generous gift I have ever received. Good-bye, my friend."

"Good-bye, Merges," said Ernest, watching Merges stroll away, more perky now and with a graceful cat gait. Is it my imagination, he thought, or has Merges grown appreciably smaller?

"Perhaps we'll meet again," said Merges, without breaking stride. "I'm considering settling in California."

"You have my word, Merges," Ernest called after him. "You'll eat well here. Roast crab—and cilantro—every night."

Darkness again. The next thing Ernest saw was the roseate glow of dawn. Now I know the meaning of a "hard day's night," he thought as he sat up in bed, stretched, and contemplated the sleeping Artemis. He felt certain that Merges would now depart from the dream dimension. But what about the rest of the cat curse? None of that had been discussed. For a few minutes Ernest considered the prospect of being involved with a woman who might, every so often, be sexually ferocious and voracious. Quietly he slipped out of bed, dressed, and went downstairs.

Artemis, hearing his footsteps, called out, "Ernest, no! Something's changed. I'm free. I know it. I feel it. Don't go, please. You don't need to go."

"Be right back with breakfast. Ten minutes," he called from the front door. "I have an urgent need for an extra-seedy bagel and cream cheese. Yesterday I spotted a deli down the street."

He was just opening his car door when he heard the bedroom window go up and Artemis's voice. "Ernest, Ernest, remember I'm a vegan. No cream cheese. Can you get—"

"I know—avocado. It's on my list."

Author's Note

In this book, I have tried to be both storyteller and teacher. On the occasions when these two roles conflicted and I had to choose between inserting a juicy pedagogical comment and maintaining the dramatic pace of the story, I almost always put the story first and attempted to fulfill my teaching mission through indirect discourse.

Readers interested in a fuller discussion may consult my Web page: www.yalom.com. There I provide relevant references to the professional literature and discuss a number of technical aspects of these six tales: patient confidentiality, the boundary between fiction and nonfiction, the therapeutic relationship, the here-and-now ahistoric approach, therapist transparency, existential therapeutic approaches, and bereavement dynamics.